Shopping

Shopping

Material Culture Perspectives

Edited by Deborah C. Andrews

UNIVERSITY OF DELAWARE PRESS
Newark

Published by University of Delaware Press
Copublished by The Rowman & Littlefield Publishing Group, Inc.
4501 Forbes Boulevard, Suite 200, Lanham, Maryland 20706
www.rowman.com

16 Carlisle Street, London W1D 3BT, United Kingdom

British Library Cataloguing in Publication Information Available

Library of Congress Cataloging-in-Publication Data

Shopping : material culture perspectives / edited by Deborah Andrews.
pages cm
Includes bibliographical references and index.
ISBN 978-1-61149-517-1 (cloth : alk. paper) -- ISBN 978-1-61149-518-8 (electronic)
1. Consumption (Economics)--Social aspects--United States. 2. Shopping--Social aspects--United States--History. 3. Consumer behavior--United States--History. 4. Material culture--United States. 5. United States--Social life and customs. I. Andrews, Deborah.
HC110.C6S536 2014
306.3'4--dc23
2014033018

∞™ The paper used in this publication meets the minimum requirements of American National Standard for Information Sciences Permanence of Paper for Printed Library Materials, ANSI/NISO Z39.48-1992.

Printed in the United States of America

Table of Contents

Acknowledgments vii

Introduction ix
Deborah C. Andrews

1 The Spaces of Shopping: A Historical Overview 1
Sandy Isenstadt

2 Woolworth to Walmart: Mass Merchandising and the Changing Culture of Consumption 33
Susan Strasser

3 Shopping Malls: Machines for Selling 57
David Ames

4 Passages: From Arcade to Virtual Arcadia 73
Lance Winn

5 The Shop Around the Corner: Change, Continuity, and the Independent Neighborhood Grocer 89
Anne Krulikowski

6 Farmers' Markets, Food, and the Architecture of Control 111
J. Ritchie Garrison

7 Living in a Bubble in the 1950s: The Material Culture of Effervescence 131
Jay Gitlin

8 A Toxic Safari in a Big Box Store 159
McKay Jenkins

9 Secondhand Learning: Using Secondhand Consumerism in the Classroom 181
Helen Sheumaker

10 In Conversation: Community, Women, and Work in the American Garage Sale 195
Gretchen Herrmann with Martha Rosler

Index 207

About the Contributors 209

Acknowledgments

Full disclosure: I've never been much of a shopper. As a tourist, I find myself drawn to cabinets of wonder in exotic places, including department stores, bakeries, markets, bookstores, and museum shops. But the more I look, the less able I am to actually *buy* anything.

However, when I was searching for a theme around which to organize a colloquium series at the University of Delaware in material culture studies during fall semester 2011, one that would draw students, I thought: shopping. That was the hook, and the presentations on shopping-related topics hooked me, too.

I would thus like to thank those colloquium presenters whose rewritten talks are included here as well as three other scholars who later contributed essays. They are indeed "colleagues in shopping," the appropriate salutation in the countless e-mails that brought this anthology into being. Their diligence, smart thinking, and good cheer resound on every page.

For generous financial support I would like to thank the Center for Material Culture Studies and the College of Arts and Sciences at the University of Delaware. In particular, Ann Ardis, deputy dean, set the colloquium and this book in motion. The anthology has also gained immeasurably from the editorial advice provided by Don Mell, chair, board of editors, University of Delaware Press; Julia Oestreich, senior editor; and the Press's two reviewers. Chapter 2 is reprinted with permission from Nelson Lichtenstein, editor, *Wal-Mart: The Face of Twenty-First Century Capitalism* (New York: New Press, 2006). Chapter 8 is excerpted with permission from *What's Gotten Into Us: Staying Healthy in a Toxic World* (New York: Random House, 2011). Chapter 10, "In Conversation: Community, Women, and Work in the American Garage Sale," originally appeared in *Garage Sale Standard, Issue 1*, a newspaper (and .pdf file) accompanying an installation at the Museum of Modern Art (MoMA) in November 2012. We are grateful to Martha Rosler, Gretchen Herrmann, and Sarah Resnick, editor, for permission to reprint this conversation as the final chapter.

Introduction

Deborah C. Andrews

> The supermarket spread before her as a place of boundless opportunity, something new and vast and exciting, the way the prairie must have looked to the first settlers of the West.
>
> —Cathleen Schine, *The Three Weissmanns of Westport*[1]

We all shop. At no time are we more thoughtful about objects and our relations with them than when we are hunting them down in a store or searching for them online and consciously weighing the merits of one or another product in relation to our own, often intimate needs and desires. The degree to which shopping, or more broadly, consumerism, is both critiqued and defended in American society only confirms the role that commercial goods play in our daily lives.

This collection grew out of a series of talks sponsored annually by the Center for Material Culture Studies at the University of Delaware. The series, which serves as a one-credit course, aims to engage undergraduate students in thinking about material culture, that is, about the relationship between people and their things. The talks are also open to the public and attended by a broad audience. Because shopping exposes significant ways in which people and things connect, it served as the theme for the series in fall 2011; speakers were asked to draw a bead on the activity from their own disciplinary and personal points of view. That was a risky premise on which to base a coherent course, but it worked. The concept of shopping provided rich shared ground for the talks while fostering diversity in the definition of that concept and approaches to studying it. The talks worked so well that we wanted to give them an afterlife in print. Some of the original presenters were unavailable to do so, and thus three additional contributions were solicited for this anthology.

Not intended as a comprehensive or chronological history of shopping, this collection provides a series of individual snapshots that depict this engaging activity from the multiple perspectives of material culture studies. The authors include several historians with diverging specialties, an art historian, an anthropologist, an environmental journalist, a geographer and urban planner, and practicing artists. Each author shows how a focus on the mutual creation of people and their things can illuminate a specific corner of consumption. While the essays center on the American scene, the context throughout is that of shopping as a global activity, especially as shopping moves to the Internet.

As in the original series of talks, these essays address a wide audience of people who shop, both students and general-interest readers. In doing so, the anthology also offers an enticing diversity of models of ways to *write* about shopping—and much else.

This introduction is not, as in traditional anthology introductions, a summary of each essay. Instead, it gives a quick preview of what's to come, as the essays take up three interconnected elements of the topic: concerns about the *spaces* in which shopping occurs; about the *experience* of shopping itself, both individual and social; and about its economic, environmental, and personal *downsides*. In short, the introduction provides background on shopping's places, pleasures, and perils. It ends with a look at how shopping has inspired artists and writers and will continue to do so. As a signal activity, especially in American culture, shopping has moved from the store and the street to the museum, the screen, the literary page, and the student paper.

A CULTURE OF CONSUMPTION

An extensive body of scholarship addresses matters of production and consumption, scholarship that in the United States and Europe increasingly focuses on consumption, "the whole question of how we relate to a world that we do not make."[2] In her essay in this collection, historian Susan Strasser examines this question from the perspective of America in the late nineteenth and early twentieth century: "People's daily routines involved making fewer things and purchasing more, while shopping and planning for consumption became major activities, pursued both as part of household work and for pleasure." Moreover, as artist and design theorist Lance Winn notes in his essay, these purchased commodities were ones in which "there is no longer anything that is supposed to remind us how it came into being." "Huge swaths of products, from plastic toys to upholstered furniture," comments environmental journalist McKay Jenkins, "report nothing about what went into making them—not the materials, not the circumstances under which they were made, not whether or not they were 'inspected,' nothing." Jenkins details the perils of such products in his essay about a "safari" in a big box store.

One significant perspective in the scholarship of consumption, stemming from Thorstein Veblen, author of *The Theory of the Leisure Class* (1899), and others, is that consumers are "pawns of capitalism." In their view, consumption represents excess, waste, and environmental plundering. Such materialism is, moreover, a devotion to things at the expense of persons. A second approach, championed by, among others, Daniel Miller, an anthropologist at University College London and a prolific writer, resists what can be characterized as this traditional academic view. Miller argues that people acquire goods "to enhance and not to detract from our devotion to other people."[3] In his yearlong ethnographic study of a commercial street in North London, for example, Miller found that "shoppers develop and imagine those social relationships which they most care about through the medium of selecting goods."[4] Looking directly at the experience of consumers, particularly women, and not simply theorizing about them, he examines the family and community rituals engaged in by consumer–citizens. Along with, for example, historian Amanda Vickery, he emphasizes the important economic and social role women's shopping plays as skilled, unpaid work that provides care and helps families thrive. It requires time and a knowledge base often overlooked in other, especially fictional, accounts of the pleasure women find in shopping.[5]

In addition to such academic studies, the mass market offers popular writings on the topic. For example, *Why We Shop: The Science of Shopping*, by Paco Underhill, in updated editions, is a four-star best seller on Amazon.com. Two of the section headings provide the flavor of the discussion: "Men Are from Home Depot, Women Are from Bloomingdales: The Demographics of Shopping" and "Screen Savers, Jet Lag and Whirling Dervishes: The Culture of Shopping." The blogosphere abounds in blogs about shopping, with advice about where to find the best products as well as narratives by those addicted to shopping and strategies for overcoming such addictions—or for turning them into profitable enterprises.

PLACES

Whatever perspective one takes on the values and broader implications associated with shopping, it is clear that as an activity, shopping is shaped by and shapes the spaces in which it takes place. In the collection's opening essay, architectural historian Sandy Isenstadt surveys the broad historical picture of shopping's architecture, noting the cycle of rise and decline in major forms of merchandising. Subsequent essays look in detail at shopping spaces of special interest to the authors.

One innovative merchandising space that figures prominently in essays by Strasser, Isenstadt, and Winn is the department store. Established in the 1860s in Europe and the United States, by the turn of the century, these "palaces of consumption" or "dream worlds" "provided customers with an array of services never before offered even by the most exclusive single-line shops: lunchrooms, tearooms, and other restaurants; public telephones, as well as telegraph and post offices; beauty parlors, child care, first aid, and lost-and-found departments" (Strasser, Chapter 2 of this book).

Reaching back from the current reinvention and flourishing of farmers' markets, historian Ritchie Garrison details the evolution of such markets, held largely outdoors, where producers sell goods directly to consumers. He traces various political, social, and ethical implications in the production and delivery of food. Historian Anne Krulikowski also looks at the distribution of food, turning our attention to the neighborhood grocery, particularly in Philadelphia and close environs, where a row house, a domestic space in the city, found a new commercial purpose. These shops eventually faced stiff competition, especially during the Depression, from chain supermarkets, which could offer a wider range of goods in big buildings located cheaply outside the city. They offered low prices to an increasingly mobile population, who parked in their large parking lots; served themselves from shelves stocked with branded, packaged items; and could shop less frequently because they had wheeled grocery carts to pile their items into as they shopped, cars to carry their goods to their homes, and refrigerators there to store them.

Along with supermarkets, department stores later moved to the suburbs, where they anchored another new shopping space: the mall. In his essay, geographer and urban planner David Ames traces the growth of the shopping mall, with a focus on the work of a major mall architect in the United States, Victor Gruen. An Austrian, Gruen looked to European town centers and shopping districts as he designed the purpose-built, enclosed structures that became a familiar presence along suburban highways in the United States during the mid-to-late twentieth century. Gruen called these structures "selling machines." Ames details the management strategies supported by the physical layout of the malls that encouraged casual visitors or those intent on a specific purchase to linger and buy more.

In the twenty-first century, however, shopping malls are in decline. The decline comes in part from the changes in mass merchandising described by Strasser. Mail order houses, such as Sears and Montgomery Ward (which also had brick-and-mortar presences in or near the malls), gave way to discount stores in the 1950s and then to the big box stores, such as Walmart and Target, founded in the 1960s.

A second reason shopping malls are becoming obsolete and abandoned is the rise of online shopping. Winn sees in that a parallel to the decline in another earlier shopping space, the arcades, nineteenth-century urban passages of iron and glass. The decline of the arcades in the early twentieth century was memorialized in lengthy notes compiled by the German literary critic and philosopher Walter Benjamin and published as *The Arcades Project*. This extensive and insightful examination of the arcade's decline in the face of competition from department stores frames Winn's analysis of the transition from the mall as the iconic shopping space to shopping online.

PLEASURES

Discussing Émile Zola's novel *The Ladies' Paradise,* set in a Parisian department store, Isenstadt notes that shopping "takes on erotic and ecstatic dimensions, as women crowd each other and swoon in surrender to achingly delicate fabrics bathed in soft light tumbling through skylights and drifting through lace to settle on the incandescent union of shoppers and merchandise." Isenstadt, Ames, and Strasser discuss the experience of shopping in such stores, whose abundance and display of goods recall the cabinets of wonders, collections of marvels assembled by elite men of the Renaissance. The name of a twenty-first century shopping mall in Beijing that features department stores among its many shops suggests this magic space: Joy City.

In a play on words, Sinclair Lewis, the American novelist, calls Americans' pleasure in their possessions, the products of their shopping, the "goods life." Henry James praised the painter John Singer Sargent for his "august capacity to portray Americans at ease among their possessions, intimately, at times gloriously, at one with the sofa, the foot stool, the screen."[6] Reflecting an aspect of that life in middle-class America in the 1950s, historian Jay Gitlin writes his essay from a personal perspective: "Born in our parents' dreams of creating new lives—ours—that might be spared the human sorrows of war and horrors of the Holocaust, our lives were shaped by the designed bubbles of suburbia." Gitlin focuses especially on children as shoppers during that child-oriented decade of "great fancy and imagination," where the lightness of new materials, products of advances in chemistry, provided such pleasures as bubble gum, bubble bath, balloons, and other "uplifting playthings." The bubble of safety and transparency in which the children, and their parents, lived in the suburbs is reflected in popular songs, films, and childrens' books.

The pleasures of shopping thread through other essays as well. Winn finds an analogy between Benjamin's flaneur of the arcades and a web surfer–shopper. For such individuals, browsing incorporates the thrill of the hunt even more than does the actual purchase. Sometimes by accident, as in corner neighborhood stores, and sometimes by design in shopping malls, the spaces of shopping provide an engaging social experience, particularly for women shoppers, as discussed by Garrison, Isenstadt, Ames, Strasser, and Krulikowski. Herrmann and Rosler see the social aspects of shopping as fundamental in their "conversation" about American garage sales. Shopping, then, can serve to enhance personal relationships, especially when shoppers meet in spaces that are aesthetically pleasing and designed to delight.

PERILS

On the other hand, not all shoppers find the experience pleasant, as noted by Jenkins, who admits to having "an intense, even neurotic, dislike of shopping," an attitude shared by many others. Shopping has downsides. One is a shift in the spaces of shopping. Arcades and department stores provided a dream world of aesthetically displayed products. Elegant stores selling clothing, foods, and other consumer goods continue to exist, but mass merchandising has shifted to big box stores. These large, undistinguished, warehouse-like buildings can seem soulless. Second, the social pleasures of shopping evaporate in cyberspace, something noted by Isenstadt and Winn. In their isolation, online shoppers are also vulnerable to the manipulative power of consumer websites. A third downside of shopping, particularly in big box stores, is a troubling abundance of cheap products, globally sourced.

Achievements in retailing and mass merchandising over the past century mean that we have ever more stuff, and cheaper stuff. Enhanced global production, particularly the "endless conveyor belt of products moving into this country from factories somewhere in China," as Jenkins describes it, adds to that abundance and encourages buyers, looking for bargains, to buy too much, more than they need. Strasser quotes a Minnesota woman who shopped at Walmart: "[S]he could 'come out with a cart full top and bottom' for the same amount of money that would fill only a bag or two at other stores. 'How great that feels.'"

From this stream of cheap goods in full carts, historian Helen Sheumaker selects for analysis cheaply produced clothing. Bought and quickly disposed of, such clothing, including the products known as "fast fashion," contributes to the "mountains of castoffs" entering a secondhand consumer market in thrift stores. There items are winnowed for resale, with the remains from that process bundled and shipped to the Third World. She argues that the flood of cheap clothing from the United States undermines manufacturing in such countries as Zambia and Haiti. American donors, thinking they are doing good by donating the clothes, are often unaware of these unintended economic consequences abroad. In her essay, Sheumaker describes how she helps students in an American studies course learn about secondhand consumerism and, more broadly, consumption patterns in the global economy through a service-learning experience in thrift shops.

Jenkins points out another peril awaiting shoppers in big box stores: multiple products harmful to the purchaser's health and harmful to the health of those who produced them. These include paints, cosmetics, pajamas, furniture, mattresses, and toys "manufactured, one way or another, from a mix of synthetic chemicals." He recounts the underside of the chemical products, including plastics, so celebrated in the world of the 1950s described by Gitlin. One pervasive synthetic chemical is phthalates, added to anything requiring soft plastic, like shower curtains and water bottles. According to Jenkins, phthalates "mimic or interfere with the human hormone system, leading to things like low sperm counts in boys or early-onset puberty in girls. . . . Nearly five million metric tons are consumed by industry every year—for a world of consumers that sees convenience, disposability, and cheapness—rather than sustainability, durability, and health—as paramount virtues."

While we think government standards and inspections provide some protection from faulty products, Jenkins disabuses us of that notion. And as they break down in landfills or are dumped into streams and the ocean, elements of these products can exist in the environment for long periods, with toxic effects.

Strasser details further downsides of the shift in retailing to big box stores. Such stores often engage in unfair labor practices, especially low wages and gender discrimination, affecting women employees. They squeeze manufacturers and other vendors to offer low prices, which puts local stores out of business. They exploit their low-wage customers with stores deliberately built in poor areas. Devastating fires and building collapses that killed hundreds of workers in Asian clothing factories only add to this picture of shopping's perils.

THE ART OF SHOPPING

Whatever its spaces or consequences, its pleasures or perils, shopping is the signal activity in our consumer culture. It is a complex, richly significant activity, one that has inspired artists and writers for years. Shopping engages audiences.

The social experience of shopping moved from the store and the street to the museum in a major art installation inspired by the garage sale, an activity that grew up in America in the 1960s. Photographer and performance artist Martha Rosler created *The Meta-Monumental Garage Sale*, an installation that in 2012 transformed the atrium of New York's Museum of Modern Art (MoMA) "into an informal cash economy—a space for the exchange of goods, accompanied by narratives and ideas—as it implicates visitors in face-to-face transactions."[7] In bringing the garage-sale model to an art space, with its foregrounding as well as denial of questions of worth and value, performance artist Rosler wanted to "engage the visitors not as observers but as participants enacting the impulse to possess things and find a bargain." She had been "struck by the strange nature of [such sales], their informal economic status and self-centeredness, but also the way they implicated the community in the narrative of the residents' lives."[8] A "conversation" between Rosler and anthropologist Gretchen Herrmann in this collection provides insights into the American garage sale as a cultural event and its transformation into art.

In addition, in a happy coincidence of timing as we edited this collection during the spring of 2013, MoMA featured an encore installation of "The Store," a landmark early work by the American artist Claes Oldenburg. In 1961, Oldenburg developed a selling space on the Lower East Side of Manhattan, for which he created brightly painted soft sculptures out of plaster and wire that, at a range of scales and odd proportions, modeled popular consumer objects, including lingerie, pastries, sandwiches, and a cash till. He stuffed the store with these items and sold them himself, at reasonable prices, to real customers in an imitation of an "everything must go" sale. That this was a way to start his career outside the gallery circuit and that these items are now in major private and public collections suggest another story. But he indeed created art from shopping.

Many playwrights and novelists also advance their plots and develop their characters with a strong eye on shops and shopping. In a similar coincidence of timing, a department store, for example, took center stage in *Mr. Selfridge*, an eight-part Public Broadcasting System "Masterpiece Classic," broadcast in spring 2013. The overview on the PBS website suggests the drama inherent in the shopping experience: an "American retail tycoon arrives to jettison fusty British tradition and open the biggest and finest department store the world has ever seen: Selfridges . . . to provide London's shoppers with the ultimate merchandise and the ultimate thrill."[9]

In the quotation that opens this introduction, novelist Cathleen Schine links the vision of abundance in a supermarket to the way the prairie must have looked to early settlers of the West. Exploring and populating new territory, a kind of shopping, is part of the American mythology. Another American novelist, Edith Wharton, whose works are often taught in high school and college courses, provides further evidence of how shopping can be transformed into art. In *The Custom of the Country*, she says of her main character: "In this world of lavish pleasures she lost what little prudence the discipline of [her small hometown] had inculcated. She could never be with people who had all the things she envied without being hypnotized into the belief that she had only to put her hand out to obtain them. . . . She knew her wants so much better now, and was so much more worthy of the things she wanted!" Acknowledging her skills at shopping, her husband suggests that her time bargaining in the shops was not intended to save money "but only to prolong and intensify the pleasure of spending."

In another novel, *Summer*, Wharton portrays the attraction of store windows in a similar vein to Zola's portrayal of the department store:

> Even the shops that were closed offered, through wide expanses of plate-glass, hints of hidden riches. In some, waves of silk and ribbon broke over shores of imitation moss from which ravishing hats rose like

> tropical orchids. In others, the pink throats of gramophones opened their giant convolutions in a soundless chorus; or bicycles shining in neat ranks seemed to await the signal of an invisible starter; or tiers of fancy-goods in leatherette and paste and celluloid dangled their insidious graces; and, in one vast bay that seemed to project them into exciting contact with the public, wax ladies in daring dresses chatted elegantly, or, with gestures intimate yet blameless, pointed to their pink corsets and transparent hosiery.

Whether in fiction or in fact, in art or in reality, shopping for goods brings us into close encounters with objects. We are shaped by them and they shape us. *Shopping: Material Culture Perspectives* offers multiple ways to make sense of these encounters. While most essays center on historical analysis, Winn grounds his in theory and allegory, Sheumaker describes an approach to teaching about the implications of shopping, Herrmann and Rosler organize their discussion as a dialogue, and Jenkins and Gitlin frame their argument in a personal, narrative approach. These essays thus provide a diversity of models of ways to look at a broad topic like shopping, develop evidence, align evidence to support a point of view, and present that evidence. In the end, readers of this anthology can learn not only about shopping but also about strategies for writing, whatever the writing is about.

NOTES

1. Cathleen Schine, *The Three Weissmanns of Westport* (New York: Farrar, Straus & Giroux, 2010), 101.
2. Don Slater and Daniel Miller, "Moments and Movements in the Study of Consumer Culture: A Dialog between Daniel Miller and Don Slater," *Journal of Consumer Culture* 7, no. 5 (2007), 6.
3. Daniel Miller, "The Poverty of Morality," *Journal of Consumer Culture* 1, no. 2 (2001), 231.
4. Daniel Miller, *A Theory of Shopping* (Ithaca, NY: Cornell University Press, 1998), 5.
5. Miller published two books directly addressing shopping: *A Theory of Shopping* (1998) and *The Dialectics of Shopping* (2001), which was based on lectures he delivered in 1998 at the University of Rochester.
6. Bill Brown, *A Sense of Things: The Object Matter of American Literature* (Chicago: University of Chicago Press, 2003), 137.
7. Sarah Resnick, ed., *Garage Sale Standard, Issue 1* (New York: Museum of Modern Art, 2012), 2. Accessed April 4, 2014. http://www.moma.org/interactives/exhibitions/2012/garagesale/garagesale1.pdf
8. Sarah Resnick, ed., "In Conversation. Martha Rosler with Sabine Breitwieser," *Garage Sale Standard,* no.1, 13. Accessed April 4, 2014. http://www.moma.org/interactives/exhibitions/2012/garagesale/garagesale1.pdf
9. Masterpiece website. Accessed April 4, 2014. http://www.pbs.org/wgbh/masterpiece/programs/series/mr-selfridge/

ONE

The Spaces of Shopping

A Historical Overview

Sandy Isenstadt

Sometime in the 1990s a new visual trope appeared. It features a woman, usually alone, but sometimes a man and a woman or two women, holding a credit card, usually unbranded, looking into a laptop computer, also unbranded, and smiling broadly (Figure 1.1). The surrounding space is always domestic in character, evident in features such as a bed, dining room table, living room sofa, or a glass or two of wine. Such images, which have since become ubiquitous, are plainly intended to suggest that online shopping is not only fun, but it is also social. The smile signifies a deep satisfaction not at the success of acquisition, for the thing purchased is not yet possessed. Rather, the smile registers a kind of engagement with the material world, despite being conducted at home and through a screen.

Clearly, such engagement is an illusion. The entire process of shopping online is, after all, automated, other than the shopper herself, and even she is by some accounts, preprogrammed to buy. The ambition of the smile, which is a requisite part of the trope's visual amalgam, is to eclipse the actual joylessness of online shopping—devoid of objects; devoid of human contact, spaceless, even airless; devoid of all presence—with the memory of what shopping had formerly been: a profoundly social experience. Online shopping is convenient, no doubt. But its convenience entails the evacuation of all the social and material aspects of shopping in a store: a passage through and orientation within the public realm; a threshold and a semipublic physical space; encounters with

Figure 1.1. Laptop—credit card—smile: a new species of visual rhetoric designed to make us believe that online shopping is social and fun. *Source: Subbotina Anna / Shutterstock.*

salespeople or other shoppers; the feel of fabrics or the heft of objects; judgments among myriad qualities; a moment of material exchange, perhaps a brush of hands, wherein the abstraction of currency or credit is transformed in a kind of everyday magic into an object possessed; and the gratification of reentering the public realm subtly renewed by a sense of successful acquisition at capturing an object of desire or at least, making a worthy journey to do so. These are all elements that comprise our contemporary understanding of shopping.

But shopping is just now undergoing momentous change. Stores remain, of course, and at the time of this writing, they are the crucible for more than 90 percent of all consumer purchases,[1] but their inevitable erosion as the leading venue for commercial exchange warrants a closer look at their effect not only on commercial transactions but also on material, social, and even urban life. For the past five hundred years or so shopping has been defined not only as the perusal and purchase of goods; it has also been defined by the particular space in which it took place. In this sense, shopping, at least since the Renaissance, is distinguished by its physical enclosure. The physical space of exchange—the shop—as well as its place within the city have set the parameters and conditioned the relations between ourselves and the things we bought, as well as relations between ourselves and others as mediated by those things.

Since the Renaissance, when retail commerce began to settle into a fixed space, goods have cost more because the space itself was seen to have value, tacitly by buyers and explicitly by merchants. The changing ways in which retail exchange was enclosed have, each in their turn, configured and codified different forms of sociability, along with mediating the manner in which goods are acquired. Even the big box self-serve stores from the last quarter of the twentieth century are laced with social relations. Today, however, with the advent of online shopping, a fixed and dedicated retail space has become superfluous. The disappearance of that space ends a long series of evolving forms of social contact.

At first glance, shopping hardly seems to warrant academic study. Indeed, the constituent parts of shopping—judging personal need, going to a store, determining quality, assessing value, reading labels, and so on—could hardly seem more trivial. Its elements comprise inattention, banal objects, ephemeral feelings, and instrumental motives so familiar as to be invisible. Yet one might say the same thing about eating, which occupies a spectrum ranging from commonplace to extraordinary, from distracted to obsessed, which varies geographically and temporally and bears on almost everything from biological necessity to cultural caprice. In a modern consumer society, shopping is no less significant. The vast majority of everyday things, whether a pack of gum or an automobile, came from a shop along a conduit of individual decisions and experience. That so many of those experiences are registered beneath the level of conscious attention argues for the necessity of scholarly assessment.

MEDIEVAL SHOPPING

The origin of the shop is lost in history. Certainly, the ancient world had shops: an enclosed, fixed space along with a more or less regular inventory. Ruins at Pompeii reveal many shops, mostly selling foodstuffs, while a soaring, multilevel, vaulted structure housed the markets of Trajan, comprising a variety of spaces for storage, offices, and living quarters, as well as shops and a central hall. Such ruins attest to a key point: fixed shops require a materially advanced, urban society such as that of the Roman Empire. When the Empire collapsed, urban living declined dramatically. Although larger towns in the Middle Ages could support makers and vendors of staples such as milled grain or bread, most people in medieval Europe would procure goods at markets and fairs.

Depending upon the size of a town, markets could be held every day, on alternate days, or weekly. They served the local population and offered simple goods, including foodstuffs. The vendor was quite likely also to be the maker. Bakers sold bread, for example, whether made from their own dough or dough supplied by their customers. Vendors operated from wooden stalls or "shambles." Since most of what could be purchased at a market was considered a necessity, such as food, prices were often regulated by town officials, who were concerned that periodic scarcity could turn into prolonged famine. Practices that risked the greater good for individual gain were thus usually proscribed. For example, a vendor who tried to corner the market in one or another commodity, often by intercepting the delivery of goods before they arrived at the stalls of other merchants, could be charged with "forestalling" and thereby fined.[2]

Further, prices were relatively stable over long periods of time, which led to the presumption that an item for sale had a single, proper price. Merchants who attempted to exploit spikes in demand, such as the need for roof tiles following a damaging storm, could be penalized and compelled to sell their goods at the normal price. The temptation on the part of merchants to exploit temporary shortages by raising prices was thereby moderated, but it was just such temptation to exploit the prevailing economy of scarcity that helped to give commerce overtones of immorality. Indeed, there were few merchants as such in the Middle Ages. Rather, most things were sold by peddlers, a class of people who are defined by selling things that they did not produce. They were generally seen as earning a living by the labor of others. A "market cross" was a common feature at many markets; it was meant to mediate the baser, self-serving impulses of commercial exchange by admonishing all to trade honestly and fairly under the watchful eye of a higher authority.[3]

In many ways, trust was the premise of medieval markets. A chronic shortage of coins meant that many trades were bartered, with both sides acceding to testaments of quality. Often a trade was concluded with a promise of repayment, that is, with debt. But without intermediaries such as banks, receiving credit from a vendor required personal contacts and a wide social network.[4] In this sense, debt could function as a kind of social glue, as relative strangers were bound to each other's fortunes by way of third parties not directly involved in a purchase. One might argue that relations with things were equally as intertwined. Because supplies of any item were always subject to the vagaries of weather, choice was limited to those items that were physically present and within reach. Also, without uniform standards for consumption, nearly everything was sold by a unique measure. Buyers expected they would bring their own containers for merchants to fill. The physical differences between a peck of coal, a quire of paper, a stone of meat, four nails of cloth, a pottle of salt, a firkin of ale, and a rundlet of wine were all tangible to buyer and seller. Weekly or biweekly markets were supplemented by seasonal or annual fairs, a word descending from the Latin *feria*, meaning holiday. Fairs would often specialize in certain types of goods, such as luxury fabrics or tools. They were often international in scope, too. Townsfolk anticipated the arrival of strangers with curious accents who would bear a range of things rarely, perhaps never, encountered.[5]

In larger towns, some workshops would sell directly to buyers. Artisans labored inside the workshop and, often, lived there. Customers rarely went inside. In the morning, wooden shutters were unfolded to form a counter or table for the convenience of workers. Leaving an item there for display might entice a customer, but it also tempted theft. A passerby might well stop and negotiate a purchase "through-the-window," as the custom came to be called. Shoes and boots, for example, were sold directly from the shop, as shown in Figure 1.2. Only in the biggest towns would merchants specialize exclusively in trade, buying wholesale from farms and selling retail to urban customers. Usually they congregated to draw crowds of potential customers. Cities like London, which were already large in the Middle Ages, bear evidence of these specialties in the names of streets, such as Wood Street, Milk Street, Poultry, Ironmonger Lane, and Bread Street, all off Cheapside, the city's historic center of shopping. Cloth Fair was situated next to Smithfield Market, the historic meat market. William Hogarth's eighteenth-century engravings of Beer Street and Gin Lane testify to this type of urban market.

Artisanal shops are the precursors to more modern spaces of shopping, defined here as taking place in an enclosed, fixed location that is open on a regular schedule, containing a steady inventory and operated

Figure 1.2. ***Effects of Good Government on the City Life*, detail. Ambrogio Lorenzetti, 1338–1339. *Source: Palazzo Pubblico, Siena, Italy.***

by someone whose specialty is selling things rather than making them. Occasional in the Middle Ages, such shops became more common during the Renaissance. Europe saw an increase in trade at this time and higher levels of production, which engendered in turn higher customer expectations in terms of both quality and choice of goods. A new class of financiers arose specifically to facilitate the greater flow of goods. A textile and cloth industry blossomed in the Netherlands during this time with advances in loom design and weaving methods, while Italian shopkeepers invented double-entry bookkeeping, a flexible and efficient accounting system useful for keeping track of the greater numbers of imports that originated in the New World to the west and the Ottoman Empire to the east. Shops proliferated both in number and in regard to the type of merchandise sold in response to these powerful currents of trade.[6]

The nature of shopping was in flux, but it remained socially complex. Shops served the distinct clienteles and social classes that emerged in Renaissance cities. For the wealthy, and especially for wealthy women, shopping was usually executed by proxy, as such women would not be expected to countenance contact with artisans or merchants; few items were ready made, as they are today, so many purchases took a great deal of time to complete; and the usual factors of supply and demand continued to affect the availability of crafted goods and the quality of constituent materials.[7] Currencies were volatile, which meant that many purchases still required a social network to facilitate them. Shops were not distinguished in architectural terms. Typically, a shop was simply a private home whose ground-floor front rooms had been converted to commercial purposes. With very little thought given to matters of display, few shops had large windows, a feature that appears to have been fitfully introduced in northern Europe starting in the sixteenth century.[8]

SHOPPING COMES OF AGE

The establishment of the Royal Exchange in London, which opened in 1571 under Queen Elizabeth I, was a milestone in commerce: its state sponsorship signaled elite approval of shopping as an activity as well as recognition of the value of heightened consumption. The Exchange consisted of a bourse, modeled on the one in Antwerp, on the ground floor for the conduct of international trade and, along a gallery above, a series of separate shops replete with goods from around the world. Richly decorated and brightly lighted "in the Italian style with coloured glass cups full of burning grease, and great wax torches burning in sconces on the walls," the Exchange swiftly became a major attraction. International traders conducted their business on the ground floor by day; in the evening on the gallery "the butterflies of fashion" would come to gawk at the panorama of exotic goods.[9] The success of the Royal Exchange inspired the construction of its rival, the New Exchange, completed in 1609 to a design most likely by Inigo Jones, then the city's most fashionable architect. Built outside the historic city walls but close to the royal seat at Westminster, the New Exchange aimed to attract well-heeled society with nearly one hundred shops. Its founder, Sir Robert Cecil, hired Jones and the playwright Ben Jonson to create a gala opening for the Exchange, which was compared at the time to theatrical entertainment. The event was one way that Cecil diffused the project's commercial premise since retailing still carried overtones of dishonesty.[10]

The seventeenth century was a period of increased consumption, especially of luxury goods, powered in part with the wealth created by new agricultural methods, as well as by greater trade, much of it now with newly established colonies. More and more novel items, such as sugar, tea, and china, began to flow to Europe from Asia and from colonies in the Americas. The English language bears testimony to these developments: terms such as "bazaar" (introduced from Persian via Italian), "calico" (named for an Indian city on the Arabian Sea), and "far-fetched" (designating an alluring, distant origin) first became familiar in the seventeenth century. In this context, shopping was becoming a way to see not only the elite of one's own city. It was also a way, during the golden age of exploration, to experience the larger globe. Shopping at the exchanges or other fancy shops was as much a way to represent oneself to society as it was to actually buy something.

As a corollary, attitudes toward consumption began to change in significant ways. The repeal in England of sumptuary laws (laws intended to restrain luxury consumption) in 1604 only acknowledged how popular shopping had already become, since the laws had not been regularly enforced for many years. A number of new retail shops opened and English theater, which blossomed in this age of Shakespeare, began to feature shops in plays where the action was sometimes set in them. Whereas luxury consumption had been limited largely to royalty, it was gradually attracting a wider clientele. To be sure, a gendered protocol of shopping prevailed. Goods for men and for women were kept in separate shops, guaranteeing that the sexes would not mix over matters of commercial exchange. Although segregated in this way, such specialized shops provided new economic opportunities for women.[11]

The success of individual shops or even the Royal Exchange or the New Exchange would vary due to changes in supplies, inclement weather, and even war, such as the British civil wars in the middle of the seventeenth century, and, of course, changes in taste. But the overall trend was by this time quite clear: shopping was not simply a way to survey and choose basic necessities; it was also, perhaps foremost, a way to assert membership in a cosmopolitan society that increasingly measured social merit in terms of material acquisitions and, just as important, knowledge about material goods. One became a citizen of all of Europe by going to the best venues and choosing from among the best objects. Indeed, with British merchant fleets dominating international trade in the seventeenth century through consortia, such as the vast East India Company, founded in 1600, customers in London shops could see themselves playing a role in global relations.

Correspondingly, commerce was more and more seen as a proper vocation for a member of urban society, and in turn, a city could be assessed for the quality of its commerce.[12] As a result, London's municipal government went out of its way to facilitate commerce, to augment international trade in goods, and even to ameliorate fluctuations in local currencies caused by an influx of gold from the New World. After the great fire of 1666, John Evelyn, the noted diarist, suggested ways to restore and improve the city, which included making it "fitter for commerce."[13] As the city was rebuilt after the fire, some smaller markets were consolidated to form larger ones, and medieval markets, such as Leadenhall Market, were rebuilt and improved. Taken together, these larger markets diverted trade from periodic markets and fairs, making them less and less viable over time. Along streets that had come to house retail shops, such as The Strand, shops were rebuilt with larger windows, presumably to attract the attention of passersby with a purposeful display of the wide array of goods available inside.[14]

As the flow of goods from around the world became steadier and more reliable, what might be called a virtuous circle ensued. Merchants competed to draw shoppers—for now we can use that term to designate those people who regularly patronize shops not only to buy but also simply to look at goods—who were attracted by novelty and variety. Thus they began more regularly to organize their wares into eye-catching and changing displays. Competition among British merchants spurred so many innovations in retailing practice in the eighteenth century as to create a "consumer revolution" running parallel with and, indeed, fueling that country's contemporary Industrial Revolution.[15] As early as 1727, Daniel Defoe noted that merchants would sometimes spend more on furnishing their shop than on the combined value of the goods inside. They would lure customers with sumptuous painting schemes, gilding, and fine decorations, as well as with elaborate displays of goods, increasingly visible from the street through larger shop windows. Such extravagance in display had formerly been uncommon, Defoe wrote, but it had since become "a rule in trade."[16] The population was growing, too, which led to yet more shops to provide for even more people. As British merchants made deeper inroads into Asia and North America, trade only accelerated. Shops had become a fixture of urban life. British shops, filled with goods from British colonies and British manufacturers, became famous throughout Europe. Although the origin and tenor of the phrase "a nation of shopkeepers" is disputed, it appeared at the end of the eighteenth century to characterize the basis for Britain's domestic economy.

Shopping was also becoming common far from cities, along frontiers of the New World, in the form of the trading post. In many ways, the trading post was the most civilized place on the frontier. Warring parties could meet up at the trading post since everyone had become accustomed to, and needful of, the same goods. Weapons were put aside while rivals perused metal tools, jewelry, or vermillion, a pigment from China that became popular with some Native American groups for use in face painting. Bartering was common at trading posts, but being far from other shops, the posts encouraged payment with convenient and easily carried items, such as valuable metals, tokens, or coins, thereby helping to habituate customers to the abstract value of currency instead of tangible goods. Still, trading posts were leading collectors of furs, which would fetch high prices back in Europe. The most valuable beaver pelts were those that had been worn by a Native American for years and had become greasy and soft; they were the height of fashion in Paris in the late eighteenth century.[17]

One figure in particular deserves special note here: Josiah Wedgwood, an industrialist who was active from the 1760s through the end of the eighteenth century. At first, Wedgwood was known for technical innovations in the manufacture of ceramics, the market for which had grown substantially in this period. But lax patent and trademark regulation and enforcement meant that many of his techniques were copied, and he saw little profit from them. He then turned his attention to selling his ceramics and in doing so, invented or popularized many marketing methods that remain in wide use today. For example, he drew from current events for his pottery designs, focusing on developments that were already of great public interest, the most notable of which were the excavations at Pompeii. He adapted antique patterns unearthed there and sold reproduction pieces that spoke of distant travel and times past. In addition, he sought wealthy sponsors, sometimes agreeing to unprofitable commissions so that he could honestly claim that fashion and taste leaders favored his works. He was then careful to display such commissions publicly before delivering them to his clients. Wedgwood had effectively invented the celebrity endorsement.

But he went even further: he exhibited new designs on narrow streets in order to guarantee crowds and generate a sense of frenzy; he planned shortages to do the same, limiting his stock so that prices would be driven higher; in a London warehouse, he set up a showroom organized so that clerks could sell expensive items to elite buyers while other customers could serve themselves from shelves arranged by price points; special showcases were fitted with curtains to create changing displays. He gave ambassadors fine objects to show to foreign royalty and generated an international trade so substantial that he developed entire lines for different countries (complete with catalogs from which to order), hiring translators to fill orders from overseas. He orchestrated prices, keeping them high for the rich at first and then dropping them before interest waned in order to entice other classes to buy. Presuming his customers' satisfaction, he even created what may have been the first money-back guarantee. He invented product placement, not only hiring leading artists to paint vases themselves but also to include a Wedgwood design in one of the artist's paintings. Artists obliged, since by rendering a Wedgwood vase, they were at the same time communicating their own taste and sense of fashion. Wedgwood, perhaps the first to do so, understood and developed the power of a brand. He realized that alongside the inherent quality of his goods, he was also engendering a sense of exclusivity for anyone who wanted to own them. Wedgwood, in short, was the Shakespeare of shopping.[18]

Shops, the setting for shopping, likewise continued to change. They began to take on nearly all the characteristics we now associate with retail spaces, including the paramount importance of display. Indeed, nearly all aspects of the shop come to be governed by the need to enhance display: more goods, better lighting, attractive and even "narrative" displays, easy access and circulation through the shop, and a much sharper division between a shop's operations, including bookkeeping, storage, and display.[19] Because industrialization often led to lower prices, many manufactured goods were increasingly affordable for a larger segment of the population, which meant that an attractive enough display might divert more and more of the people walking past a shop.

At the same time, industrialization also lowered the manufacturing cost of construction materials, the most important of which, for shopping, was flat glass. Glass was once a great luxury, subject to regulation and taxation, but with mass production in the early nineteenth century, it became a common material, available in larger and larger sheets. Large panels of glass allowed shops to open wide, making more and more of the interior visible to the street. Another late eighteenth-century innovation, gas lighting, made shop interiors visible at night, too. Indeed, shops, along with theaters, were among the first places to make use of gas lighting. Doing so only continued an earlier custom whereby municipalities often required lights outside shops as a form of street lighting in those places where the public might be expected to gather. The architectural profession noticed, and architects began to include shops in their practices. Henry Holland, for example, gained a reputation as a shop designer; he also designed the Royal Theatre in London, which featured shops along the street front.[20]

In turn, whole urban districts were designed or remodeled to accommodate shopping, which was by now well along in the transformation from being a means of procuring necessities to a form of urban entertainment. Commercial thoroughfares were already established, with London's The Strand and Cheapside among the best known, and "High Street," the common name for shopping corridors in many English towns. The first purpose-built shopping street in London was Regent Street, designed beginning in 1811 by John Nash, a society architect who would soon become the favorite of George IV when he was still prince regent. The street was intended to link Charing Cross, a center of London social life, with a series of residential terraces, also built to Nash's designs, lining Regent's Park, to the north. Although the development required government approval, it was financed almost entirely by private developers, who hired other leading architects to design individual buildings to guarantee the street would conform to leading fashions.

In designing the rows of shop fronts, Nash and other architects faced a conundrum. Then current classical taste and, indeed, millennia of architectural convention dictated that a building had to appear dignified or, at the very least, sturdy and stable. But merchants increasingly wanted their shops to be wide open to the street so that passersby could gaze upon the artfully displayed goods and be lured inside. How could the responsible architect reconcile this conflict between wide open intervals at the base of classically costumed buildings above? Porticoes, such as those at The Quadrant, a curving portion of Regent Street, could screen the shop fronts, while also affording shelter for pedestrians. But the most common solution was to emphasize vertical lines, whether as piers or pilasters, running the full height of the building or springing from deeply rusticated bases, which transmitted a sense of compression and weight even when the intervals between piers were relatively wide (Figure 1.3). Many buildings also disguised their mass with a strong cornice line about two-thirds of the way up, to visually diminish the building's height. The result was a continuous street façade that emphasized the horizontal length of the shopping street rather than the sometimes wobbly looking support of any one building. In fact, many of the buildings proved structurally suspect and were later rebuilt more sturdily and with even larger shop fronts. In any case, Nash's designs were well timed: iron was coming into greater use to support wider spans in buildings, and glass was becoming available in larger sizes to fill the shops' widened windows.[21] As if in concert, the 1815 Congress of Vienna defused political tensions following the French Revolution, Napoleon's defeat, and the dismantling of the Holy Roman Empire and so ushered in a period of accelerated trade throughout Europe, which, in turn, fueled the appearance of even more shops.

This emerging urban reality soon found its way into the cultural imagination as various representations appeared that captured the proliferation of new commercial streets. Entrepreneurs put together lists of local businesses, often charging merchants for the privilege of appearing in their directory. These would in turn be sold to out-of-town vendors or buyers seeking to find specific sorts of merchandise in the city. In time, some directories were pictorialized, providing striking images of whole urban corridors given over to commerce. Taken together, these pictorial

Figure 1.3. A recent photograph of a section of Regent Street, London, showing the long, uniform building edge lined with ground-floor shops. *Source: CC by Marcio Cabral de Moura.*

directories, often with lively activities depicted in the foreground, create a tableau of multiple urban hubs, each of which was extending tendrils of trade to outlying areas to form vast regional and, often, international circuits of commerce.[22] To observers at the time, the twin currents of goods moving in and out of the city and people, often strangers, chasing after those goods, flowed into one another to form a characteristic feature of modern urban life: thronged streets and a new sort of rushed experience, where people and things merge into torrents of frenetic impressions. William Wordsworth captured this hybrid energy wonderfully in a section of his "Prelude," composed at the start of the nineteenth century, regarding the time he spent in London. He saw flowing an "endless stream of men and moving things!"

> On strangers, of all ages; the quick dance
> Of colours, lights, and forms; the deafening din;
> The comers and the goers face to face,
> Face after face; the string of dazzling wares,
> Shop after shop, with symbols, blazoned names,
> And all the tradesman's honours overhead.[23]

Wordsworth was hurtling through a city full of shops full of things and, seemingly, all of humanity shopping there. In doing so he recorded an urban vision born of commerce: intense activity comprised equally of distracted people and diverting things—"face to face,/Face after face; the string of dazzling wares,/Shop after shop"—coursing irresistibly along city streets.

A GOLDEN AGE OF SHOPPING

As goods surged through the marketplace in the wake of the industrial and consumer revolutions, other types of dedicated shopping streets appeared. The most novel of these is the arcade: a linear pedestrian passageway, covered by a glass roof, faced on both sides with shops and usually passing through the interior of a city block. Just as the shop is defined by its physical enclosure of the act of shopping for any one item, so too did the arcade enclose shopping more generally, understood as the act of moving from one shop to another. Although large-scale industrial production was more advanced in England than in France, arcades, or *passages* in French, appeared first in Paris. The French Revolution had conclusively broken the influence of guilds, which, despite their declining power, had still affected French commerce through the eighteenth century. Paris grew quickly in the years following the revolution, and pedestrian, carriage, and cart traffic filled its mostly unpaved streets. The arcade was free of the congestion and filth of crowded streets and, by virtue of a glass roof, assured a temperate climate year round. Evincing the very latest in new construction materials, iron and glass, and filled with goods from around the world, arcades became some of the most fashionable spots in the city. They were often the first public or semipublic place to be illuminated with gas lighting. The late eighteenth century witnessed the construction of several arcades, but most were built in the first half of the nineteenth century.

Quickly becoming a favored commercial venue for the city's burgeoning middle class, there were about fifty arcades in Paris by the mid-nineteenth century. Travelers to the city were charmed by the arcades and brought home excited news of them. Dozens were then built elsewhere in Europe and several in the United States. Since the use of iron minimized the supporting structure, grand arrangements of goods blossomed in shop fronts, uninhibited by the heavier architectural frames that bordered stores on the boulevards. In turn, arcade shoppers took special delight in admiring one large and well-appointed window display after another in a continuous visual experience that we call today "window shopping."[24] While individual shops had already been emphasizing the display of goods, the arcade, in a sense, emphasized the display of the shops themselves (Figure 1.4). They created an entire world of shopping. To put it another way, the industrial and consumer revolutions that so powerfully altered everyday encounters with the material world found their spatial corollary in the arcade.[25]

By all accounts the greatest single moment in the nineteenth century for the visual display of commercial goods occurred at the Great Exhibition of the Works of Industry of All Nations, held in London in 1851 (Figure 1.5). The exhibition was contained within a building stretching over a third of a mile and built entirely of iron and glass, which earned it the nickname of the "Crystal Palace." The appearance of a vast, light-drenched interior filled with tens of thousands of goods gathered from around the world and arranged in evocative pavilions displaying novel machinery or representing foreign countries was unprecedented and the subject of countless discussions throughout Europe. Not only was it the world's largest commercial space for the span of the six months it was open; it was also the first time that the world's nations staged a competition with one another in terms of their commercial output, a display of national shops, so to speak. The Exhibition also demonstrated the extent to which window shopping was deeply gratifying in itself, for, in fact, nothing was actually available for sale while the Exhibition was open.

Figure 1.4. Providence Arcade, Providence, Rhode Island, c. 1885. The fashion for arcades reached the United States in 1828, when a grand two-story arcade opened in Providence. Rather than being assembled from easements at the interior of a block, it was built as a freestanding building. *Source: The Arcade, circa 1885, in Virtual Exhibits, Item #197.* http://sos.ri.gov/virtualarchives/items/show/197.

Following its close in October 1851, however, nearly every one of the numerous items was purchased in just a few days by eager buyers.

The Crystal Palace sparked the tradition of world's fairs, occasional global showcases of national and corporate genius. It also likely inspired Aristide Boucicaut, founder of a small shop in Paris in 1838. Prior to the Exhibition, he had already expanded his store, named Le Bon Marché, with additional "departments," zones dedicated to selling certain classes of goods. Such "department stores" had appeared even before this time, but they comprised a building type whose full potential was only first recognized by Boucicaut as he attended a large exhibition in Paris in 1855 that was modeled on the Crystal Palace. Many of the traits of shopping familiar to us today were pioneered or developed by Boucicaut. Possibly the most important of these was fixed pricing. Commonplace now, fixed prices were a crucial innovation. They lubricated sales by eliminating negotiations between customers and a store's owner, who was then free to turn his attention elsewhere, as multiple sales clerks could now manage the actual transactions. It also meant that clerks were easier to train, since they had less to do to clinch a sale, and they could each therefore handle more customers over the course of the day. In turn, the store

Figure 1.5. Thomas De La Rue Printer and Stationer, exhibit at the Great Exhibition of the Works of Industry of All Nations. ***Source: Lithograph, Lloyd, London, 1851. © Victoria and Albert Museum, London.***

could expand more readily since it was no longer limited to the number of clerks on the floor.

In addition, Le Bon Marché allowed customers to return unsatisfactory merchandise, with the promise of an exchange or money-back guarantee. Boucicaut stressed friendly service; offered free delivery, even to foreign countries; and hired multilingual correspondents who could take orders from overseas. He also took advantage of the trend in ready-to-wear items, and with increased sales, he exploited economies of scale, negotiating lower prices by buying in bulk and then turning around to sell more goods at lowered prices, resulting in a virtuous commercial cycle that raised profits even as prices dropped. He trusted the power of advertising and assembled an entire public relations department. Perhaps most significant, he believed in the idea of shopping as a form of entertainment, making it appear to customers as if sales were only one of many reasons to visit his store.

In 1867 Boucicaut opened a new store, engineered by Gustave Eiffel, with advanced building techniques and featuring an interior so open and grand that the vast array of merchandise could be seen all at once, the visual experience introduced so convincingly at the Crystal Palace. This open construction was made possible by new technologies that proffered a spectacle of goods drawn together from all parts of the nation and far reaches of the world. In-store events were held in this interior space, including concerts that filled the store with live music. Customers could walk past smaller rooms and niches in which demonstrations were being given or English lessons conducted. Displays were placed directly on the showroom floor rather than behind a counter, to encourage browsing. Customers could even join guided tours of the store, which further suggested it was a world in itself, populated only by goods rather than people and distributed over a varied and continually unfolding landscape. Le Bon Marché became more than simply the city's dominant retailer. It became a leading institution of middle-class culture, a place where to a large extent, middle-class culture was powerfully and persuasively imagined and inhabited (Figure 1.6).[26]

Within a few years, other department stores opened in Paris and, indeed, elsewhere in Europe and the United States. Large cities would have several of them. They were effectively enormous machines, with advanced technologies, such as electric lighting, elevators, or internal pneumatic delivery systems. They employed a large and diverse staff. They often featured dining rooms, kitchens, and living quarters as well as variously sized offices and storage, shipping, and transfer facilities, and they were powered by literally tons of mechanical equipment. But aside from some of the staff, all of this was hidden from the customers, who instead saw only a vast and spreading interior laced with fabrics, exotic goods, and elaborate displays adorning and veiling architectural elements, such as columns or walls. Department stores contained luxurious

Figure 1.6. Central Stairway, Bon Marché, Paris, 1892. The image makes vivid the unfolding and palatial character of the Parisian department store. Souvenir of the Bon Marché, Paris Plan of Paris. Paris: E. Plon, Nourrit and Co., 1892. ***Source: Courtesy, John Hay Library, Brown University Library.***

amenities, such as well-appointed lounges or public reading rooms that would make them destinations in themselves. As such, they functioned as a kind of social condenser, attracting a wider range of social classes than any other type of shop. Even an elevator, so commonplace today, would have been a radically new space at the time. It offered an unaccustomed sense of vertical movement along with its unprecedented convenience. People from different social classes and all walks of life wanted to ride one and would willingly compress themselves into the uncomfortable space, unthinkable in any other situation.

Most important, the department store was one place where women could safely appear in public without male accompaniment and without damage to their reputation, since shopping was deemed to be a largely female activity and the store was a safe environment. A preponderance of female customers meant that department stores were *the* pseudo-public place for women. In Émile Zola's *The Ladies Paradise,* which is set in a Parisian department store, shopping even takes on erotic and ecstatic dimensions as women crowd each other and swoon in surrender to achingly delicate fabrics bathed in soft light tumbling through skylights and drifting through lace to settle on the incandescent union of shoppers and merchandise.[27] There was no comparable building in any city with such boisterous commercial life or overscaled visual, even emotional, effects. In the United States, women became prominent at the close of the nineteenth century in the City Beautiful movement, an effort to make cities more congenial. In a sense, they sought to extend to the city at large the sort of controlled environment they knew from department stores. They argued explicitly for the value of economic development of downtown areas, with an eye toward genteel improvements of benefit to all.[28]

By 1900 there were large and lavish department stores in virtually every large city in Europe and the United States. Paris alone had half a dozen: Les Galeries du Louvre, La Samaritaine, Galeries Lafayette, Le Palais de la Nouveauté, Les Grands Magasins Dufayel, and Printemps, in addition to Le Bon Marché. They featured ornate architecture; extensive art programs that encompassed statuary, paintings, and decorative arts; and public events, sometimes held in purpose-built theaters seating thousands and exploiting flamboyant lighting and new visual technologies such as cinema. They extended credit and encouraged installment purchases. As a corollary, they also became adept at developing financial data on their customers since, in many instances, they became responsible for collecting debts. They were often leading advertisers in any city and, certainly, major employers. Department stores were, in short, pioneers in the formation of a consumer society.[29]

With their cornucopia of goods and amenities and their sheer scale, department stores bred a novel sociability that reached far into the civic realm. They recalled the city in their multifariousness but were clean, safe, and gracious. In many ways, they proffered visions of a better city, characterized by circulation and variety yet open to all and presenting none of the dangers—dirty, crowded streets; malevolent figures; Spartan amenities, if any; even the threat of rain or cold—so frequent in the city outdoors. They became powerful institutions within the city, well-known urban landmarks, and a kind of public museum. Le Bon Marché, for example, produced a labyrinth game that featured the store as part of an urban circuit traversing the city of Paris and its best-known and best-loved landmarks. The city was reimagined as a social space whose benefits flowed naturally from its commercial premise. No purchase was necessary to linger in this urban vision. Rather, the department store held a purchase on the civic imagination, as it demonstrated that private control of what was easily supposed a public space could result in benefits to all. It advanced the logic of a consumer society in two key ways. First, it suggested that commercial motivations might well be a satisfactory basis for a full civic life, and second, it further distanced the production of goods from their consumption by interposing a great circus of shopping.

SHOPPING WITH THE CAR

The automobile, perhaps more than anything else, changed everything. With its unprecedented mobility the car allowed customers to chase after the best goods or the lowest prices, wherever they might be found. Merchants, in turn, found that they could lower their costs by moving outside the city, where rents were cheaper, and then lower prices which, in turn, attracted more customers. As the quality of manufactured goods generally improved and the middle class grew larger and better positioned to afford them, low prices became a shopping magnet not only luring customers but, in the end, anchoring large commercial centers. This model of decentralized shopping was most effective in cities that were young and still developing, with an apron of cheap land surrounding them. The strip, a new venue for shopping, was born when suburban stores began to locate adjacent to one another as a way to draw ever more mobile shoppers away from central shopping districts and to emphasize convenient parking as much as they touted their goods (Figure 1.7). Indeed, the automobile service station was a model for the suburban strip. It was a new building type that in city settings, broke with the longstanding continuity of building façades as a way to accommodate drive-in customers. Some stations started selling necessities, such as food, while motorists waited for their tanks to be filled. As more drivers came to shop, parking areas grew in size, and eventually, store façades were oriented to a parking area within the building lot rather than to the street. Los Angeles was a pioneer in this regard as "superstations," gas stations with plenty of other items for sale, would advertise their location rather than their particular lines of goods.[30]

With lower prices growing more important as a means to lure shoppers, stores began to innovate in cost-cutting methods. Minimizing the store's labor force, comprising largely clerks and stock boys, was a key part of this effort. Previously, most goods were kept behind a counter; a customer asked to see an item, and a clerk retrieved it so that the customer could weigh the merits of the possible purchase firsthand (Figure 1.8). Even in department stores, customers may have inspected an item at a display on the sales floor, but a clerk was still needed to fetch it from stock. In other words, clerks mediated the relationship between customers and the goods for sale. Eliminating clerks meant finding a way to have the object speak more directly to the customer and if possible, make a compelling sales pitch.

This was the role played by packaging (Figure 1.9). Packaging had been a familiar element of retail for centuries, in fact. Printed labels were used in seventeenth-century London, most commonly in pharmacies, where they were placed on bottles of drops or boxes of pills and powders, although most other goods were sold in bulk. A major step forward arrived with technical advances in canning food as a way to retard spoil-

Figure 1.7. ***Park and Shop*, exterior with parked automobiles, an example of an early strip marketplace featuring shops set back from the property edge to allow for easy parking of cars. Theodor Horydczak, ca. 1920. *Source: Horydczak Collection, Library of Congress Prints and Photographs Division Washington, D.C.***

Figure 1.8. Meat counter at Fred Gouer's grocery store, Baltimore, Maryland, 1920s. The clerk retrieves most of the merchandise for the customer and puts bulk items into smaller containers. *Source: Theodor Horydczak, c. 1920. Horydczak Collection, Library of Congress Prints and Photographs Division Washington, D.C.*

age and facilitate transportation. Better preservation led in turn to greater acceptance of canned foods by the public, and it was especially useful to the military. Early packaging also began to be promoted for sanitary reasons (open barrels of, say, grains often attracted rodents) and increasingly for convenience since a premeasured and prepackaged product meant that no time was lost while a clerk scooped, weighed, and wrapped up some oats. With no access to their insides until they were opened, however, cans and boxes required labels that were both descriptive and reliable.

Packaging grew in popularity for a number of reasons by the end of the nineteenth century. For one, printing labels had become far less expensive, and new machinery could rapidly cut, fold, and glue together cardboard boxes or produce glass bottles, which formerly had to be hand blown one at a time. For another, the general public was increasingly literate, which meant that more customers could read and appreciate labels. Manufacturers began to notice that good packaging could mean the difference between the success and failure of a product. Lifesavers,

Figure 1.9. Father and son shopping in a cooperative store, Greenbelt, Maryland, 1942. Customers have learned to read packages that describe their own contents. *Source: Farm Security Administration—Office of War Information Photograph Collection (Library of Congress).*

for example, were not a popular candy when first introduced in 1912; they tended to taste of the glue used to assemble the boxes they were sold in. Repackaged in foil and, importantly, routinely positioned at the point of sale, Lifesavers swiftly became a best seller. The shiny cylinder of a stack of Lifesavers remains a landmark in packaging and surely occupies at least a little real estate in the mind of anyone reading this essay.[31]

Manufacturers also noticed that customers who bought their products repeatedly were effectively being exposed to a brand and, by a reciprocal logic, the brand might be promoted as much as the product itself. Thus, manufacturers turned to advertising agencies that specialized in marketing rather than just placing notices of availability in local newspapers, which had long been the mainstay of the advertising business. Large companies, such as Proctor & Gamble, even began to hire in-house brand managers early in the twentieth century, and trade organizations arose to help regularize and enhance the marketing power of packaging as much as its technical performance. Packaging as a result became far more sophisticated and ambitious. The enlarged role of packaging might even have influenced the industrial design profession, which emerged in the 1920s to prepare commercial products, ranging from small appliances to automobiles, for the mass market. With annual style changes in automobiles, for example, designers could signal progress in performance or comfort with a new package, so to speak, whether or not anything had actually improved under the hood.

Packaging clearly has important practical roles to play in retail: it protects contents from damage or contamination; facilitates the transportation of goods; can make storage more efficient; can make it easier for the customer to pick up an item and carry it; and can make it easier for a clerk or cashier, a new and specialized type of clerk, to ring the item up. Boxed soap flakes, for example, meant the customer no longer had to bring her own container to the store and ask a clerk to measure out a pound or two.

Packaging created a seismic shift in shopping. It made possible the self-service store, where customers could roam aisles, read labels, and choose items on their own. In terms of sociability, the self-service store was a space of discourse between a shopper and a series of manufacturers' proxies, the package. The closest precedent for such a space would be a museum, where visitors serially encounter objects that would be identified and possibly explained by a label. The best-known self-service stores were the variety, or "five-and-dime," stores pioneered by F. W. Woolworth in the late-nineteenth century. By purchasing directly from manufacturers rather than through wholesalers and by creating a self-service environment, Woolworth's was able to undercut competing retailers and establish one of the most successful retail enterprises of the entire twentieth century. These stores were filled with many different types of goods, and with many different manufacturers competing to sell to self-service stores, prices were kept as low as possible.

Sales strategies such as those of Woolworth's, which relied for its success on bulk purchases, became the foundation of the chain store. Driven by new economies of scale, along with packaging, automatic bottling, product branding, and strengthened trademark protections, not to mention improved transportation, manufactured goods could be distributed from central plants with far greater magnitude than previously. Self-service and chain stores effectively created national markets. Moreover, chain stores developed structured routes through their aisles, making displays ever more important. A shopper would therefore not only find the same products in distant cities, she—the pronoun is used in the rest of this chapter since shopping had become a mainly female enterprise—also would find them in the exact same spot within the different stores. Chain stores were mightily resisted at first since they transferred some portion of a community's wealth to a corporate headquarters, but the values they offered at the level of the individual customer were too great to withstand. Similar to the manner in which mass-produced goods prevailed in the marketplace over handmade objects, despite often being of lower quality, so too did chains displace independent or mom-and-pop stores. In effect, chain stores industrialized consumption as surely as conveyor belts accelerated production. It is at this point that we can begin to freely use the term "consumer" rather than customer, in the sense that the shopper is, at least in the eyes of manufacturers, advertisers and retailers, no longer an individual so much as she is herself a commodity. The sociability of shopping in older types of stores, it turned out, slowed down sales.

As packaging was extended across all categories of products, the act of shopping changed dramatically. Self-service stores were visually dense, almost predatory in nature: a shopper might imagine herself hunting the aisles for goods, but in a very real sense, the packages were jostling to arrest the shopper's attention. With no clerk, or for that matter, butcher, baker, or grocer, to intervene, manufacturers could speak directly to customers through their packaging. As brand consciousness developed, packages began to do more than just relate what was inside the wrapper. They promoted beliefs, even systems of belief. Picking up a package meant inviting a conversation. As the shopper scans the package, she, in effect, asks questions of it. In short order, the shopper finds herself in visual and linguistic dialogue with an inanimate thing.

The package, in other words, encourages commercial discourse with itself; the package is a container that has learned how to talk. It performs the merits of a product while the shopper attends to that performance. In many ways, the package is a kind of expert on itself. It speaks not only about its specific components and general quality but also about its uses and storage, and it provides testimonies to its unique attributes. It conjures a world comprising ritual and attitude about itself, modest, to be sure, but sufficient to impel it across the threshold of ownership from shop to shopper. Once it is visually engaged, the package becomes a philosophy of self-endorsement, with a passion and subtlety that could hardly be expected of any clerk. In this way, self-service stores might be understood to be equally as sociable as earlier stores, although the relationships within the store develop between a shopper and an item and, with the "comparison shopping" required by a mature marketplace replete with different brands of the same product, as a kind of contest of fealty between goods, all of it overseen by the acquisitive eye of the shopper.[32]

All of these developments converge seamlessly in the supermarket, which must count as one of the most successful and fastest developing retail environments ever introduced. Ralph's, in Southern California, is a prime example of a store founded upon packaging, pricing, and parking. It was already a successful chain in the late-nineteenth century, but, in 1925, store managers experimented with self-service shopping. They noticed that customers bought more with each visit if they were allowed to make their own selections. Ralph's moved toward a self-service format and provided baskets for customers, which encouraged them to buy even more at one time. With faster merchandise turnover, Ralph's was able to lower its profit margin on any one item but increase profits overall, adding new stores in underserved areas until it became the dominant grocery retailer of the entire region. This model has since become standard for nearly all grocery stores.[33] At the same time, automobiles made it possible for shoppers to haul even more goods from the store while ice boxes and, starting in the 1920s, electric refrigerators gave shoppers a place to put them once they got home. In fact, customers were explicitly advised to visit grocery stores to learn strategies for effective storage and attractive display within their own homes. In this sense, the refrigerator functioned as off-site inventory storage for the growing food industry as relations of capital infiltrated the domestic sphere more and more deeply.[34]

Suburban population skyrocketed in the United States in the postwar years, and stores moved to the city peripheries to service it. The suburbs were based on the automobile and so too were the stores that located there, many of them aggregated next to one another in shopping centers. Shopping centers swiftly began to take on specific forms that maximized their commercial premise, resulting in the shopping mall, the mid-twentieth-century contribution to retail consumption. At the Northgate Mall, for example, opened in Seattle in 1947, two department stores anchored a corridor of shops between them to form the first "dumbbell plan," which became the most common plan type for the mall. The first mall to be enclosed was built in Minneapolis in 1956, which, like nineteenth-century arcades, protected shoppers from bad weather.[35] Victor Gruen, the best-known mall designer of the postwar period, articulated the mall's spatial logic. Tenants would come and go, he noted; consequently, the mall had to be flexibly designed and built of materials that could be easily and quickly renovated. It should also be designed to maximize circulation past the greatest number of shop fronts and thereby encourage people to go into many stores rather than just the one they may have been planning to visit. But since it was a "shopping center" rather than a "selling center," he wrote, it ought to have amenities, including community buildings, landscaping, art, and programmed activities.

Shopping, implied Gruen, was not only about getting things. It was in itself a deeply social activity. Like its forebears in the Greek agora or the medieval marketplace, the mall was ultimately a civic space and therefore should have a public countenance.[36] Currently, there are tens of thousands of shopping malls in North America alone—countless more around the world—some of them serving a few towns; some of them "super regional," drawing customers from several counties away; and some, like the Mall of America, which opened in Bloomington, Minnesota, in 1992, or the Golden Resources Shopping Mall, Beijing, 2004, affectionately known as the Great Mall of China, global tourist destinations themselves.

In social terms, malls indeed have come to function as public places. They encourage face-to-face contact, with rows of smaller shops staffed by clerks and shoppers assured of help from someone on the sales floor, even if anchor stores garner the majority of sales. And the common areas of the mall seem to return an air of ease, comfort, and civility to the act of shopping. Indeed, like the earlier arcades, the shopping mall is essentially an enclosed street and invites a leisurely stroll. Like the expositions, the shopping mall creates its own world with its grand scale and cornucopia of goods, and, like the department store, malls feature amenities for comfort and amusement. But while possessing all the attributes of the civic realm, malls are privately owned, which means they have the right to exclude certain individuals or activities. In fact, in recognition of their semblance to public spaces, the courts have been asked to adjudicate limits on the mall owners' power to control speech or behavior, to consider whether or not the mall actually is a public place. At the same time, of course, the postwar suburban shopping mall is an explicit rejection of the city, the origin and model for the civic realm. The mall was premised on cheap land outside the city but close to motorized shoppers and, with its moat of parking, dissociated even from its suburban context. Perhaps the greatest irony of all is that suburban malls were so successful that in the 1970s cities themselves started developing commercial "urban entertainment destinations"—shopping malls with programmed activities and scripted architectural charm—as a way to draw suburbanites back downtown, if only for an afternoon.[37]

Malls were very successful shopping venues, but that did not make them the least expensive. The magnet of low prices continued to draw economically minded consumers. A spate of discount stores was founded in the 1960s, notably Walmart, Kmart, and Target. They came to be called "big box" stores since they were effectively enormous warehouses that shoppers drove to and through which they circulated. Although they offered better-known national brands of goods, they focused increasingly on generic products, sometimes manufactured in the same plant as the better-known item but appearing under a different label for a lower price. As with grocery stores before them, the big box stores relied on narrow profit margins adding up through large sales volumes. Soon, in an effort to keep down costs, the big box stores began to vertically integrate: they developed their own store brands for many product lines, operated their own trucking companies, advanced lines of store credit, and paid closer attention to the physical retail environment to create a pleasant and imageable or distinct shopping experience. Big box stores took a big bite out of regional shopping malls; together, they continued to drain the life from downtown commercial centers.[38]

Shopping in a big box store offers an intensified version of self-service. It is largely a private affair (for a narrative about shopping in such a store, see Chapter 8). With loyalty dissolved by the corrosive power of low prices, shoppers hold little expectation of a long-term relationship with any single store, which explains the great effort big box stores put into advertising, or in the case of Walmart, the use of "greeters" to put a face on an otherwise anonymous experience of commodity acquisition. Another indication of the evacuation of social relationships is the extended warranty. Essentially a bet against quality, warranties have become important "profit centers," an industry phrase designating a sector of trade that has a high profit margin relative to other aspects of a company's business. The warranty promises repair in the event of some malfunction, but it also serves as a token of trust. Trust, which in the commercial realm once inhered in a bond between a customer and a retailer, has been commodified. Formerly, if something went wrong with your purchase, you brought it back for repair to the store, which was aiming for a long-term relationship with you. In an advanced consumer society, extended warranties also underscore that many items are expected to be as evanescent as our loyalty to any one commercial institution. However, although big box stores overstep any single proprietor's particularities (after all, a Target is a Target is a Target), they are nonetheless brimming with encounters in time and space between individuals and material objects, and they are governed by culturally distinct rules, making them bastions of sociability when compared to Internet shopping.

SHOPPING REMAINDERED

If shopping as we have come to understand it is defined by the spatial enclosure of commercial acquisition, then it ends with the rise of the Internet: everywhere all at once and all the time. The idea of purchasing goods while remaining at home and having them delivered soon afterward was already in the air in the mid-twentieth century, presaged even earlier by catalog shopping, such as that promoted by Aristide Boucicaut. But widespread virtual shopping is possible only with the computer, the Internet, and graphical web browsers, all of which are buoyed on financial, transportation, and communication infrastructures that facilitate low-cost shipping, secure money and credit transfers, and abundant information regarding items for sale. We may continue to call online shopping "shopping," but the shop itself has been displaced by the website on screen.

With the Internet, the act of shopping is no longer enclosed. Indeed, it can hardly be said even to occur in physical space. Consequently, the stages of acquisition once contained by the shop have splintered. Learning about an item, physically encountering it, comparing it to other items, assessing quality and value, perhaps getting someone else's opinion, buying it, and then taking possession of it are neither co-spatial nor cotemporal. Finding a shop is superseded by dropping keywords in a search box, and handling an object to learn about it is displaced by reviewing images sorted by one of several factors, such as price or "most popular," whatever that might mean. With virtual carts, shoppers can choose their items one day and buy them weeks later, maybe at three in the morning, dressed only in pajamas.

With the disappearance of the shop, sociability changes as well. Typically, the only face-to-face interaction in online shopping is to say thanks to the person who delivers the package, and even that can be avoided. People can interact—if that is the right word for it—by offering feedback online, although the ensuing string of comments tends to focus on product quality or else on inflection points in online shopping, that is, on an item's transition from onscreen appearance to in-hand presence, with consumer satisfaction residing in the accuracy of digital representations. However mediated one's encounter with merchandise was formerly, it was usually social in nature, for social rules govern our relations with material objects as well as with other people. The shop, in other words, is a social space because it is bound by social rules that can adjust to technological change. The Internet, in contrast, is governed by technological parameters that can accommodate social conventions.

At the same time that shopping has diminished in social complexity, it has become a model for social interactions more generally. Citizens of a consumer society have learned to approach all interactions in terms of a choice made from a range of options that is then concluded with a transfer of currency. Politicians, eager to learn what will earn the voters' currency—their votes—make use of marketing tools, such as focus groups, a survey technique developed in the 1950s to investigate consumer preferences and thus determine what issues they will emphasize or "sell."[39] They realize, as did manufacturers decades before, that branding—the creation of an identity that distinguishes a good, or persona, from its competitors—could displace actual content. Consumer–voters are encouraged to think about differentiating features in one or another candidate's program or simply their appearance. In retrospect, the spaces of shopping have turned out to be so many incubators for consumer society.

The swift growth of online shopping has been powered by its convenience, selection, and competitive prices, leading Netscape founder Marc Andreessen to prophesy the end of retail stores altogether: "Software eats retail," as he put it.[40] But the shop is not only a place of material exchange but of social exchange as well. It is a place to learn about contemporary social values through the channels of human enterprise. It answers a deeply human need to be part of a public sphere, even when the immediate premise is acquisition. Despite the rise of e-commerce, stores will remain important shopping venues, although, of course, they will inevitably change.

Shopping likely will become an amalgam of e-commerce and physical interaction. Already, it is a common practice to order an item online and pick it up at a nearby store. Shoppers increasingly bring their smartphones with them to stores to compare products and prices from other retailers or to get more detailed information regarding sizes and styles. Initially, stores frowned upon this activity, but many now accept and try to exploit it since digital media open up new channels of communication with shoppers. As a result, retailers have placed screens inside stores for online browsing and to offer more information about items, including details of their composition or production or suggestions for their use. Displays can show items in action or present in-store commercials to excite a customer's imagination and to encourage the purchase of accessory items. By doing so, stores offer far richer interactions with goods than can be achieved just through a computer screen at home. In keeping with the idea of an "experience economy"—an economy wherein not just goods are traded but experience itself is commodified and sold—stores may become the scaffolding for immersive experiences, and in turn, goods may become souvenirs of those experiences.[41]

In this view, the future of shopping may very well depend upon the physical shop. A space for interaction with the shopping public is exactly the asset that online retailers do not possess. The inherent value of such a space is demonstrated by media conglomerates such as Apple and Disney, which maintain retail outlets. Such stores appear more as stages for the performance of corporate identity than as conventional shops. They aim to build brand loyalty more than to generate immediate revenue. Apple, for instance, staffs its stores with enthusiasts; paid a salary rather than a commission, they are motivated by a passion for technology, not profit, thus reflecting a facet of Apple's corporate persona. In addition, customers might be motivated to rush to a store through a "flash sale," a brief markdown advertised only to a select group, such as those who have "liked" a store on Facebook or who "follow" it on Twitter. Loyalty on a social media platform can nourish in-store sales and vice versa. In turn, shoppers can post reviews of their experience at the store, thereby generating more followers online and more foot traffic on Main Street at the same time.

In this context, shops may come to be dominated by brands. The discounts of the big box store or the wide selection of a shopping mall can be replicated by e-commerce, but brands have long been premised on their value proposition—their statement of what makes them unique, unlike any other product in the same category. Brands have also been successful at extending that proposition from a core item to a family of goods, from soap, for instance, to a range of skin-care products. Brands appear now to be colonizing commercial space, too, with the distinctive themed experiences they can provide for customers. The store, in other words, may become another component of brand value. If this comes to be the case, then shops will remain a leading arena for social interactions with material objects. As this essay has argued, stores have always served as much more than sites of mere acquisition.

NOTES

1. "Quarterly Retail E-Commerce Sales, 3rd Quarter 2013," *U.S. Census Bureau News*, CB13-187 (Washington, DC: U.S. Department of Commerce, 2013) and U.S. Census Bureau, *Statistical Abstract of the United States: 2011* (Washington, DC: U.S. Department of Commerce, 2011), Table 1047. Retail Trade—Establishments, Employees, and Payroll: 2006-2007, 659.

2. Molly Harrison offers a concise overview of medieval shopping in *People and Shopping* (London: Ernest Benn, 1975), 10–31. For more on the economic role of markets, see Mark Casson and John Lee, "The Origin and Development of Markets: A Business History Perspective," *The Business History Review* 85 (Spring 2011): 9–37. David Clark argues that fixed shops were more common than has been presumed in "The Shop Within?: An Analysis of the Architectural Evidence for Medieval Shops," *Architectural History* 43 (2000): 58–87.

3. Further discussion of the "just price" for goods can be found in John Baldwin, "The Medieval Theories of the Just Price: Romanists, Canonists, and Theologians in the Twelfth and Thirteenth Centuries," *Transactions of the American Philosophical Society*, New Series, 49, no. 4 (1959): 1–92.

4. See Craig Muldrew, "Interpreting the Market: The Ethics of Credit and Community Relations in Early Modern England," *Social History* 18, no. 2 (May 1993): 163–83, and Keith Wrightson, *Earthly Necessities: Economic Lives in Early Modern Britain* (New Haven: Yale University Press, 2002).

5. See Craig Muldrew, *The Economy of Obligation* (New York, 1998). Christopher Dyer uses debt records to reconstruct class-based social relations in "The Consumer and the Market in the Later Middle Ages," *The Economic History Review*, New Series, 42, no. 3 (August 1989): 305–27.

6. For more on changes to shopping and the European economy in the Renaissance, see Dorothy Davis, "New Beginnings in Retail Distribution," and "Shopping for Pleasure in London," in *A History of Shopping* (London: Routledge & Kegan Paul, 1966), 55–71, 100–126.

7. Evelyn Welch, *Shopping in the Renaissance: Consumer Cultures in Italy 1400-1600* (New Haven: Yale University Press, 2005).

8. A. E. Richardson, "Shops and Shopkeeping Throughout the Ages," *Journal of the Royal Society of Arts* 102, no. 4928 (June 25, 1954): 610–27.

9. Alfred Edward Woodley Mason, *The Royal Exchange* (London: Royal Exchange, 1920), 21–24.

10. See Janette Dillon, *Theatre, Court, and City, 1595-1610: Drama and Social Space in London* (Cambridge: Cambridge University Press, 2000); Linda Levy Peck, *Consuming Splendor: Society and Culture in Seventeenth-Century England* (Cambridge: Cambridge University Press, 2005), and Jean Imray, "The Origins of the Royal Exchange," in *The*

Royal Exchange, ed. Ann Saunders (London: London Topographical Society, 1997), 20–35.

11. For more on women and commerce at this time, see Steve Rappaport, "The Status of Women," in *Worlds Within Worlds: Structures of Life in Sixteenth-Century London* (Cambridge: Cambridge University Press, 2002), 36–42.

12. Werner Sombart traced the shift in attitudes toward shopping to the seventeenth century. Discussed in Christopher Berry, *The Idea of Luxury. A Conceptual and Historical Investigation* (Cambridge: Cambridge University Press, 1994).

13. Peck, 4–12.

14. Richardson, 612.

15. See N. McKendrick, J. Brewer, and J. H. Plumb, *The Birth of a Consumer Society: The Commercialization of Eighteenth-Century England* (London: Europa, 1982); and J. Brewer and R. Porter, eds., *Consumption and the World of Goods* (London: Routledge, 1993). Helen Berry offers an overview of the rich literature of the consumer revolution in "Polite Consumption: Shopping in Eighteenth-Century England," *Transactions of the Royal Historical Society* 12 (2002): 375–94.

16. From 1727. Cited in Wolfgang Schivelbusch, *Disenchanted Night: The Industrialization of Light in the Nineteenth Century* (Berkeley: University of California Press, 1995), 144.

17. See Carolyn Gilman et al., "The Trading Post," and "Parisian Women's Dogs" in *Where Two Worlds Meet: The Great Lakes Fur Trade* (St. Paul: Minnesota Historical Society, 1982), 46–80.

18. McKendrick et al. (1982), 100–145.

19. See Nikolaus Pevsner, "Shops, Stores and Department Stores," *A History of Building Types* (London: Thames & Hudson, 1976), chapter 16.

20. For more on glass and shop design in the eighteenth century, see Richardson, 619–20; Claire Walsh, "Shop Design and the Display of Goods in Eighteenth-Century London," *Journal of Design History* 8, no. 3 (1995): 157–76; and Wolfgang Schivelbusch, "Shop Window." On Henry Holland, see Dorothy Stroud, *Henry Holland: His Life and Architecture* (London: Country Life, 1966).

21. For changes in English shop design more generally, see Kathryn Morrison, *English Shops and Shopping: An Architectural History* (New Haven: Yale University Press, 2004).

22. Jeffrey A. Cohen, "A Streetscape Named Desire: Long Views Through the Emerging Bourgeois City," in *Portraits of the City: Dublin and the Wider World*, eds. Gillian O'Brien and Finola O'Kane (Dublin: Four Courts Press, 2012), 22–34.

23. William Wordsworth, "Residence in London," *The Poetical Works of William Wordsworth* (London: Oxford University Press, 1913), 689.

24. See Rosalind Williams, *Dream Worlds: Mass Consumption in Late Nineteenth Century France* (Berkeley: University of California Press, 1982).

25. For more on the architecture of arcades, see Johann Friedrich Geist, *Arcades: The History of a Building Type* (Cambridge, MA: MIT Press, 1982).

26. The best resource on Le Bon Marché remains Michael Miller, *The Bon Marché: Bourgeois Culture and the Department Store, 1869-1920* (Princeton: Princeton University Press,1994).

27. The nearly erotic pleasure of shopping runs throughout Zola's novel, originally serialized and subsequently published as a novel in 1883 titled *Au Bonheur des Dames.* It is available in a number of editions. Erika Rappaport examines parallel developments in regard to women and shopping in London in *Shopping for Pleasure: Women in the Making of London's West End* (Princeton: Princeton University Press, 2000). Elizabeth Kowaleski-Wallace looks at the role of women more broadly at this time in *Consuming Subjects: Women, Shopping and Business in the Eighteenth Century* (New York: Columbia University Press, 1997).

28. Alison Isenberg, *Downtown America: A History of the Place and the People Who Made It* (Chicago: University of Chicago Press, 2005).

29. For more on American department stores and modern consumer society, see Jan Whitaker, *Service and Style: How the American Department Store Fashioned the Middle Class* (New York: St. Martin's, 2006).

30. Richard Longstreth, *The Drive-In, the Supermarket, and the Transformation of Commercial Space in Los Angeles, 1914-1941* (Cambridge, MA: MIT Press, 1999), 1–30.

31. Thomas Hine discusses Lifesavers' packaging and much more in *The Total Package: The Secret History and Hidden Meanings of Boxes, Bottles, Cans and Other Persuasive Containers* (Boston: Little, Brown, 1995).

32. In a crowded store, of course, packages compete with each other, and the result can be confusing, a situation addressed by "honest brokers," allegedly objective authorities such as *Consumer Reports* or other shopping guides. Discussed in Sharon Zukin, "Consumer Guides and the Invention of Lifestyle," *Point of Purchase: How Shopping Changed American Culture* (Routledge, 2004), 169–96.

33. Longstreth, 77–128. For more on grocery stores, see Daniel Boorstin, *The Americans: The Democratic Experience* (New York: Random House, 1974), 117–18, 443–44, and William Walsh, *The Rise and Decline of the Great Atlantic and Pacific Tea Company* (Secaucus, NJ: Lyle, Stuart, 1986).

34. For more on refrigerators in this context, see Sandy Isenstadt, "Visions of Plenty: Refrigerator Design in America around 1950," *Journal of Design History* 11, no. 4 (Autumn 1998): 311–21.

35. The literature on the shopping center and the shopping mall is voluminous. Meredith Clausen discusses the origin of shopping centers in "Northgate Regional Shopping Center—Paradigm from the Provinces," *Journal of the Society of Architectural Historians* 43, no. 2 (May 1984): 144–61. The tension between shopping centers and malls is discussed throughout Richard Longstreth, *City Center to Regional Mall: Architecture, the Automobile, and Retailing in Los Angeles, 1920-1950* (Cambridge, MA: MIT Press, 1998). The political economy of the mall is the subject of Lizabeth Cohen, "From Town Center to Shopping Center: The Reconfiguration of Community Marketplaces in Postwar America," *American Historical Review* 101 (October 1996): 1050–81. The mall's place in American culture is treated by Paco Underhill, *Call of the Mall: The Geography of Shopping* (New York: Simon & Schuster, 2005).

36. Victor Gruen and Larry Smith, *Shopping Towns USA: The Planning of Shopping Centers* (New York: Reinhold Publishing, 1960). For more on Gruen see Jeffrey Hardwick, *Mall Maker: Victor Gruen, Architect of an American Dream* (Philadelphia: University of Pennsylvania Press, 2010).

37. Margaret Crawford, "The World in a Shopping Mall," in *Variations on a Theme Park: The New American City and the End of Public Space*, ed. Michael Sorkin (New York: Noonday Press, 1992), 3–30.

38. The history of big box stores is outlined in Sharon Zukin, "From Woolworth's to Wal-Mart," in *Point of Purchase: How Shopping Changed American Culture* (New York: Routledge, 2004), 63–88. The effect of big box stores on local retailers is the subject of Troy Blanchard, et al., "Suburban Sprawl, Regional Diffusion, and the Fate of Small Retailers in a Large Retail Environment, 1977-1996," *Sociological Focus* 36, no. 4 (November 2003): 313–31.

39. For the history of market research, see Jean Converse, *Survey Research in the United States: Roots and Emergence 1890--1960* (Berkeley: University of California Press, 1986).

40. Sarah Lacy, "Andreessen predicts the death of traditional retail. Yes: Absolute death," *Pandodaily*, accessed January 7, 2014, http://pando.com/2013/01/30/andreessen-predicts-the-death-of-traditional-retail-yes-absolute-death/

41. The experience economy was defined by James Gilmore and Joseph Pine in "Welcome to the Experience Economy," *Harvard Business Review* 76, no. 4 (July-August 1998): 97–105, and *The Experience Economy: Work Is Theatre & Every Business a Stage* (Boston: Harvard Business School Press, 1999).

TWO

Woolworth to Walmart

Mass Merchandising and the Changing Culture of Consumption

Susan Strasser

"We must have cheap help or we cannot sell cheap goods," wrote Frank W. Woolworth to his store managers in 1892, when his business was still young and many of the managers were not employees but old friends and mentors, full partners in their branch stores. "When a clerk gets so good she can get better wages elsewhere, let her go—for it does not require skilled and experienced salesladies to sell our goods. You can get good honest girls at from $2 to $3 per week and I would not give $3.50," he went on. "It may look hard to some of you for us to pay such small wages but . . . one thing is certain: we cannot afford to pay good wages and sell goods as we do now, and our clerks ought to know it."[1]

Walmart is not unusual among big retailers in basing low prices in part on low wages. As Frank Woolworth discerned, mass merchandising depended from the start on sacrificing workers' interests to low prices. Nor was Walmart the first amazingly dominant retailing firm, a description that could easily apply to other predecessors, including the Sears, Roebuck mail-order business and the A&P grocery chain, as well as to Woolworth. Like Walmart, the early mass merchandisers—the department stores, chain stores, and mail-order houses of the late nineteenth and early twentieth centuries—lured customers away from neighborhood shopkeepers they may have known all their lives. Like Walmart, the successful leading firms of mass merchandising's first fifty years spawned organized resistance because they threatened local grocers and small merchants as well as large regional and national wholesalers and manufacturing corporations. Even the Walmart greeter has precedents: the manual for the Riker-Hegeman drug chain, which had 105 stores in New York in 1914, instructed the store manager to stand at the entrance and welcome every customer who entered. Walmart, in other words, can best be understood at least in part as a highly successful exemplar of the principles of mass merchandising, patterns that have operated for more than a century. Still, this contemporary juggernaut differs from its predecessors in some critical ways, which are also essential to understanding the Walmart phenomenon.[2]

Controlling costs was crucial for Frank Woolworth, who built his business on fixed prices. As in today's dollar stores, everything literally sold for a nickel or a dime at his 5 (and later 5&10) Cent Stores, so there was no way for him to make up for increased costs by raising prices. The burgeoning consumer economy of the 1890s offered few of the brokers of closeouts, factory seconds, and excess merchandise from other retailers that service the dollar stores, although undoubtedly manufacturers attempted to get whatever money they could from selling their surplus. Woolworth's strategy for preserving his pricing plan lay in seeking out and promoting small, cheap goods—the safety pins, combs, mops, and other quotidian products newly made possible by that growing mechanizing and industrializing economy. The low wholesale prices of the massive depression that began in 1893 enabled him to add new lines such as leather goods to his stock. Now a nickel or a dime could buy belts and pocketbooks as well as stove polish, hairpins, and knitting needles. Everybody could use these products, and most people could afford them. Building big stores in downtown locations, Woolworth's company grew by servicing a wide range of urban workers and suburban consumers who shopped in city centers. In 1924, when Woolworth became one of the first two retailers to join the list of corporations whose stock prices went into the Dow-Jones Industrial Average, the company comprised 1,356 stores.[3]

Men like Frank Woolworth, Richard Sears (the guiding spirit of the other Dow-Jones retailer), and the A&P grocery chain's John Hartford were pioneers of mass merchandising. During the last decades of the nineteenth century and the first decades of the twentieth, they established innovative methods and systems that could handle the huge new output of mechanized factory production and organize distribution across a continent, among thousands of manufacturers and millions of consumers. As the United States shifted from an agricultural to an industrial society, modern organizational systems and advanced technologies for production and distribution transformed industry itself. Standardized, uniform products that cost money were manufactured in highly mechanized factories, many of them organized for efficiency as defined by Frederick Winslow Taylor and Henry Ford, and operated by large corporations that sold goods over long distances. Decision-making at those companies was increasingly driven by marketing more than by production. Industrial managers learned from the developing advertising profession that they could make more money by creating demand, not merely by manufacturing products and then trying to sell what they had made.[4]

Markets were growing in any case due to demographic change: population increase (much of it from immigration), urbanization, and a decrease in household size. These trends alone could account for substantial market growth in consumer goods. Simply put, the more people and households, the more demand for household goods, and people in cities had less time and space for home production. The economic effects of these demographic changes were compounded with a general rise in disposable income, with the rising expectations and standards of living promoted by the new products and by the developing advertising industry, and with the triumph of a culture of mass consumption.

Increasingly, Americans satisfied their needs entirely through the market. It was literally a consumer culture, in the anthropological sense. People's daily routines involved making fewer things and purchasing more, while shopping and planning for consumption became major activities, pursued both as part of household work and for pleasure. Factories poured out goods that once had been made at home. New classes of human activity became commodities as folk culture was commercialized, and experiences became something to buy. The young adopted new ways sooner than the old, and the rich quicker than the poor, but the new culture came to encompass everybody. Even the families of low-paid urban workers, who had little land for gardens and insufficient time for handcrafts, joined the expanding market for manufactured goods, and people in the most remote rural areas shopped from the Sears and Montgomery Ward catalogues.

As production moved out of households and artisans' shops, an ever-expanding market for manufactured goods was not only an economic abstraction. New products from new companies—indeed, new kinds of products from new kinds of companies—found their way into those stores, and into people's homes and daily routines. Prepared foods, ready-made clothes, and factory-made furniture and utensils altered the texture of daily life. They replaced the various makeshifts of most people's subsistence, and began to substitute for much of the massive productive and maintenance work once done by housewives and servants. Electric and telephone wires, water and gas pipes literally joined the private household to the public world. New technologies made old ones obsolete, as, for example, electric lights replaced oil lamps. Americans of all classes began to use products that nobody had ever made at home or in small crafts shops—products like toothpaste, corn flakes, safety razors, and cameras. These provided the material basis for new habits and the physical expression of a genuine break from earlier times.

The foundation for this transformation had been laid throughout a long period of change. Beginning with the textiles of the Industrial Revolution, new products came sooner to the cities than to the farms, and wealthy people enjoyed more benefits from economic growth than did the poor. But in both city and countryside, economic development had brought an ever greater proportion of Americans into the money economy. Business cycles brought depressions regularly, each graver than the one before, as more people depended on wages and manufactured products and as more businesses engaged in trade over longer distances.

As long as production was generally local and small-scale, distribution could be carried out by rural peddlers and general stores, by single-line urban shops (such as grocery, dry goods, hardware or shoe stores), and by the wholesalers who serviced these retailers. Big wholesaling firms held the power in this arrangement. They took bids from manufacturers on unbranded white soap or tenpenny nails, and they decided what and how much choice to offer the shopkeepers who were their customers. Wholesalers' traveling salesmen crisscrossed the country on the railroads; they visited the corner grocer, the Main Street hardware dealer, and the crossroads general store keeper, introducing these retailers—and, through them, their customers—to the thousands of new products. Eventually, the increased flow of merchandise from high-output factories to individual kitchens and parlors, and the new advertising, branding, marketing and retailing techniques that developed to handle that flow, created new retailing and wholesaling institutions that grew big enough to overtake the old ones.

Beginning in the 1880s, branding altered the balance of power in the chain of distribution, offering manufacturers a new kind of control by establishing direct relationships with end users. Previously, wholesalers took bids for white soap from manufacturers and promoted what they bought to retailers, who sold it to their customers. But when customers and retailers began to ask for Ivory, a product that could only be obtained from Procter and Gamble, wholesalers had to buy from that company. To the extent that manufacturers could convince people to rely on advertising rather than on grocers' opinions, branding offered them a more predictable and controllable market, with protection against competition and industry price fluctuations. By 1910, many now familiar national brands—Ivory, Kellogg, Colgate, Singer, Heinz, Kodak, Wrigley, and others—were established in American consumers' minds.[5]

Branded, standardized products came to represent and embody the new networks and systems of factory production and mass distribution, the social relationships that brought people the things they used. Formerly *customers*—purchasing the objects of daily life from familiar craftspeople and storekeepers in networks of relationships based in villages, small towns, and big-city neighborhoods—Americans became *consumers*. Buying and using factory-made goods, they participated in a complex network of distribution, a developing global market that promoted individuals' relationships with big, centrally organized companies. They got their information about products not from the people who made or sold them, but from advertisements created by specialists in persuasion. These changes were accelerating processes that had taken firm hold on the American way of life by the time the economy crashed in 1929.

It was in the context of these decades of cultural change that mass merchandisers—department stores, mail-order houses, chain stores, and supermarkets—developed the many successful methods of operation that Sam Walton was to inherit in 1945 when he opened his first Ben Franklin variety store franchise. Those methods, in turn, rested on such fundamental principles as fixed prices, rapid stock turn, low overhead, and low markup—principles that are at the core of all mass marketing.

DEPARTMENT STORES: THE FIRST MASS MERCHANDISERS

The first tenet of mass marketing to develop historically—a rule of operation easy to take for granted today, but an essential principle for employers who rely on low-paid workers—was fixed prices. Nobody bartered or bargained with Woolworth or Sears. Nineteenth-century peddlers and general store keepers had often traded teakettles, papers of pins, clocks, and other manufactured goods for eggs, animal skins, medicinal herbs, and other products of farm and wilderness, or for recyclable materials like rags and bones. Country general stores continued to barter well into the twentieth century; 87 percent of those reporting to a 1919 Harvard study exchanged cash, merchandise, or credit for farm produce, especially eggs and butter. In urban downtowns before the Civil War, and in immigrant neighborhoods to the end of the century, merchants more often bargained for cash; they marked goods with secret price codes to remind them of their own buying prices as they haggled, often with customers who had grown up bargaining at European markets.[6]

Bargaining and bartering, however, could be entrusted only to the most reliable employees. "The old dicker and bargain policy" of the old-fashioned store, wrote marketing professor Paul Nystrom in 1915, "required salespeople with considerable skill in handling customers." New York City's A.T. Stewart, proprietor of a huge dry goods emporium, the "richest dry goods house in the city," was one of the first retailers to institute the one-price system, at least as early as 1846, when he opened his four-story "Marble Palace" at Broadway and Chambers Street. Stewart was explicit about the relationships between fixed prices and cheap labor. "Not one of them has his discretion," he maintained, referring to the 1,000 clerks who staffed the new store he opened at Ninth Street and

Broadway in 1862. "They are simply machines working in a system that determines all their actions."[7]

Stewart's establishment, which served tens of thousands of customers a day during the 1860s, has sometimes been described as the first department store. More accurately, it was a departmentalized dry goods store, with both merchandise and clerks organized into departments that sold only textiles and clothing. During the 1860s and 1870s, other successful dry goods stores did evolve into full-fledged department stores, both in the United States and in Europe. Rowland H. Macy, for example, began to expand his stock beyond dry goods around 1860. By 1877, his twenty-four departments sold china, toys, house furnishings, flowers, and books, among many other goods.[8]

For Macy, as for Stewart before him and the many department store owners who followed him, departmentalization offered a structure for developing specialized buyers and clerks and sophisticated accounting systems. By putting different kinds of merchandise in separate departments, merchants could audit the contribution that individual departments and even single pieces of merchandise made to overall profits, and they could drop unprofitable goods and lines of goods. Departments also helped managers to compare employees, evaluating them and their departments with numerical measures of performance.

Macy's and other big-city department stores, writes historian Neil Harris, represented "mass encounters with the art and objects of the modern world, dramatic, persuasive, self-consciously designed to produce a maximum effect." For the affluent women of the "carriage trade," these stores offered levels of service, luxury, and excitement that have prompted historians to describe them as "dream worlds" and "palaces of consumption." Department stores drew crowds with their displays, using mirrors, electric lighting, and colors to create a festive atmosphere. By the turn of the century they provided customers with an array of services never before offered even by the most exclusive single-line shops: lunchrooms, tearooms, and other restaurants; public telephones, as well as telegraph and post offices; beauty parlors, child care, first aid, and lost-and-found departments. Some department stores featured live music, some sponsored lectures and plays, some housed branch libraries. Telephone service and delivery made it possible to extend the dream world to customers' homes. In 1907, Wanamaker's in Philadelphia took orders around the clock.[9]

Less has been written about the development of department store services for the "shawl trade," the immigrants who patronized the bargain basements more easily recognized as Walmart progenitors than the upstairs departments. Marshall Field's inaugurated the bargain basement in 1879; Boston's Filene's made basement shopping central to its mission, opening its "automatic" basement thirty years later—the first air-conditioned space in the store, decorated with a colored glass floor and mirrored ceilings. Historian Susan Porter Benson describes the new basements of the early twentieth century as a "device for turning an unattractive area into a revenue producer." But selling bargains was not new with the basements, nor was opening the store to a clientele that included both rich and poor. A.T. Stewart had introduced the clearance sale as a means of moving old stock as early as 1837, when depression conditions pressured merchants to innovate or close their doors. Stewart also sold fabric remnants that were said to bring poor women elbow to elbow with the affluent.[10]

Selling old stock and bringing in new goods was the essence of rapid stock turnover, another crucial principle of mass merchandising developed by Stewart and the department store merchants. Small storekeepers tended to let unsold goods sit on the shelf for months or years. Successful mass merchandisers, in contrast, understood that shelf space could be used over and over again by stock that sold quickly, and that capital tied up in unsold wares could reap continual profits if it were invested instead in things that people would buy. A simple textbook explanation of turnover concerned a pushcart peddler; if he sold his goods by noon, reinvested his money in more stock, and sold out again by the end of the day, his original investment earned twice as much. The concept was a profound departure from the basic idea of marking up merchandise enough to cover a proportion of expenses and yield a profit. By increasing turnover, mass merchandisers made fortunes not from high markups on individual products, but from volume sales of products with lower markups.[11]

Rapid turnover of massive quantities of stock created economies of scale. The biggest department stores were huge: the stores that Marshall Field's and Macy's completed in 1902 each had over a million square feet of floor space, more than four times the size of a Walmart supercenter. Such stores had thousands of employees; in 1904, Marshall Field's employed eight thousand to ten thousand workers and served a quarter of a million customers a day in high season. Department store merchants therefore also had massive buying power. They could and did serve as their own wholesalers, and some also became middlemen for small-town merchants; Marshall Field's, especially, was one of the biggest general wholesalers to the developing West.

Small, single-line urban merchants understood that they could never compete with huge companies that were economic forces in themselves. During the 1880s and 1890s, some urban retailers tried to keep department store growth in check, demanding taxes on, or laws that would restrict, the number of lines of merchandise a store could handle. These efforts, easily defeated by the department store merchants and their friends in government, presaged more popular and powerful protests, conducted later against mail-order houses and chain stores, which would call on the loyalty of small-town customers to small-town merchants.[12]

More successful campaigns were waged against department store labor policies. Like A.T. Stewart in the middle of the nineteenth century, many of the managers of these big operations treated sales workers as "machines working in a system that determines all their actions." Department store saleswomen earned low wages in comparison with other jobs available to them; they spent long hours on their feet; they were strictly disciplined with inspections, fines, and dismissals; and their employers based this treatment on the widespread assumption that women workers only worked temporarily. In 1890, the New York City Consumers' League was founded by a group headed by Josephine Shaw Lowell, described by historian Kathryn Kish Sklar as "New York's most politically powerful woman." At an early mass meeting of the League, packed with fashionable women, a charismatic department store clerk named Alice Woodbridge described long hours of standing, compulsory overtime without pay, and bosses who rewarded "fidelity and length of service [with] only the reward of dismissal," in the words of Maud Nathan, a leader of the League. The next year, the Consumers' League began to issue a "white list" of department stores that met the "standard of a fair house," avoiding the legal difficulties of blacklisting and boycotting. They published the list—compiled with regard to wages, hours, physical conditions, management-employee relations, and child labor—in New York newspapers. The New York organization was instrumental in creating the National Consumers' League; under the energetic Florence Kelley, who came to New York to head the national group in 1899, the department store White List evolved into the famous White Label campaign, a twenty-year-long movement against sweatshop production.[13]

The Consumers' League was not alone in investigating department store working conditions. Other women's social reform organizations, including the Women's Trade Union League and the Young Women's Christian Association, helped to develop a bill of particulars that encompassed bad ventilation and unsanitary toilets, grueling systems of rules and discipline, and low pay. "The critique of the department store," writes Susan Porter Benson, "became so widespread and was so easily verified by the concerned public that even relatively favorable articles included the Consumer League's indictment of department-store practices." In response to this pressure, as well as to internal financial demands, the more progressive store executives instituted new policies that promoted training and decent treatment, lunchrooms and other welfare programs, and various kinds of bonuses and incentives that rewarded sales in the pay envelope.[14]

MAIL-ORDER HOUSES: THE TECHNOLOGY OF RETAIL FACTORIES

Mail-order businesses, not dependent on expensive downtown display space, offered an even wider range of products than department stores, although the distinction is not precise because most big department stores issued their own mail-order catalogues. Montgomery Ward, the first of the big firms that initially sold only by mail, began in 1872 as a way to eliminate middlemen and get good prices for members of the Grange, the leading national farmers' organization. In a nation with a substantial agricultural population—in 1900, three-fifths of the population still lived in places defined by the census as rural—the success of the mail-order merchants rested on making the entire range of new factory-produced goods available to people who could not get to stores. Ward's 1884 catalogue ran 240 pages and listed nearly ten thousand items; that number more than doubled by the early 1890s, thanks to a new warehouse. By that time the company had serious competition from Sears, Roebuck, which was eventually to surpass it. Sears's 1897 catalogue, 786 pages long, claimed, "Nearly everything in merchandise can be found in this book."[15]

Mail-order houses offered what Internet shoppers would now recognize as a convenient, private shopping experience; these stores provided no services, only products. But for mail-order to succeed, people had to learn to visualize merchandise without actually seeing it—photographic reproduction was still far too expensive for use in catalogues—and to put their trust in merchants they had never met. "Any one who has had experience in learning to read a plan or blueprint or in forming a mental conception from written words," a popular magazine writer explained in 1916, "will realize how difficult it has been to accustom those who were used to buying after actual inspection of the thing bought to make their choice from a catalogue." At the outset, Montgomery Ward sent merchandise on a cash-on-delivery basis, and customers paid only if they were satisfied with what they had received. "Send No Money," Sears advertised, so often that one of the firm's leading executives used the phrase to title his memoirs.[16]

Even the skeptical might well be tempted to try the mail-order houses because—as at Walmart—their prices were so low. The 1897 Sears catalogue offered sewing machines, for example, at $15.55 to $17.55, and Ward's prices were approximately the same. In contrast, Singer and the other big-name firms sold machines on the installment plan for at least double, and often many times, that price. Alvah Curtis Roebuck, who soon left the business although his name remains, remembered that during the depression years of 1894 and 1895, the two partners discussed the possibility of cutting prices radically, but did not believe they could increase sales sufficiently to do so. By September of 1897, however, they were ready to slash the middle-priced machine by more than $3. The standard scholarly history of the company tells a tale with distinct parallels to Walmart strategies:

> Orders deluged the company . . . Sears was intoxicated. He persuaded the manufacturer to lower his price to the company by one dollar per machine, down to $9.50. Then Sears, Roebuck likewise dropped its price—to $12.50. In October 19,000 orders made their way to the company; even after cost of advertising and order-handling this represented a profit of $19,000.

Prices were consistently lower in the catalogues. A 1916 estimate suggested that at local retail stores, consumers paid average markups of about 75 percent over the prices charged by manufacturers; those who purchased the same goods from "an honest and well-managed retail mail order house" paid only 37 percent more than the manufacturer's price.[17]

The big mail-order houses did not simply squeeze manufacturers; they owned many of them. To some extent, their lower prices could be attributed to vertical integration. Richard Sears, especially, had developed a strategy for getting merchandise in the large quantities he needed: he helped finance the expansion of manufacturing firms that promised to sell him their entire output, loaning them money and purchasing shares in initial public offerings. By 1906, Sears held a major interest in sixteen manufacturing plants, including factories producing stoves, furniture, agricultural implements, plumbing equipment, and cameras.[18]

Like Walmart, the great mail-order houses achieved low prices also by applying technology and system to the distribution process, at a level that most contemporary Americans imagine had to wait for the invention of the computer. In 1906, Sears moved to a new distribution plant in Chicago. It covered forty acres, with miles of pipes, wires, railroad tracks, and underground tunnels connecting the buildings. The building where the merchandise was handled included a clothing factory, and could receive a sixty-car train. Railroads, telegraph companies, the express companies, and the post office all managed branches on the grounds. The goal was to achieve a smooth flow of goods through the system, much like a factory adopting conveyer belts to move goods through the production process. Two thousand people processed more than nine hundred sacks of mail every day. With the scheduling system inaugurated at the new plant, Sears could ship merchandise within forty-eight hours of receiving an order. Special machines opened twenty-seven thousand letters per hour; the factory was equipped with "elevators, mechanical conveyors, endless chains, moving sidewalks, gravity chutes, apparatus and conveyors, pneumatic tubes and every known mechanical appliance for reducing labor," in the words of the 1905 catalogue. As early as 1911, Sears maintained a card index that showed what every customer had ever bought, which it used to decide who would get which specialized catalogues. By 1915, Sears and Montgomery Ward kept files on 4 million to 6 million customers.[19]

When the Sears plant opened in 1906, the company employed nearly eight thousand workers, a hundred times the staff of 1895. Personally influenced by Chicago's famous social reformer Jane Addams, personnel manager Elmer Scott turned Sears, Roebuck into one of America's model firms for employee welfare. The company established a plant hospital, disability benefits financed by employee contributions, a night school, five restaurants, employee discounts, paid vacations, and other benefits. Nonetheless—and despite an official policy against night and Sunday work (the standard work week was 57 hours)—department managers regularly violated the overtime rules, and "the company paid wages only as high as necessary to maintain its work force."[20]

Like Walmart, mail-order houses met considerable opposition from local business interests and attacks in local newspapers. Small-town businessmen organized "trade-at-home" clubs, and during 1906 and 1907, Midwestern commercial associations banded together in the Home Trade League of America. In 1912, in the middle of an Iowa winter, the Cedar Falls Commercial Club paraded through town, marching to band music under banners that proclaimed, "We thought we were buying cheaper, but we know better now." After the parade, club members converged on the town square for a catalogue bonfire. Other groups fought in the marketplace: Peabody, Kansas merchants urged customers to bring their catalogues to the stores so that merchants could match mail-order prices.[21]

Some historians have described the protests as inevitably futile, the ineffectual actions of men whose old-fashioned way of life was threatened by technological and organizational change in a developing economy. But small-town businessmen usually led their communities' forces for local economic development. Their associations promoted road-building, sewer systems, train depots, and irrigation projects; they crusaded not only against mail-order houses but also against peddlers and other less-established business people. They attempted both to defend their immediate financial interests and to expand their horizons. Still, they failed to see that the good roads they promoted and the mass-merchandising techniques they attacked were two sides of the same coin, a sweeping cultural transformation.[22]

The protests were effective enough to demand a response from Sears and Montgomery Ward. Both companies courted consumers directly. "This book tells you just what your storekeeper at home pays for everything he buys," the cover of the 1899 Sears spring catalogue stated, "and will prevent him from overcharging you." In 1902, Ward's catalogue reprinted an agricultural paper's declaration that farmers were "tyrannized over by the country merchants." Sears promised in 1908 that goods would arrive from Chicago in plain wrappers because "many people object to having the name of the shipper spread across every box or package, so that when it is unloaded at the station or express office everyone can see what they are getting and where they buy it. . . . We have learned that thousands of our customers need the protection that the omitting of our name affords. This applies especially to townspeople."[23]

THE CHAINING OF AMERICA: SYSTEM AND OPPOSITION

Two decades later, shopkeepers joined a campaign in opposition to chain stores that echoed the anti-mail order protests, with local merchants again urging patrons to trade at home, battle big business, and save the American way of life. The mail-order houses had remained a generally rural phenomenon until the 1920s, when Sears and Montgomery Ward built bricks-and-mortar stores in urban areas. Along with chain stores selling groceries, drugs, variety merchandise, and other specialties, these new outlets again threatened the businesses that lined small-town Main Streets and urban neighborhood shopping streets. As historian Lizabeth Cohen has shown for Chicago, chains did not conquer urban retailing all at once. At least until the Depression made the expanding chains' low prices irresistible, immigrant communities stayed loyal to ethnic businesses, the face-to-face personal relationships that went along with retail credit, and the delivery and other services that small retailers provided.[24]

In some states, chains enjoyed tax advantages unavailable to independents, a major issue for legislative reform as opposition to chain stores developed. In others, opponents attempted to enact legislation specifically taxing chains. The first such bill was introduced in Missouri in 1923 but did not pass; four years later, anti-chain bills were introduced in thirteen states, and succeeded in Maryland, North Carolina, Georgia, and Pennsylvania. The chains went to court, and while the cases were on appeal, more states passed taxes on chain stores. The Supreme Court accepted such taxation in 1931, prompting the introduction of hundreds of bills in state legislatures; the peak was 1933, when 225 anti-chain bills were introduced in forty-two states, and thirteen passed. During the same period, the Federal Trade Commission, directed by the Senate to investigate the chains in 1928, issued thirty-three interim reports; its final statement, issued in 1935, confirmed many allegations against the chains. The Roosevelt administration also initiated antitrust actions, most notably in 1939, when the Justice Department filed a suit against A&P, which the company lost seven years later.[25]

Both sides of the chain-store debate mobilized public opinion during this period of legislation and litigation. During the late 1920s, homegrown trade-at-home campaigns were organized in small towns; the first anti-chain mass meeting was held in Petersburg, Virginia, in 1926. The owner of a Louisiana radio station, with sufficient wattage to broadcast his opinions across the Midwest and the South, organized a national group, the Merchants' Minute Men, which coordinated local trade-at-home campaigns in more than four hundred towns by 1930. That year, chain stores were the national college and high school debate topic. To combat the small merchants and their organizations, the chains hired public relations firms. The National Chain Store Association funded a campaign that targeted more than four hundred thousand editors, marketing teachers, state officials, legislators, and libraries. Other chain groups, and individual chains, mounted public relations efforts over the next decade, culminating in a three-year publicity program that A&P began in 1937.[26]

A&P—the Great Atlantic and Pacific Tea Company—was the largest, oldest, and best established of the chains. In 1930, it reached a peak of 15,737 outlets, more than four times the number of Walmarts (including supercenters and Sam's Clubs) in the United States in 2004. That year, its sales totaled $1.066 billion, more than one percent of the gross domestic product. The next largest chain grocery, the Kroger Grocery and Baking Company, had peaked the year before at a fraction of A&P's size, with 5,575 stores and $286 million in sales.[27]

A&P founders George F. Gilman and George Huntington Hartford had opened their New York tea store in 1859; by 1865 they ran twenty-five stores as well as a widely advertised mail-order tea and coffee business. They began to expand into other grocery lines during the 1880s and 1890s, and by the turn of the century, A&P operated nearly two hundred grocery stores in twenty-eight states and the District of Columbia. Other grocery chains remained much smaller; for example, the Great Western Tea Company of Cincinnati—later the Kroger Grocery and Baking Company—was founded in 1882 and ran thirty-six stores in 1902. Nongrocery chains also began during the same period. Woolworth opened his first successful five-cent store in 1879, had fifty-nine stores in 1900, and purchased thirty-seven more in 1904, in a significant expansion. McCrory's had twenty stores in 1900, and Kress had eleven, but S.S. Kresge, which would become the second largest variety chain, was still a single store. Drug chains lagged behind, probably because many pharmacists considered themselves professionals more than businessmen. Still, at the turn of the century, distribution was for the most part confined to single stores operated by individual merchants, and chain operations were small by later standards.[28]

By 1912, the biggest chains (especially A&P and Woolworth) had grown significantly and were under attack as part of the Progressive movement to protect the public from the excesses of big business. Critics charged that Wall Street interests dominated the chains. Indeed, Woolworth's directors included Henry Goldman, of Goldman, Sachs and Company; Philip Lehman, of Lehman Brothers; and the chairman of the board of the Chase National Bank. These three men also served together on the boards of Sears and two other companies. "When a man with a business investment of three thousand dollars is told to compete with a man having a business investment of three million dollars—he is told to do the impossible," a representative of the National Association of Retail Druggists told a Senate committee. "Unrestricted competition . . . is nothing short of a cruel joke."[29]

Like department stores and mail-order houses—and like Walmart—chains depended on innovative systems that rested on the fundamental principles of mass merchandising. Unlike most small stores, they practiced modern accounting, organized their merchandise into departments, and turned stock frequently. The United Cigar Stores, with more than nine hundred outlets in 1914, required daily reports from each store; men from headquarters appeared without notice to check on their accuracy. The company claimed to turn the stock fifty times a year, in contrast to even the most prosperous and up-to-date independent tobacco stores, which turned stock fifteen or twenty times. Chain-store locations were chosen systematically, and real-estate specialists negotiated sales and leases. Child's restaurants, with eighty outlets around the country, waited as long as five years for specific locations, chosen on the basis of detailed data. United Cigar employees stood on street corners counting pedestrians; the company's real-estate subsidiary bought whole buildings to secure good locations, and reaped substantial income renting office space. Inventory management enabled chains to know what was selling and to move it efficiently from boxcar to shopping basket. By the interwar period, A&P managers filled out standardized order sheets twice a week, to be processed at warehouses that arranged the goods in the order they were listed on the sheet.[30]

Unlike mail-order houses, which built massive plants staffed with workers who interacted more with management than with the public, chain stores brought the principles and techniques of centralized mass merchandising to many stores in multiple locations, operated by clerks and low-level managers working far from company executives. Still, like A.T. Stewart in the mid-nineteenth-century and Walmart today, the chains developed methods that enabled them to operate with low-cost labor. "The Philadelphia grocery chains," reported the weekly advertising trade journal *Printers' Ink* in a 1914 series on chains, "hire immigrants at low salary . . . because the work has been methodized to the point where it requires the least possible amount of instruction, supervision and personal initiative."[31]

Intent on controlling their systems and keeping labor costs low, the chains at first resisted unionization. The union movement, in turn, joined forces with the chains' opponents. But, suggests historian Richard Tedlow, the grocery chains (already under attack by so many levels of government during the New Deal) eventually chose to court unions in order to garner political support. A&P signed collective-bargaining agreements with American Federation of Labor unions in 1938 and 1939.

In return, the unions—representing large numbers of members who were also consumers, interested in low prices—opposed anti-chain legislation. Centrally-managed chains were formidable, but could be organized more easily than tens of thousands of small stores. The president of the Amalgamated Meat Cutters claimed that chains paid better and were easier to work with than independent merchants, and pointed out that unions would be threatened by the demise of the chains because old-fashioned independent proprietors had fewer employees.[32]

Systematized and massive buying power enabled chains to make new kinds of demands on manufacturers and wholesalers. Like Sears and Montgomery Ward, some chains eliminated wholesalers completely, and invested in manufacturing plants. When they bought merchandise from others, they asked for and got extra discounts; they demanded—and sometimes simply took —extensions of time for payment, financing operations in part on the credit of the wholesalers and the manufacturers. The creditors "don't like it," wrote the *Printers' Ink* investigators, "but what would you have them do? Once they have tasted the chains' money, it is twice as hard to refuse." As critics charged, chains had access to Wall Street financing. And like Sears, the biggest chains integrated backward into manufacturing: A&P's subsidiaries baked bread, ran canneries, packed beans and cereals, and in 1930 functioned as the world's largest coffee merchant.[33]

Such financial advantages enabled chains to offer better prices than independent merchants on branded, nationally advertised products, threatening manufacturers' power and alarming small retailers forced to sell identical goods at higher prices. Price-cutting challenged the central marketing strategy used by successful mass producers, who aimed to establish brand loyalties strong enough to overcome price sensitivity, belief in the qualities of Kellogg's or Ivory that would convince customers to pay whatever they cost. If the 10¢ cornflakes sold for 8¢, they feared, consumers might conclude that Kellogg's was worth no more than cheaper brands.

Not all chains cut prices. The five-and-tens rarely followed the practice; drug chains all did. While A&P "is not a rabid price-cutter," *Printers' Ink* wrote in 1914, most other grocery chains were. In theory, chains could advertise trademarked goods as loss leaders, and then encourage clerks to "substitute," pushing private brands at the counter by claiming that the unadvertised products (on which the merchants made more money) were just as good. But, the authors explained, most chains did not substitute; independents were far more guilty of the practice.

> The chain theory of merchandising is to give the public exactly what it wants. If it can satisfy the customer and bring him back again and again, it will make many profits that will outweigh the one large one that might possibly be secured from substitution. . . . The Owl Drug

> Company, of San Francisco, has a sign posted in its stores threatening with dismissal any clerk who shall substitute. . . . This is contrary to the general impression of chain methods, but it is thoroughly in line with modern merchandising principles.

Still, after the sale was made, the Owl clerk was supposed to suggest the private brand for the customer's *next* purchase.[34]

Concerned that their brands would be undermined, some manufacturers refused to sell to chains that cut prices, and had to defend themselves when chain stores filed suit. Other manufacturers mobilized small retailers and their organizations into support for retail (or resale) price maintenance, a policy whereby manufacturers set prices not only to wholesalers, but also to retailers and consumers, sometimes by printing a price on the package. Known as fair trade to its friends and as price-fixing to its foes, price maintenance has a legislative and legal history that is long, complicated, and still ongoing. The Supreme Court ruled it illegal under the Sherman Antitrust Act in 1911, in a case concerning the Dr. Miles Medical Company, a patent medicine firm. Almost all of the states passed legislation permitting price maintenance within their borders during the early years of the Depression. These laws were reinforced by the Miller-Tydings Act (1937), which amended the Sherman Act to give federal sanction to retail price maintenance in interstate trade. Along with the Robinson-Patman Act (1936), which limited the discounts available to chain stores, this law built the anti-chain legal edifice. In 1975, Miller-Tydings was repealed by the Consumer Goods Pricing Act, which legitimized the pricing practices of Walmart and other discount stores and was essential to their further expansion. But the details of price maintenance were still being debated (and part of the law was once again reversed) as late as 1997, when the Court held that manufacturers could set maximum prices in *State Oil Company v. Barkat U. Khan*.[35]

THE RISE OF SELF-SERVICE

For all its many outlets and its efficient warehouses, A&P did not operate supermarkets until the late 1930s. Its small stores were run by clerks who stood behind counters and retrieved goods for the customers. During chain merchandising's first decades, most chain groceries offered the same services that independent groceries typically provided: credit, delivery, and telephone ordering. Although top management was unlikely to help rural districts through bad harvests or workers through strikes the way the old-fashioned grocer or general storekeeper did, in other ways chain stores resembled the independents in the early years. Many chains supplemented store income by operating peddler wagons, and later automobiles; as many as twenty salesmen worked out of each store, soliciting sales on commission. The A&P had thousands of peddler routes, Grand Union more than 3,500.[36]

In 1912, A&P instituted "Economy Stores," an innovation that would kindle the rapid expansion of the chain. Operated by one manager and one assistant—who closed the store to go to lunch—Economy Stores eliminated services and functioned strictly on a cash-and-carry basis. The resulting savings were passed on to shoppers, who paid lower prices at the new, uniform red-fronted stores than at older A&P outlets. Under the new policies, the company opened hundreds and even thousands of stores every year until it reached its peak in 1930. But while some other chains followed suit and abolished credit and delivery, many still offered these two essential (and typical) services of turn-of-the-century independent grocery stores.[37]

At least as early as 1909, writers in business magazines were suggesting that the old-fashioned method of hiring clerks to wait on customers was less than ideal. An expert on store fixtures dreamed of "a fixture from which the customer can select goods without assistance, pay the cashier and leave the store." The first successful self-service operation is generally credited to Clarence Saunders, who opened his Piggly Wiggly store in Memphis in 1916. The next year he was granted a patent on the design: customers carried baskets through a maze of aisles that exposed them to all the merchandise, and they exited at checkout stands. The Piggly Wiggly chain ultimately had 2,660 stores, and by 1926 sales at the average Piggly Wiggly were well over twice those at the average A&P.

Supermarkets, which brought the advantages of self-service to fruition, were a direct result of the Depression. As Richard Tedlow writes, "The supermarket was built on price appeal." Although there were earlier precedents, several variations on what are now recognizable as supermarkets began business during the 1930s. Their imaginative entrepreneurs understood the new conditions of a consumer culture in crisis: a population accustomed to branded goods, increasingly equipped with automobiles and refrigerators, and looking for low prices as the Depression deepened. Supermarkets were built outside major urban areas, on big tracts of cheap land or in empty factory buildings. In their huge spaces, manufacturers mounted big displays that made self-service an effective merchandising technique for branded, packaged goods. With ample acreage devoted to parking lots, supermarkets could serve customers from miles away. With carts on wheels—a significant innovation over baskets—and with cars to carry groceries home, shoppers were not constrained by the amount they could carry. With refrigerated storage in their kitchens, they could even buy perishables in great quantities, contributing to the supermarkets' high volume and fast turnover.[38]

By the 1950s, half of American grocery purchasing was done in supermarkets, but numerically they were still only 5 percent of the grocery stores. The successful chain grocery companies had converted into supermarket chains; A&P had made this strategic decision in 1938. Their stores grew by broadening the merchandise mix, expanding to include lines of merchandise carried by variety stores. Many of the successful independents, in contrast, served in essence as nonchain convenience stores. Individual proprietors were willing to work long hours, and small neighborhood stores provided frequently used, highly perishable foods—especially milk and bread—within walking distance.[39]

During the 1950s, new kinds of discount stores applied supermarket principles to more lines of goods; with the exception of E.J. Korvette, most were too short-lived to be remembered by name. Making money by means of high volume and low overhead, and despite low markups, they specialized in brand-name semidurable goods such as luggage, sporting goods, cameras, jewelry, and appliances. Discounters assailed state and federal fair trade laws in word and in deed, selling branded goods below the manufacturers' "suggested retail price." They operated with minimal labor and offered minimal service, growing by expanding their merchandise lines to encompass most of those retailed by department stores, which were opening outlets without bargain basements in suburban malls. Some "closed-door discounters" charged membership fees and courted particular groups, such as government employees or union members.[40]

In 1962, two huge variety store companies, Kresge and Woolworth, inaugurated discount chains Kmart and Woolco; a Minnesota department-store chain opened its first four Target stores; and Sam Walton opened the first Walmart in a sixteen-thousand-square-foot building in Rogers, Arkansas. Twenty-five people worked there. Clerks earned considerably less than minimum wage. The logo included the slogans "We sell for less" and "Satisfaction guaranteed." Advertisements explained that Walmart could lower prices because it bought directly from the manufacturer, and indeed, the store charged as much as 50 percent off items like Sunbeam and General Electric appliances, and Polaroid cameras. The grand opening drew "tens of thousands" of customers, according to Walton. The success in Rogers almost immediately fostered expansion, for both the store and the company.[41]

WHAT'S NEW ABOUT WALMART?

History, Mark Twain reputedly declared, does not repeat itself, but sometimes it rhymes. Sam Walton stood on the shoulders of retail giants. We comprehend his achievements better if we recognize theirs; we understand his company's success better if we grant its similarities to its predecessors. Still, Walmart is without doubt a unique retailing phenomenon. What, then, is new and different about it?[42]

First, sheer size. In 2004, the company's annual revenues were 2.3 percent of the United States' gross domestic product; it did 20 percent of the retail toy business, and sold 14 percent of all groceries; it was the world's largest corporation. Walmart was so vast, investment banking advisor Peter J. Solomon explained in 2004, "that the principal strategic question for every American retailer and consumer goods manufacturer is: 'What's my relationship to Wal-Mart?'" Arguably, this was once equally true of A&P and the packaged-food industry, but never before has one retailer so dominated retailing and manufacturing in virtually *all* consumer goods lines, nor have the dealings of a single retailer so impacted the entire economy.[43]

Along with the other discount giants that also emerged in 1962, Walmart had the advantage of timing, expanding initially during a period of prosperity that promoted the flowering of a culture of consumption. Americans simply have—and buy—more stuff than they had when Woolworth and Sears were in their heyday, and vastly more stuff than during the Civil War years, when A.T. Stewart was at his peak and A&P was first getting started. We no longer make our clothing or prepare a large quantity of our food, nor do we know the people who do it for us. Purchasing and amassing standardized products, individual consumers create "lifestyles" that come as close to fulfilling their needs and representing their taste as their budgets, and their time and tolerance for shopping, allow.

While many of the marketing methods and consumption patterns of the early twenty-first century are extensions of earlier trends, the world of consumer goods retailing is qualitatively different than it was a century ago. Retailing has become more standardized; the business districts of small towns and urban neighborhoods once reflected regional differences, ethnic heritages, and distinctive personalities. Consumption is held to be a source of identification and satisfaction that surpasses work for most people, and rivals it for everybody. Clothes are labeled on the outside; consumers advertise beer and vacation resorts on their T-shirts. Brands have become individual statements about status with respect to other individuals, whether ghetto youth flaunting their sneakers or Wall Street traders brandishing their watches.

In such a culture, consistently low prices on a wide range of products are a powerful draw for most people, who never earn enough to satisfy their desires. And while the Walmart shopping experience may appear to be the opposite of the luxurious dream worlds of early-twentieth-century department stores, the chain distinguished itself from the start by its similarly customer-oriented policies toward both merchandise and workers. It attunes its stock to its clientele; its Supercenters enable working families to do one-stop shopping. In other words, customers are powerful at Walmart. As one Minnesota woman wrote to her local paper, she could "come out with a cart full top and bottom" for the same amount of money that would fill only a bag or two at other stores. "How great that feels."[44]

The company has many time-honored strategies for keeping overhead low. Like Frank Woolworth, who let good clerks go when they could get better wages than he was willing to pay, Walmart managers have favored customers' financial interests over those of their workers. Like Richard Sears, who bought and sold his suppliers, they are famous for squeezing manufacturers, sacrificing good relations with producers on the altar of low price. Like the mail-order companies, which were publicly subsidized by rural free delivery beginning in 1901 and parcel post in 1912, Walmart has developed extraordinary expertise at getting government subsidies. It builds stores and distribution centers with public assistance: help with land purchases and financing deals; infrastructure construction, such as water lines, sewers, and access roads; property tax breaks, state corporate income tax credits, and tax exempt bond financing; enterprise zone status; and job training and worker-recruitment projects.[45]

The company developed during—and has helped contribute to—a change in the power structure of distribution. By the time Sam Walton started Walmart in 1962, retail price maintenance was effectively in decline, as a variety of discount outlets simply ignored manufacturers' price limitations. From the start, Walmart distinguished itself by offering low prices on branded goods. After the 1975 Consumer Goods Pricing Act legally ended retail price maintenance, warehouse discounters flourished, and were increasingly able to pressure manufacturers for good deals based on their size. More recently, Walmart has held additional power with respect to manufacturers simply because manufacturing has become less important to the American economy—a trend that Walmart has contributed to, by forcing manufacturers to go offshore.[46]

In part, the power shift has resulted from the company's control of information. Like Sears and the A&P, Walmart has effectively applied technology to problems of merchandising. It did so during a period accurately described as an information revolution. It was one of the first companies to adopt Universal Price Code scanning, and was thereby able to gather (and manipulate) information about merchandise and about consumers instead of depending on manufacturers' market research. In 1988, Walmart completed the largest private satellite communication system in the United States, linking all stores and distribution centers with the Arkansas headquarters, with two-way voice and data transmissions and one-way video. More recently, the company has ordered its top suppliers to invest in radio frequency identification (RFID) technology, applying tags to pallets and cases so that merchandise can be tracked at every stage in the distribution process.[47]

Finally, Walmart has done an exceptionally good job of targeting particular markets. As clearly as the mail-order houses went after the rural market during the 1890s, Walmart set out to serve small towns in poor areas. A 2000 study by economist Andrew Franklin found "a significant negative relationship between median household income and Wal-Mart's presence in the market." In the words of the lead plaintiff in the sex-discrimination case against the company, "They are promoting themselves to low-income people. . . . They don't lure the rich. . . . They know the haves and have-nots. . . . They don't put Wal-Mart in high-end parts of the community. They plant themselves right in the middle of Poorville." Within that market segment, the company has done a particularly good job of creating a retail environment attractive to working women with families, who can buy everything they need in one place at good prices, saving both time and money.[48]

Successful companies not only drive weak competitors out of business; they foster new competition. "The last dominant retailer to have such influence," Peter J. Solomon explained in 2004, was Sears. As that company expanded during the 1920s from a catalogue house into a bricks-and-mortar chain sanctified by Dow-Jones, local department stores merged to create such major new competitors as Federated Department Stores, which still operates many department store chains, including Macy's. Similarly, wrote Solomon, "Wal-Mart's success is stimulating countervailing forces," mergers among Walmart suppliers. He did not mention the many other kinds of opposition developing as he wrote, from unions and community groups.[49]

Those groups have developed a critical analysis of Walmart that ranges from low wages to gender discrimination to the cultural impoverishment of communities dominated by big box stores. As Walmart opposition has developed, it has focused increasingly on globalization, incorporating pressing issues of the environment, the global labor force, and human rights. History provides no simple answers or explanations for the questions raised by these critiques. Indeed, a historical perspective generally complicates matters. But it also provides a viewpoint from which we may evaluate the present: things change, it was not always like this, and what we see now will develop into something different. Companies have life cycles: transitory phenomena, they rise and fall. Both a "template for 21st century capitalism" and a spectacularly successful practitioner of 19th century principles of mass merchandising, Walmart is no more eternal than the Sears catalogue, which dominated American merchandising in its day. But it is also part of an enduring trend, the development of a culture of consumption dominated by giant enterprises.

NOTES

1. John K. Winkler, *Five and Ten: The Fabulous Life of F. W. Woolworth* (New York: Robert M. McBride, 1940), 109–110.

2. Charles W. Hurd and M. M. Zimmerman, "How the Chains Are Taking Over the Retail Field, IV," *Printers' Ink*, October 8, 1914, 35.

3. Godfrey Lebhar, *Chain Stores in America: 1859–1959* (New York: Chain Store Publishing, 1959), 38.

4. Not all the new goods were, technically speaking, mass produced. Philip Scranton has broadened historical understanding of the massive quantities of consumer goods produced during the decades after 1880 by explaining the importance of the many small firms that did "batch work," making consumer products like fashion apparel, jewelry, and furniture that came in many styles, so were not amenable to the requirements and strictures of mass production. See Scranton, "Diversity in Diversity: Flexible Production and American Industrialization, 1880-1930," *Business History Review* 65 (Spring 1991): 27–90, and *Endless Novelty: Specialty Production and American Industrialization, 1865-1925* (Princeton, NJ: Princeton University Press, 1997).

5. This argument about branding is developed in my book *Satisfaction Guaranteed: The Making of the American Mass Market* (New York: Pantheon, 1989; Washington: Smithsonian, 2004).

6. For more on the two-way system of distribution, see Susan Strasser, *Waste and Want: A Social History of Trash* (New York: Metropolitan Books, 1999), 69–109. Harvard study: Harvard University Bureau of Business Research, *Management Problems in Retail Grocery Stores*, Bulletin No. 13 (Cambridge, MA: Harvard University Press, 1919), 47–48. On secret price marks, see Strasser, *Satisfaction Guaranteed*, 74.

7. Paul H. Nystrom, *The Economics of Retailing* (New York: Ronald Press, 1915), 192; Deborah S. Gardner, "'A Paradise of Fashion': A.T. Stewart's Department Store, 1862-1875," in *A Needle, a Bobbin, a Strike: Women Needleworkers in America*, ed. Joan M. Jenson and Sue Davidson (Philadelphia: Temple University Press, 1985), 63; Stewart quoted in Harry E. Resseguie, "Alexander Turney Stewart and the Development of the Department Store, 1823-1876," *Business History Review* 39 (Autumn 1965), 314.

8. Gardner, "Paradise of Fashion," 64.

9. Neil Harris, "Museums, Merchandising, and Popular Taste: The Struggle for Influence," in *Material Culture and the Study of American Life*, ed. Ian M.G. Quimby (New York: W.W. Norton, 1978), 149; Rosalind H. Williams, *Dream Worlds: Mass Consumption in Late Nineteenth-Century France* (Berkeley: University of California Press, 1982); Susan Porter Benson, "Palace of Consumption and Machine for Selling: The American Department Store, 1880-1940," *Radical History Review* 21 (Fall 1979), 199–221; Alphonsus P. Haire, "The Telephone in Retail Business," *Printers' Ink*, November 27, 1907.

10. Meg Jacobs, *Pocketbook Politics: Economic Citizenship in Twentieth-Century America* (Princeton, NJ: Princeton University Press, 2005), 24; William Leach, *Land of Desire: Merchants, Power, and the Rise of a New American Culture* (New York: Pantheon, 1993), 78; Susan Porter Benson, *Counter Cultures: Saleswomen, Managers, and Customers in American Department Stores, 1890-1940* (Urbana: University of Illinois Press, 1986), 46. Gardner, "Paradise of Fashion," 65.

11. Strasser, *Satisfaction Guaranteed*, 205–206.

12. Benson, "Palace of Consumption," 201; Ralph M. Hower, *History of Macy's of New York, 1858-1919: Chapters in the Evolution of the Department Store* (Cambridge, MA: Harvard University Press, 1943), 156; Alfred D. Chandler, *The Visible Hand: The Managerial Revolution in American Business* (Cambridge, MA: Belknap Press, 1977), 229.

13. Susan Porter Benson, "The Cinderella of Occupations: Managing the Work of Department Store Saleswomen, 1900-1940," *Business History Review*, 55 (Spring 1981), 7; Benson, *Counter Cultures*, 22–24; Kathryn Kish Sklar, *Florence Kelley and the Nation's Work: The Rise of Women's Political Culture, 1830-1900* (New Haven, CT: Yale University Press, 1995), 146–147. Kathryn Kish Sklar, "The Consumers' White Label of the National Consumers' League, 1898-1918," in *Getting and Spending: American and European Consumption in the Twentieth Century*, ed. Susan Strasser, Charles McGovern, and Matthias Judt (New York: Cambridge University Press, 1998).

14. Benson, *Counter Cultures*, 135–165, quotation on 135; Benson, "Cinderella."

15. Rural population calculated from U.S. Bureau of the Census, *Historical Statistics of the United States, Colonial Times to 1970* (Washington, DC: Government Printing Office, 1975), 11–12. Boris Emmet and John E. Jeuck, *Catalogues and Counters: A History of Sears, Roebuck and Company* (Chicago: University of Chicago Press, 1950), 213; Fred L. Israel, ed., *1897 Sears Roebuck Catalogue* (New York: Chelsea House, 1968), 786.

16. Theodore H. Price, "Big Business Junior in America: The Mail Order Business," *The Outlook*, January 26, 1916, 227. Emmet and Jeuck, *Catalogues and Counters*, 74; Louis Asher and Edith Heal, *Send No Money* (Chicago: Argus Books, 1942).

17. Emmet and Jeuck, *Catalogues and Counters*, 67. Price, "Big Business Junior in America," 229.

18. Emmett and Jeuck, *Catalogues and Counters*, 118–119.

19. "A Great Mail-Order Plant," *Printers' Ink*, April 18, 1906, 20–23. Emmet and Jeuck, *Catalogues and Counters*, 132, 461–464; Price, "Big Business Junior," 165.

20. Emmet and Jeuck, *Catalogues and Counters*, 137ff; quote on 144.

21. "A Mail Order Bonfire," *Grocers' Magazine*, April 1912, 8. For other protests involving the destruction of catalogues, see Emmet and Jeuck, *Catalogues and Counters*, 151; "Some Live Wire Retailers," *Grocers' Magazine*, May 1912, 26.

22. See Emmet and Jeuck, *Catalogues and Counters*, 150; Daniel J. Boorstin, *The Americans: The Democratic Experience* (New York, Random House, 1973), 111.

23. Emmet and Jeuck, *Catalogues and Counters*, 160. Joseph J. Schroeder, Jr., ed., *Sears, Roebuck & Co., 1908 Catalogue No. 117, The Great Price Maker* (Chicago: Follett, 1969), 8.

24. Lizabeth Cohen, *Making a New Deal: Industrial Workers in Chicago, 1919-1939* (Cambridge, UK: Cambridge University Press, 1990), 106–113, 116–120, 235–238.

25. Lebhar, *Chain Stores in America*, 120–132; Richard S. Tedlow, *New and Improved: The Story of Mass Marketing in America* (New York: Basic Books, 1990), 218.

26. See F. J. Harper, "'A New Battle on Evolution': The Anti-Chain Store Trade-at-Home Agitation of 1929-1930," *Journal of American Studies* 16 (December 1982): 407–26; Carl G. Ryant, "The South and the Movement Against Chain Stores," *Journal of Southern History* 39 (May 1973); Emmet and Jeuck, *Catalogues and Counters*, 606–621; Lebhar, *Chain Stores in America*, 159–160; M. A. Adelman, *A&P: A Study in Price-Cost Behavior and Public Policy* (Cambridge, MA: Harvard University Press, 1966), 80; Richard S. Tedlow, *Keeping the Corporate Image: Public Relations and Business, 1900-1950* (Greenwich, CT: JAI Press, 1979), 91–96.

27. Lebhar, *Chain Stores in America*, 25, 29; GDP from http://www.census.gov/statab/hist/HS-32.pdf, accessed January 12, 2005.

28. Harper, "'A New Battle on Evolution,'" 407; Federal Trade Commission, *Chain Stores: Final Report on the Chain-Store Investigation* (Washington, DC: Government Printing Office, 1935), 4–5; Roy J. Bullock, "The Early History of the Great Atlantic & Pacific Tea Company," *Harvard Business Review* 11 (April 1933): 298; Bullock, "A History of the Great Atlantic & Pacific Tea Company Since 1878," *Harvard Business Review* 12 (October 1933): 59–69; Lebhar, *Chain Stores*, chap. 2, "The Birth of the System," 25, 35.

29. Charles W. Hurd and M. M. Zimmerman, "Chain Store Advantages in Organization and Financing, VII," *Printers' Ink*, October 29, 1914, 78.

30. Hurd and Zimmerman, "How Big Retailers' Chains Outsell Independent Competitors, XI," *Printers' Ink*, November 26, 1914, 66–68; Hurd and Zimmerman, "Chains Picking Up the Best Sites, IX," *Printers' Ink*, November 12, 1914, 58–62; Tedlow, *New and Improved*, 209.

31. Charles W. Hurd and M. Zimmerman, "Taking the Chains by Fields and Their Number in Each, V," *Printers' Ink*, October 15, 1914, 80.

32. Tedlow, *New and Improved*, 221.

33. Hurd and Zimmerman, "Chains Outclass Individual Dealers in Buying Advantages, X," *Printers' Ink*, November 19, 1914, 64. Tedlow, *New and Improved*, 210–213.

34. Hurd and Zimmerman, "Taking the Chains. . .V," 72, 29; "How Big Retailers' Chains Outsell Independent Competitors, XI," *Printers' Ink*, November 26, 1914, 72. On substitution, see Strasser, *Satisfaction Guaranteed*, 83–87.

35. For a recent summary, see Stephen Martin, Industrial Economics Fall 2004 Course Materials, "Price Discrimination and Vertical Restraints,"http://www.mgmt.purdue.edu/faculty/smartin/courses/461F04/VRPD.pdf, accessed December 29, 2004. See also Strasser, *Satisfaction Guaranteed*, 270–284.

36. Charles W. Hurd, "How Shall the Advertiser Regard the Newly Forming Chains?" *Printers' Ink*, December 28, 1916, 88–89; see also Bullock, "Great A&P Tea Company Since 1878," 62.

37. Tedlow, *New and Improved*, 191–193, 203–204.

38. Tedlow, *New and Improved*, 231–235.

39. Sharon Zukin, *Point of Purchase: How Shopping Changed American Culture* (New York: Routledge, 2004), 79; Tedlow, *New and Improved*, 241.

40. Sandra S. Vance and Roy V. Scott, *Wal-Mart: A History of Sam Walton's Retail Phenomenon* (New York: Twayne Publishers, 1994), 24–28.

41. Ibid., 30–45.

42. I have not seen this quotation attributed to anybody else, but have not been able to find a source among Twain's writings, and it does not appear onwww.twainquotes.com

43. Peter J. Solomon, "A Lesson from Wal-Mart," *Washington Post*, March 28, 2004, B7; Simon Head, "Inside the Leviathan," *New York Review of Books*, December 16, 2004, 80.

44. Quoted in Liza Featherstone, "Down and Out in Discount America," *The Nation*, January 3, 2005, 13.

45. See Philip Mattera and Anna Purinton, *Shopping for Subsidies: How Wal-Mart Uses Taxpayer Money to Finance Its Never-Ending Growth* (Washington, DC: Good Jobs First, 2004).

46. See David W. Boyd, "From 'Mom and Pop' to Wal-Mart: The Impact of the Consumer Goods Pricing Act of 1975 on the Retail Sector in the United States," *Journal of Economic Issues*, 31 (March 1997): 223–233; see also Charles Fishman, "The Wal-Mart You Don't Know," *Fast Company* (December 2003); http://www.fastcompany.com/magazine/77/walmart.html

47. See Walmart timeline,http://www.walmartstores.com/wmstore/wmstores/Mainnews.jsp?pagetype=news&categoryOID=-8769&template=DisplayAllContents.jsp, accessed December 31, 2004; Bridget McCrea, "Tag You're It: Wal-Mart Is Forcing Its Suppliers to Adopt This Emerging Technology," *Logistics Management*, 43 (February 2004), 44–48.

48. Both quoted in Featherstone, "Down and Out in Discount America," 11.

49. Solomon, "A Lesson from Wal-Mart."

THREE

Shopping Malls

Machines for Selling

David Ames

Store designers call it the "pinball effect." Goods are dispersed around a store in a deliberate design that bounces shoppers like balls throughout the store. The first bounce comes at the front, where display windows preview attractions for sale inside to bring pedestrians into the consumption game. Small windows and entrances usually mean pricy goods—the diamond ring in the tiny cube window, for example. Bigger entrances and windows often mean lower-priced goods. Inside, there are three zones: the "front line" at the entrance is the "power display" or "grabber" of featured fashionable things to buy to entice customers into the store; the "departmental center" is the heart of the marketing, displaying the store's main product lines with primary and secondary focal points; and the third zone is "the wall" at the back of the store designed to be a magnet to draw people through the entire store. In supermarkets, dairy is often at the back because many come only for milk; in electronics stores the "wall" may be a media wall of turned on televisions. Clear sight lines from the "front line" to "the wall" are critical because designers want customers to focus on merchandise in the "department center" from a distance and appreciate it more as they are drawn through the store. The store is also laid out for "rightness." Because Americans usually move automatically to the right, prime goods are placed at the front right of the store. Shelves are often stocked for the ease of those who are right handed.[1]

In its design, a single store aims to pull shoppers from item to item, from purchase to purchase. In the United States in the 1950s, a bigger retail pinball machine, combining several stores, appeared: the enclosed regional shopping center.

This essay traces the evolution of the shopping center as a major feature of the landscape of the United States in the twentieth century. Underlying this discussion is the development of the management and marketing concepts that fostered the design of these new spaces in support of a new shopping experience. Changes in that experience, especially accompanying new roles for women in American society and the arrival of the Internet, led to the decline and sometimes abandonment or repurposing of the American shopping mall. But in their prime, they played a significant role in how Americans shopped.

CENTERS OF SHOPPING

Retail stores as we know them today stem from the mid-nineteenth century when new forms of retailing emerged to meet the growing demand for consumer goods. Stores clustered in downtown shopping districts. A major new marketing form was the department store, developed in France in the 1850s and later in the United States. Each store needed a minimum number of customers to be profitable, and as stores grouped together the number of customers they needed increased. Before the 1880s, customers traveled to stores by foot or horse, including horse-drawn omnibus. The greatest concentration of stores was thus in large cities with concentrations of people; commercial districts grew at the centers of cities, reachable by a short walk or horse ride.

Advances in transportation technology changed the retailing picture. Scholars usually identify four stages in these advances: the walking city before the 1800s, the streetcar city from the 1880s to the 1920s, the automobile city from the 1920s to the 1950s, and the freeway city, the current stage.

In the walking city, workers had to live near enough to where they worked to be able to walk there from home or take a horse-drawn omnibus in a reasonable amount of time, say 20 to 30 minutes. This meant that commercial, residential, and industrial land uses were mixed in the walking city. Commonly, for example, shopkeepers lived above their stores.

The streetcar changed that picture. Invented in the 1880s, streetcar lines radiated out from the city center to newly developing residential districts, spreading the city's growth to its edges. They moved people quickly to the center, thus contributing to the formation of department stores. Important examples are Wanamaker's in Philadelphia, Macy's in New York City, and Marshall Field in Chicago. At the same time, streetcars fostered the development of "streetcar suburbs," single-purpose residential neighborhoods. Developers bought land along and at the end of the lines, laid out a subdivision plan, added roads and some other improvements, and then sold lots to new suburban owners to build on.

While streetcars brought customers to central department stores, they also opened up opportunities for retailers to follow their customers to the suburbs. The first retailing clusters sold groceries and other convenience goods, which workers picked up before walking home. Later, supermarket grocery chains replaced country stores and led the way to further suburban retail development. Although streetcars initiated suburbanization, the automobile accelerated it by freeing commuters from fixed rail lines and opening more land to residential development. A second technological development led to the rapid growth of suburban stores: the electric refrigerator. With cars to carry large amounts of goods and refrigerators in which to store them, residents could stock up, changing grocery shopping from a daily to a weekly trip.

PROTOTYPE COMMUNITY SHOPPING CENTERS: 1900–1930

The streetcars and early automobile in prosperous times also made possible new, large-scale, middle- and upper-income residential developments or subdivisions. For these, builders constructed community shopping centers to serve their residents and express the character of the new communities. Two influential prototypes for future centers were Roland Park near Baltimore (1907) and County Club Plaza, built near Kansas City in the 1920s. The 1920s have been called the "suburban decade" because, for the first time, suburban population growth outpaced that of central cities with the rise of high-quality residential areas.

The Roland Park Center, in an exclusive, high-income streetcar suburb on the north edge of Baltimore, broke new retailing ground as a site with buildings that were architecturally uniform, set back from the street, and under common management, features that would come to define the suburban center. Its timing coincided with the explosive growth of automobiles led by the mass-produced Model T Ford.[2]

Country Club Plaza, built in 1922 on the outskirts of Kansas City by developer J. C. Nichols, foreshadowed modern malls through the "themed approach" of its developer, who oversaw the center's Mediterranean architectural design and retailing composition with a strict, overarching management approach. The main shopping center for an ambitious 4,000-acre community, Country Club Plaza was bisected by public streets, which integrated it into the community. Like later self-contained centers, it offered such features as small gardens, fountains, benches, public art, and community activities.[3] Nichols followed the traditional street-facing placement of stores for high visibility and access to foot traffic. Parking was provided by garages and on the streets. Nichols formed the Urban Land Institute (ULI), which became an influential advocate for shopping centers.

REGIONAL SHOPPING CENTERS: 1930–1950

The 1930s saw the continued development of community shopping centers tied to upscale residential developments. But after 1945, with new prosperity and the suburbs booming, the most significant innovation was the regional shopping center.

The community center of Highland Park in Dallas (1931) broke new ground as a planned center. Not bisected by public streets, it is architecturally unified around a courtyard and unified as well in its management, which has allowed it to remain competitive today.[4] Another influential center was the River Oaks Center in Houston, which pioneered tenant rent based on sales performance and the careful orchestration of tenant mix and common services.

With returning prosperity after World War II came a pent-up demand for housing to overcome an acute housing shortage. Many middle-class city residents moved to the suburbs. In addition, millions of returning veterans married, had children, and sought new homes in the suburbs. Federal policy spurred outward growth because both the Veteran's Administration and the Federal Housing Administration would make loans only for new construction, not for existing houses, and their new houses were in the suburbs.

For a time, department stores resisted the opportunity to follow this population to where they lived. They assumed that their shoppers, primarily women, would continue to seek the pleasures of shopping in these large downtown emporia. Sales, however, declined. At first, to protect their downtown stores, retailers built smaller branch stores in the suburbs. When that strategy failed, some tried building full-line, stand-alone stores in the suburbs, but that approach also failed. In the 1950s, major department stores, including Bon Marche in Seattle, Hudson's in Detroit, and Dayton's in Minneapolis, were instrumental in developing a new type of regional shopping center to showcase their stores and regain their competitive edge.

In early centers, stores faced the street to attract passing customers; as demand grew and parking spaces became more limited, parking garages were built behind the stores. But more or less by the accident of topography at a center in California, retailers set their stores back from the street and provided parking in front. This arrangement had the unexpected benefit of attracting customers by advertising available parking and started a rapid shift to large car lots in front of stores. From large front lots, the next step was the clustering of stores in the center of an extensive gridded lot, which minimized and equalized the walk to the stores. Developers then turned the stores inside out to face inward on an enclosed space reserved exclusively for pedestrians. Encouraging shoppers to walk past all the stores rather than parking in front of them, the enclosed pedestrian area allowed shoppers to see all of the stores without the interference of a street or cars. Although there was more work to do, the basic pattern was set: the regional shopping center became a pedestrian shopping mall.[5]

THE PEDESTRIAN MALL 1950–1960: THREE VARIATIONS

Given a central pedestrian area and a complex of stores surrounded by extensive grade-level parking, designers varied features in three ways. The first was arranging stores in an irregular pattern to offer a variety of experiences and sight lines. The second was a "dumbbell" plan: the mall was anchored at each end by a different department store. Third, the stores were centralized around a single large department store.[6] Four pioneering shopping centers built in the early 1950s demonstrate these variations as well as other innovations in the form. The Forest Park Shopping Center near Chicago represented the first type; Shopper's World in Framingham, Massachusetts, was an example of the second type; and Northgate, near Seattle, Washington, and Northland, near Detroit, represent the third.

The Forest Park Shopping Center, south of Chicago, was built with stores facing an interior plaza. "The layout of the shopping center, though rational and roughly symmetrical in overall organization, was deliberately made irregular to offer a variety of spatial experiences along the interior mall."[7]

Shopper's World was an example of the dumbbell variation, with two department stores. They were placed at opposite ends of a linear 665-foot mall of facing stores. It was also the first two-level mall, a feature billed as "a double-decked main street." Finally, it was distinctive architecturally. With one of the anchor department stores topped by a domed roof, it was described in *Architectural Digest* as "almost that of a spacecraft that had landed in a clearing within the woods."[8]

Northgate Shopping City and Northland Regional Shopping Center are examples of centers organized around a single, large department store. One of the first postwar suburban malls in the United States, Northgate, built in 1950, introduced a number of innovations in shopping center planning. Designed by John Graham for Allied Stores, it was the first to conceive of the shopping center as "more than a collection of stores," the first to be anchored by a full-line department store and most important, the first to arrange the stores along a pedestrian street so that shoppers turned their backs on their cars. But the pedestrian area was too narrow to allow the shopper to linger. They were, in effect, pushed past the stores.[9]

Opening in October 1954 as the largest shopping center ever built, with fifteen acres in buildings and sixty-eight in parking, Northland Regional Shopping Center featured a large anchor department store—Hudson's. On two levels, it occupied more than a million square feet of space and provided 7,500 parking spots.

The drive to larger and larger shopping centers reflected a marketing principle called "Reilly's Law of Retail Gravitation." First stated by economic geographer William Reilly in the 1920s, it "posits that all factors being equal, shoppers will patronize the largest shopping center they can get to easily—bypassing smaller centers on the way."[10] It led to the locational model of ever-larger centers near exits of the new generation of limited-access highways. Another strong influence in the development of Reilly's law was the role of women. In the context of retailing and especially shopping centers, women are the major consumers. According to a study from the Boston Consulting Group, in 2008, women in the United States controlled over 70 percent of household spending.[11] Their desires and needs shaped the design of department stores, and the evolution of the shopping mall, too, is a story of how to woe female customers. In his research in the 1920s, Reilly focused on the way that middle-class American women enhanced their sensitivity to style as they were exposed to the latest fashions through magazines, movies, newspapers, and radio. Moreover, the improved standard of living gave women more time to shop, and the automobile—and good roads—allowed them to shop farther afield. They could not be taken for granted as unthinking about where they shopped. Because of his unsettling conclusions, female shopping behavior became the subject of scientific study, which continues to the present.[12]

VICTOR GRUEN: MALL ARCHITECT

Perhaps the most prominent architect driving the evolution of the American shopping mall during the 1950s to the 1970s was Victor Gruen (1903–1980). Born in Vienna, Gruen emigrated from Austria to the United States in 1938. He began his career in retailing architecture and merchandising design with plans for stores along Fifth Avenue in New York. After World War II, he followed the migration of retailing to the suburbs. Between 1952 and 1956, he designed the Northland Regional Shopping Center in Detroit, mentioned earlier, and then the innovative Southdale Shopping Center in Edina, Minnesota, outside Minneapolis, the first enclosed shopping center.

Gruen helped to invent a new aesthetic for retailing based on the simple idea that the retailing environment could entertain as much as any show, and the more time consumers spent enjoying themselves in a retailing environment the more money they would spend.[13] This became known as the "Gruen effect"; his stores were "machines for selling," where the ensemble was a stage to induce purchases. To accomplish this, he reduced the store to a windowless box and the mall itself to a disorienting space displaying a cornucopia of choices with no hint of the outside world. A desired result of the Gruen effect was the "Gruen transfer," "the moment when a 'destination buyer' with a specific purchase in mind is transformed into an impulse buyer."[14] One role of mall design was to prolong the shopper's time in the mall. The following discussion of the Northland and Southdale malls illustrates this new retail aesthetic, which Gruen codified in his manual of shopping center design, *Shopping Towns USA*, which became the key text for center developers.[15]

At Northland, Gruen dramatically enlarged the "pedestrian street" common in earlier malls. He modeled it on the wide corridor of the arcades, nineteenth-century shopping spaces that were a prominent feature of major European cities. His goal was to achieve a pleasant space that would encourage shoppers to linger like the flaneurs of the arcades. (The introduction of food courts in the 1980s is an example of this attempt to encourage lingering.) Gruen summarized his approach: "More people for more hours means cash registers ringing more often and for longer periods."[16]

In *Shopping Towns USA*, Gruen described how in designing Northland he used a $200,000 art budget to create the right atmosphere for women. Predicting that Northland would be visited primarily by them and their children, he themed sculptures to their assumed aesthetic as well as philosophical inclinations to humor, color, movement, and lightheartedness. He felt that men's propensity to drama, heroism, or tragedy had no place in the predominately female atmosphere.[17]

The interior of Northland was laid out in a cluster or pinwheel of a series of inward-facing shopping pavilions around Dayton's, the anchor department store. Within this design Gruen created public open spaces of courts, mall, terrace, and lanes with fountains, sculpture, and vegetation to encourage lingering and enjoyment. At the same time, the shopper's path from the parking lot to Hudson's department store was quite clear: gravitating to the Hudson, shoppers would pass the pavilions and be exposed fully to the retailers there. While the mall was open to the elements, covered colonnaded walks connected the spaces and provided some protection.

Southdale Center in Edina, Minnesota, which opened in 1956, demonstrated an even more revolutionary design. It was the first fully enclosed, climate-controlled shopping center. It also was the first to incorporate two competing department stores in a single retailing complex. The Dayton Company invited primary competitor Donaldson's into the center because it wanted the competition, as in the downtown. But it relegated

Donaldson's to a second tier status, allowing it only 70 percent of the size of the Dayton store. A third would be added. Southdale became the icon of the enclosed shopping center replicated across the American suburban landscape by the thousands by the end of the century. Although it may sound counterintuitive, enclosing and air conditioning a monumental interior retailing space was actually practical and cost effective. It removed the need for doors and windows for ventilation within individual stores. With fewer elements exposed to the weather, especially in Minnesota, where only one day in three was suitable for outdoor shopping, it was cheaper to build and maintain.[18]

But the primary marketing goal of enclosing open spaces and controlling temperature was to isolate the shopper from any connections to the mall's surroundings. The shopping mall, like the department store and the arcades of Europe, became a fantasy world. Enclosed with a glass roof, the pedestrian space also featured sculptures, water features, and potted trees as well as café tables and chairs and streetlamps. "Winter or summer," Gruen noted, shoppers, "even though they are protected, they must feel they are outdoors, because one of the court's chief functions is to provide psychological and visual contrast and relief from indoor shops."[19] "On a typical subarctic winter's day in Edina, visitors were confronted with a summer's atmosphere complete with tropical palms, ice cream kiosks, and bright, bold summer patterns."[20]

Reflecting on remembered forms of shops in the market squares of European towns, Gruen designed side streets for stores away from the main square. The end-located department stores had the largest and most elaborate entrances from the parking areas. Once inside, shoppers were encouraged to explore secondary stores and then move to the other magnet store, which provided a new destination.

Most important, Gruen emphasized the difference between the exterior and the enclosed interior space, reflecting, as one historian notes, "[a] basic mall trope: an inverted space whose forbidding exteriors hid paradisiacal interiors."[21] As would become common, mall exteriors tended to be solid concrete with only occasional entryways. In 1939, a Sears store in California became the first windowless shopping space since the development of windows. Others followed. The interior represented a sanitized version of a real marketplace. "Architects manipulated space and light to achieve the density and bustle of a city downtown—to create essentially a fantasy urbanism devoid of the city's negative aspects—weather, traffic and poor people."[22]

A problem with two-tiered shopping centers had been encouraging customers to move from floor to floor. Gruen solved this problem externally by placing parking lots at both levels and internally with escalators in the central court enhanced with art that showcased them. Notes one critic: "Glass enclosed elevators and zigzagging escalators added dynamic vertical and diagonal movement to the basic horizontal plan of the mall."[23] From the court, too, shoppers could see the stores above and were drawn to them.

When Southdale opened its doors in the fall of 1956, it created a national sensation. Journalists from top magazines, including *Life*, *Fortune*, and *Time*, wore out superlatives attempting to capture the feeling of Southdale. The "Splashiest Center in the U.S.," *Life* proclaimed.[24] And in fact, it was "a catalyst for retail change; it provoked a proliferation of shopping malls across suburban America and contributed to the decline of many inner cities and Main Street areas across the country."[25] So influential has Southdale been that it was ranked seventh among the ten most influential buildings in America in a 2013 Public Broadcasting System television program.[26]

THE GOLDEN AGE OF THE MALL: 1960–1980

The passage of the Interstate Highway Act of 1956 led to the creation of a national grid of high-speed highways; the automobile city became the freeway city as these highways expanded suburban development. Most significantly for the future of shopping centers, the 1973 Amendments to the act called for the construction of "spoke and wheel" highway systems in metropolitan areas. A highway around the city, the wheel, was crossed by highways radiating outward. By the 1980s, the intersections of the spoke and the wheel had become centers of a new urban place, called "edge cities." And at the heart of these edge cities were regional shopping centers. They not only revolutionized retailing and shopping, but they also radically changed the American metropolitan landscape.

The period from 1960 to 1980 is considered the golden age of the mall. In 1962 there were 5,000 shopping centers in the United States generating 55 billion USD in sales, 25 percent of all retail sales. By 1980 the number of centers had quadrupled to 22,100. This growth reflected an exploding suburban market that tripled to sixty million people during the same period.[27] As one developer put it, "[E]veryone was running around like hell throwing a shopping center up."[28] By the mid-1960s, enclosed malls had become the industry standard, with almost every example after 1960 containing dual anchors: at least seventy-two had three, and at least eight had four.[29] Two major factors thus led to the growth of malls: improved and expanded highways and the shear growth of the suburban market.

MARKETING AND MALL DESIGN: THE PINBALL MACHINE

In spite of the population increase, however, the growth of malls began to fall off in the late 1970s as the market became saturated. The composition of the market also changed dramatically as the Baby Boomers, those born between 1946 and 1964, came of age, creating a much more diversified and segmented market. As a result, sophisticated market analysis became a necessity for mall design to foster the Gruen transfer and encourage the pinball effect as shoppers were drawn through the mall spaces.

This market research went beyond income and spending patterns to examine shoppers' life styles and motivation for spending what they do on what they purchase.[30] The goal was to aid retailers in expanding their markets by finding specialized niches. A major marketing consultant divided the American population into several consumer groups based on psychographic profiles, each of which has a shopping pattern that matches its lifestyle.[31] Researchers also discovered that people live in "lifestyle enclaves" with similar people. The implementation of the ZIP code system by the post office in 1963 allowed marketers to identify these lifestyle enclaves in some detail. For example, the "Achievers" in young white suburbia could be divided into lifestyle groups such as "Furs and Station Wagons," "Blue Blood Estates," and "Young Suburbia," among others. Each had a profile of preferred purchases.[32] From this very precise data, market areas could be delimited. Thus, "developers learned with experience that more markets were suited to shopping centers than they might have thought . . . [and] that certain markets could support multiple centers and smaller (or secondary markets) could support centers too."[33]

At the same time, in response to a splintering mass market, new kinds of retail chains were emerging that would come to challenge the mall's anchor department stores. Many, like GAP clothing stores, were oriented to youth as the seventy-six million children born between 1945 and 1964 came of age as consumers. Rejecting the conservative department stores and their atmosphere, they had an outsized impact on society. Another important factor in expanding demand was the wide acceptance of bank credit cards in the 1960s. This freed consumers from department store charge cards, allowing them to shop anywhere.[34]

Marketing research was also applied to the mall's interior design. While the original Gruen effect and the Gruen transfer derived largely from their author's intuition, the new emphasis on rational marketing led to what Crawford calls the "science of malling." This approach subjected shopping behavior to social science research to understand the dynamics of the Gruen transfer and how to trigger it. Researchers actually observed that when the Gruen transfer occurs and the destination shopper becomes an impulse shopper, it is signaled visually by a shift from "a determined stride to . . . a meandering gait."[35] This finding and others made the planning of malls to achieve the Gruen transfer more sophisticated. "Basically then, a mall design is a highly calculated plan to stimulate unplanned purchases."[36] In simple terms, get consumers to the mall, keep them walking past as many stores and goods as possible in an entertaining environment to convert the impulse buyers, and keep them there as long as possible to promote more purchases.

Mall design begins long before the first customer walks in. Highly sophisticated marketers identify the market and determine the mix of goods that will best attract and serve that market. Mall developers work on the three cardinal rules of real estate: location, location, and location. A good mall location must provide easy access by automobile for its target population and visibility from the highway. The ideal location for regional and superregional malls is at the intersection of two interstates, called the "Golden Link" in the trade. Once there, shoppers encounter impressive entrances to the mall building, signaling the exciting world of goods ahead, especially for upscale malls. The *Shopping Center Handbook*, for example, suggests that granite and marble signals upscale shops and orientation to fashion and expensive goods.

The iconic strategy for moving shoppers through the mall is to place large magnet anchor department stores at the ends and specialty stores in between, called "interceptor stores," to intercept passing customers. To draw customers inside, stores must have strong merchandise displays in their windows and in the first ten feet of floor display. Mall planners locate specialty stores carefully since they draw traffic. Planners try to increase the attraction by creating "little merchandise worlds" of complementary goods, for example, children's outlets near women's stores. Mall designers also move people with enticing focal points such as water attractions, statues, and art (which Walt Disney called "weinies").[37]

As pioneered at Southdale, central atriums can also draw people toward the mall's center. Escalators, important to move people though a multilevel mall, are also vertical design features that draw customers past every floor, unlike elevators, which allow destination shoppers to skip floors.[38] Moreover, customers are far more willing to take escalators to upper shopping floors than elevators. During the 1960s and 1970s these principles of mall design further reinforced the mall as a retailing pinball machine.

A HIERARCHY OF SHOPPING CENTERS

The differentiation of shopping centers based on marketing research led to a hierarchy of such spaces: neighborhood, community, regional, and, emerging in the 1970s, superregional.[39] These included both nonenclosed and enclosed malls. Neighborhood and community centers were nonenclosed and basically "strip malls." A supermarket usually anchors neighborhood centers, while community centers are anchored by a small department store. Regional malls, which have at least two department stores, attract customers from as far away as twenty miles. With up to five department stores, superregional malls, which evolved in the late 1970s, draw customers from one hundred miles and more.[40] Centers may contain as few as six units or as many as two hundred or more outlets. Regional malls can be found in cities as small as 25,000 to 50,000.

As shopping centers diversified in the 1970s and 1980s, some catered to more specialized markets, allowing a more precise match between goods and consumers and differentiation in the shopping experience. The regional mall was split into upmarket and midmarket malls, with upmarket defined as "fashion malls anchored by a high-end department store."[41] Midrange malls appealed to the middle market, with anchors such as Sears and Penny's.

IN-TOWN MALLS

Some malls that were developed in this period took advantage of their location in a unique, often historic, environment. Ghirardelli Square, opening in 1964 in an old chocolate factory near the San Francisco waterfront, was an "early exception to typical suburban development and a pioneer of the tourist-oriented specialty retail complex."[42] It was also one of the country's first adaptive reuse projects. Developer James Rouse combined the Ghirardelli example of reusing an in-town historic building with Gruen's enclosed mall concept to create what came to be called "festival markets." The first of these was Faneuil Hall in Boston, which also opened in 1964. Rouse created a "meeting point and social space . . . and tourist destination . . . [that] is more about the experience than the goods for sale [and] relies more on impulse buying and tourist trade . . . with informal entertainment."[43] Although these festival markets exhibit the characteristics of an enclosed mall, they lack department stores and emphasize specialty shops. In the 1980s there were some thirty-one in-town festival markets, but they declined after that.

Beyond the use of historic buildings, festival markets also represented the application of the shopping mall concept to downtown revitalization, a new trend in the development of malls. As a result of suburbanization many downtowns were declining by the 1960s. Because shopping centers were so successful in the suburbs, many cities decided to incorporate the shopping center approach into their downtown redevelopment strategies. They took two approaches. One was to turn their main shopping streets into pedestrian malls by eliminating automobiles and providing parking nearby. The streets were redesigned to be pedestrian friendly with street furniture, plantings, and other elements found in enclosed malls. Cities that took this approach included Baltimore, Boston, Buffalo, Denver, Louisville, and Philadelphia. Such malls did not meet expectations, and most have been dismantled.[44]

The second approach was to build a new enclosed mall downtown. Turning his attention from suburban malls, Gruen "championed the enclosed shopping center as a means to re-develop the congested and disorganized downtown areas."[45] In Rochester, he designed Mid-Town Plaza, the first enclosed downtown mall in the United States. Opening in 1962, it was a large, vibrant enclosed mall with many of the features of Southdale. A substantial addition to downtown, the mall sat on a three-story underground garage and was topped by a thirty-story office block. However, the introverted building design cut it off from the surrounding streets and factored in its demise. Like Southdale, and with Gruen at the height of his fame, Mid-Town Plaza received national press attention when it opened. Although successful for some time, by the 1980s it was losing out to suburban malls; it was demolished in 2008. Many other cities experimented with more vertical downtown malls, such as the 1976 Water Tower Place in Chicago, "which is still one of the best mixed use projects in the country. By exploring the synergies of residential, retail, office and hotel activity, developers minimized the risks of inner city development."[46]

MIXED-USE MALLS AND MEGAMALLS

Two other types of malls emerged during the shopping center boom: the mixed-use center and the megamall. The mixed-use center was built in both the central city and suburbs. In addition to retailing, the mixed-use center incorporated offices and housing, making it a community center as well as a commercial one. The largest became supermalls. One of the first mixed-use malls, which evolved into a supermall, is the Galleria in Houston, Texas. Opened in 1971 and expanded in 1976, today the Galleria contains five anchor department stores, 375 stores, two hotels, and three office towers.[47]

The large mixed-use mall also became more common in the suburbs because from the 1960s to the 1980s, the land use composition of the suburbs changed dramatically, reflecting a transition from bedroom communities to places with more fully developed economies. As suburbs grew outward they consumed new territory at a faster rate than their population grew. Suburbanization took place in stages, akin to a land use invasion from the city. First, in the 1950s and 1960s, the suburbs were primarily residential—bedroom communities to the central city. Then retailers followed to capture these new consumer markets. Indeed, the whole development of shopping centers and malls in the 1950s represents that second stage of development. Part of that change involved retailing shifting from following suburban development to leading it.[48]

In the third stage, from the 1960s to the 1980s, office space grew more than at any other time in US history, mostly in the suburbs. Jobs followed the people there. By the 1980s, as suburbs became more diverse economically and demographically, they became city-like entities. "Developers quickly realized that the people would flock to the mall whether it had social or cultural facilities or not, and that they would travel great distances from their communities to seek it out."[49]

It was in this context that the large-scale, mixed-use, superregional shopping center came to the suburbs and became the megamall, reflecting not only great differences in scale as the malls led suburban development but, even more, the role of interstate highways in fostering that scale.

The interstate highway system developed rapidly, with much of its mileage completed from 1960 to 1970, creating potential mall locations. The Interstate Highway Act of 1956 authorized 41,000 miles of interstate highway. By 1965, 20,000 miles of interstate were open to traffic; by 1970, there were 30,000; and by 1980, there were 40,000 miles, helping to stimulate the mall boom.[50] Planners for the interstate system projected population and land use patterns useful for shopping center developers. The result was that new shopping centers leapfrogged beyond the existing suburbs and attracted development to them—speeding the outward dispersal of residential development. Geographer Pierce Lewis argues that the interstate highway system revolutionized the American settlement pattern, creating what he calls a "Galactic Metropolis": "an altogether new form of city doing all of the things that cities have traditionally done but arranging them in a new geometric form . . . where all the traditional urban elements float in space like stars and planets connected by the Interstate system."[51]

AN AMERICAN SUCCESS STORY?

One scholar of malls calls them an American success story. Among their positive traits, he includes their economic importance, social roles, frequent beauty, and embodiment of American values of individualism and choice. On the other hand, this same scholar also laments that the flash and glitter of the mall hide negative aspects of our consumer culture: "shopping centers are, in fact, the showplace of environmental catastrophe."[52] As examples of their catastrophic effect he includes the depletion of natural resources, the decline of animal habitats, and the poisoning of air, water, and soil. The same enclosure that makes the Gruen effect possible and spurs consumption also cuts people off from the larger environment.

Beyond environmental impacts, the decentralized spread of shopping centers has also been seen as an important contributor to suburban sprawl. Ironically, Victor Gruen originally wanted to create community centers that would be antidotes to suburban sprawl. "He visualized the shopping mall as an enclosed city, based on the landscape of European cities."[53] Indeed, Gruen "first conceived of Southdale as the social and commercial center for a five-hundred acre 'blight free' neighborhood."[54]

For this he completed a plan that, in addition to the shopping center, included apartment towers, office buildings, and a medical center. As developers stripped out some of the community and cultural spaces, which Gruen had included in both Northland and Southland, he denounced the shopping mall and retired from his company. Today, however, communities and developers are returning to Gruen's concept of the mall's cultural and community roles as they integrate public space, libraries, and churches into new mixed-use centers that will replace the standard regional shopping mall.

NOTES

1. James Farrell, *One Nation Under Goods: Malls and Seductions of American Shopping* (Washington, DC: Smithsonian Institution, 2003), 60–61. For the reader who may want to explore further the history of shopping malls, here are the key publications on which I relied in addition to Farrell. The most comprehensive treatments of the regional mall is Richard Longstreth's *City Center to Regional Mall: Architecture, the Automobile, and Retailing in Los Angeles, 1920-1950* (Cambridge: MIT Press, 1997). Although focused on Los Angeles, Longstreth places Los Angeles's malls in a national context. The most concise overview of malls is Margaret Crawford's chapter "The World in a Shopping Mall," in *Variations on a Theme Park: The New American City and the End of Public Space*, edited by Michael Sorkin (New York: Noonday Press, 1992). Two other books provide comprehensive, very readable histories of the American mall: Lisa Scharoun, *America at the Mall: The Cultural Role of a Retail Utopia* (Jefferson, NC: McFarland, 2012) and Lisa Cohen's *America's Market Places: The History of the Shopping Center* (Lime, CT: Greenwich Publishing Group, 2002).
2. See Scharoun, 7, and Farrell, 6.
3. Truman A. Hartshorn, *Interpreting the City: An Urban Geography* (New York: John Wiley and Sons, 1980), 372.
4. Hartshorn, 273.
5. Cohen, 28.
6. Peter G. Rowe, *Making a Middle Landscape* (Cambridge: MIT Press, 1991), 3.
7. Rowe, 124.
8. Rowe, 127.
9. Scharoun, 10.
10. Farrell, 23.
11. Michael J. Silverstein and Kate Sayre, *Women Want More: How to Capture Your Share of the World's Largest, Fastest-Growing Market* (New York: Harper Business, 2009), 31.
12. Alison Isenberg, *Downtown America: History of the Place and the People Who Made It* (Chicago: University of Chicago Press, 2004), 90–91.
13. Jeffrey Hardwick, *Mall Maker: Victor Gruen, Architect of an American Dream* (Philadelphia: University of Pennsylvania Press, 2002), 3.
14. Crawford, 14.
15. Victor Gruen and Larry Smith, *Shopping Towns USA* (New York: Reinhold, 1960).
16. As quoted by Cohen, 31.
17. Isenberg, 177.
18. Farrell, 10.
19. As quoted in Scharoun, 12.
20. Scharoun, 13.
21. Crawford, 22.
22. Crawford, 22.

23. Crawford, 22.
24. Hardwick, 145.
25. Scharoun, 13.
26. http://www.pbs.org/program/10-buildings-changed-america/
27. Cohen, 55.
28. Cohen, 56.
29. Richard Longstreth, *The American Department Store Transformed, 1920-1960* (New Haven: Yale University Press, 2010), 246.
30. Farrell, 27.
31. Farrell, 18.
32. Michael Weiss, *The Clustering of America: A Vivid Portrait of the Nation's 40 Neighborhood Types—Their Values, Lifestyles and Eccentricities* (New York: Harper & Row, 1988), 46.
33. Cohen, 56.
34. Cohen, 56.
35. Crawford, 14.
36. Farrell, 23.
37. Farrell, 29.
38. Farrell, 29.
39. Hartshorn, 377.
40. Scharoun, 15.
41. Scharoun, 15.
42. Cohen, 61.
43. Scharoun, 42.
44. Longstreth, 248.
45. Scharoun, 35.
46. Hartshorn, 372.
47. Galleria Mall, Houston, www.simon.com/mall/the-galleria
48. Rowe, 130.
49. Scharoun, 14.
50. Wendell Cox and Jean Love, *The Best Investment a Nation Ever Made: A Tribute to the Dwight D. Eisenhower System of Interstate and Defense Highways* (Washington, DC: The American Highway Users Alliance, 1996), 4. Accessed April 14, 2014, http://www.publicpurpose.com/freewaypdf.pdf
51. Pierce Lewis, "The Galactic Metropolis," in *Beyond the Urban Fringe: Land Use Issues of Nonmetropolitan America*, eds. R. H. Platt and G. MacKinder (Minneapolis:University of Minnesota Press, 1983), 35.
52. Farrell, 263.
53. Scharoun, 9.
54. Hardwick, 154.

FOUR

Passages

From Arcade to Virtual Arcadia

Lance Winn

> What the intellect gives us back under the name of the past is not it. In reality, as happens with the souls of the departed in certain popular legends, each hour of our lives, as soon as it is dead, embodies and conceals itself in some material object. It remains captive there, forever captive, unless we meet with that object. Through the object we recognize it, we summon it, and it is released.
> —Marcel Proust, *Contre Sainte-Beuve* [1]

In *The Arcades Project* (*Das Passagen-Werk*), German literary critic, cultural theorist, and philosopher Walter Benjamin (1892–1940) uses the arcades of Paris to tell a story about the Industrial Revolution and modernity. The arcades figure in a lengthy allegory he constructs about the West's confidence in progress and the realities that coexisted with the beliefs supporting capitalism. Benjamin experienced the arcades in decline during the twentieth century. He believed that things could finally become visible when they had exceeded their use value, or were no longer used for what they were initially designed for. The arcades of Paris, enclosed passageways between buildings reconfigured to create additional spaces for merchants, had been the first spaces uniquely designed to accommodate the flood of new industrially created goods produced for a growing consumer class in Paris in the 1800s (Figure 4.1). As Anne Friedberg notes in her book *Window Shopping*, "The passage was a fitting paradigm for all of modernity. A public space made possible by the recent advances of iron and glass architecture, the arcade was lined with luxury items produced in the economies of the newly industrialized textile trade."[2] The arcades, however, were quickly surpassed as sales spaces by the new department stores, which were purpose built to be larger and even more extravagant.

The allegory Benjamin sets in the rise and fall of the arcades derives from his much larger analysis of how art—visual, architectural, poetic—has been transformed by economic forces, especially capitalism. His work is wide ranging and prolific. *Passages* is in effect a long (over 1,000 pages) series of notes written between 1927 and 1940, when he committed suicide while trying to escape the Nazis in France. It was not fully published until 1972–1989. Although his commentary can be highly complex, deeply philosophical, often fragmentary, and ambiguous, it can provide rich insights into this otherwise seemingly mundane activity: shopping. Benjamin's insights into the transition from arcades to department stores suggest ways to understand later transitions from department stores to suburban mall, from malls to other shopping spaces, and on to cyberspace. Those insights frame this chapter.

"DIALECTICS AT A STANDSTILL"[3]

Like Marx and Engel, who famously proposed a dialectical view of history, Benjamin saw a dialectical pattern in the promises and failures of capitalism made visible in the arcades. For Benjamin, the arcades were the defining architecture of modernity: metropolitan, technologically advanced in the use of glass and steel, a world in themselves, containing their own climate within. As Christopher Rollason writes in *The Passageways of Paris,* "Arguing that the arcades constitute 'the most important architecture of the nineteenth century,' Benjamin reads them as a phenomenon of extreme cultural ambivalence." Rollason continues, "[W]hat [Benjamin] calls the 'ambiguity of the arcades' constitutes them as, in the suggestive term employed by his associate and commentator Adorno, a 'dialectical image,' pointing in two directions at once and expressive of both oppression (by the ideology of consumption) and liberation (into a utopia of plenty)" [original in-text citations omitted].[4]

Benjamin saw dialectics, instead of advancing culture, as being at a standstill, reflecting the situation he found himself in during the twentieth century, sandwiched between World War I and World War II. Benjamin's dialectical model is based on his questioning of what determines "progress," which had been brought into full relief, as the most advanced industrial technologies were now being used to create products of destruction beyond what humans had previously been able to imagine. The mood is described by Susan Buck-Morss in her study of the *Arcades Project,* in which she notes Benjamin's citation of a passage from the French philosopher Pierre-Maxime Schuhl, writing about the use of air attacks in the Spanish Civil War: "The bombers remind us of what Leonardo da Vinci expected of man in flight: that he was to ascend to the skies 'in

Figure 4.1. Paris. Passage des Princes. An arcade is (usually) a glass-enclosed space between buildings to create additional space for merchants. ***Source: Wikimedia Commons***

order to seek snow on the mountaintops and bring it back to the city to spread on the sweltering streets in summer.'"[5] The extraordinary development of human flight that Leonardo dreamed of was now being used as the primary device for mass destruction.

An ambivalent relationship to progress led Benjamin to a dialectical method that did not result in a simple folding of ideas into a broader narrative of human improvement but instead focused on objects that reflected both the dream of a potential future and the real conditions of the physical world, time, and history. "Dialectics at a standstill" references what is lost in the wake of progress alongside potential gains. Instead of being grounded in a set of ideas, the "standstill" was more naturally found in the realm of objects and images—things meant for one use that, when their use had run its course, could be reflected on, *and* reflect, the dream of their design against the reality of their passage through time.

Benjamin thus saw the arcades of Paris as representing both the dream and the reality of capitalism and consumption. At first, the arcades were at the center of a new economy and the developing leisure class. Later, as they deteriorated, they became host to the more base items of human desire. That trajectory contained within it a truth about progress and a truth about the complexity of human yearning.

AN ALTERNATE UNIVERSE OF CONSUMPTION

Enabling streets to be enclosed and natural light to fill public spaces that had been reclaimed for a new purpose, the arcades created a passage that became the impetus for new ways of being as well as shopping. At their best, the arcades provided a near utopia of plenty. They were safe, well-lighted, aesthetically pleasing spaces, an alternate universe of consumption that blurred outside and inside while avoiding the bad weather and noise of the external environment. The collection of shops provided a vast choice of goods from around the globe to be compared and considered, if not at one's fingertips, then at least within arm's reach. The long passageways allowed a kind of virtual travel and fostered a new form of shopping described by Friedberg as "a more leisurely examination of the goods . . . more directly determined by desire than need."[6]

It also fostered a new kind of shopper: the flaneur, made famous in the works of the contemporary French poet Charles Baudelaire (1821–1867), about whom Benjamin wrote at some length. While accommodating buyers, the arcades also accommodated those less interested in buying and more interested in observing the people and things in the city. On his leisurely stroll, the flaneur, a tourist in a world of goods brought from far places to one exotic site, could allow his mind to engender correspondences between the people, products, and images that displayed themselves in this environment.

Benjamin sees the flaneur as particularly attracted to the dilapidated arcades of the early-twentieth century, where "a bookshop makes a palace for manuals of lovemaking beside devotional prints in color; next to the memoirs of a chambermaid . . . one comes upon types of collar studs for which we no longer know the corresponding collars and shirts."[7] The flaneur delighted in such surrealistic scenes and resisted capitalistic productivity. One sign of their clash with the pace of modernity is the often cited predilection of the flaneur, at the height of this lifestyle, for walking with pet turtles on leashes. Strolling, assessing, noting, and other nondirected activities happened only in a place of comfort. The turtle on a leash is just one particularly perverse outward form of a new repossession of one's time against the forces of capitalism's demand for efficiency. The flaneur is able to take advantage of the variety of goods created by new methods of production without the anxiety of needing to make choices about what best to buy.

In his writings about Baudelaire, Benjamin cites more broadly the poet's call, as in *Le Peintre de la Vie Moderne,* for "new urban forms of aesthetic expression which will reflect the rhythms of modern life: '*La modernité, c'est le transitoire, le fugitif, le contingent*' ['Modernity is the transitory, the fugitive, the contingent']."[8] Indeed, according to Rollason, "The great achievement of Benjamin's reading of Baudelaire is, precisely, to show how art throws up new strategies of survival to adapt to the changed conditions imposed by industrial society."[9]

THE CINEMA OF VERTICAL DISPLAY

In its reflection of the rhythms and transitory nature of modern life, Benjamin saw the arcade as a kind of pre-cinema, a spectacle presenting itself to the strolling audience. Built into the cinematic model was a new kind of vertical display. As Isenstadt notes in Chapter 1 of this volume, "[A]rcade shoppers took special delight in admiring one large and well-appointed window display after another in a continuous visual experience that we call today 'window shopping.'"[10] The thin, narrow passage, as opposed to the more horizontal extension of other stores, necessitated the stacking of goods and information. Individual shops that lined a street one after another could spread goods out on tables at the appropriate height to be inspected and handled. But shops in the arcades were forced to create a flat, perpendicular model of display, premised on the shelf rather than on the table (Figure 4.2).

In addition, Friedberg claims that "shopping, like other itinerancies of the late nineteenth century—museum- and exhibition-going, packaged tourism and, of course, the cinema—relied on the visual register and helped to ensure the predominance of the gaze in capitalist society."[11] In the enclosed public space of the arcades, space itself became a commodity, and merchants invented ways to draw the consumer's gaze. Working within the constraints of the arcade's architecture, they designed a layering of signs (literal and semiotic), creating multiple visual intersections to attract attention. The arcades hint at how the larger space of the contemporary world would become promotional: blimps and planes write messages in the sky, billboards along highways address a captive audience of drivers in their cars, and motorists can rent their cars for wraparound advertising signage. Guy Debord examined this shift almost half a century ago, declaring that "in societies where modern conditions of produc-

Figure 4.2. Flat, perpendicular display and heightened perspective. Caen. Passage Bellivet. ***Source: Wikimedia Commons.***

tion prevail, all of life presents itself as an immense accumulation of spectacles. Everything that was directly lived has moved away into a representation."[12]

LEFTOVER SPACES

The arcades were surpassed as a model for shopping by the department store, extravagant and massive spaces designed specifically to create the ideal shopping experience under one roof. Benjamin experienced the arcades as spaces that had lost their original purpose only to become containers of the goods and services that did not make it to the department stores. They had come to represent, in Adorno's terms cited earlier, "oppression (by the ideology of consumption)." The arcades were repositories for cheap goods, mechanically reproduced not to meet real needs but to serve newly developed wants that the arcades helped to invent. And this is where the dialectic is revealed in the form of the arcade. The spaces, in their very nature, harbor their own demise. The precise form of progress that they embodied ensured their failure. The heightened sense of perspective and condensed space created by the long passage created the illusion that there is no end to the arcade, no end to the goods available. The form of display and the structure had built into it the demand for an increasing range of products to select from, a mandate for availability and choice. This demand would be filled, however, by the department store, architecture designed—not invented, like the arcades, out of the ingenuity of merchants—specifically for the expectations of the modern consumer.

With the rise of the department store, the arcades became, as Benjamin read them, left over spaces for shadier forms of consumption, housing brothels, palm readers, and other forms of entertainment. Quoting Benjamin, Friedberg notes, "What were sold in the Passages were souvenirs [*Andenken*]." They were its "form of commodity." Interpreting Benjamin's statement, Friedberg continues, "*Andenken* translates as souvenir, but also as memory; memory was the commodity-fetish retailed in the arcade, a 'world in miniature.'"[13] Moreover, to Benjamin, the arcades physically embodied the modern psyche, as argued by philosopher Marshall Berman:

> Modern environments and experiences cut across all boundaries of geography and ethnicity, of class and nationality, of religion and ideology: in this sense, modernity can be said to unite all mankind. But it is a paradoxical unity, a unity of disunity: it pours us all into a maelstrom of perpetual disintegration and renewal, of struggle and contradiction, of ambiguity and anguish. To be modern is to be part of a universe in which, as Marx said, "all that is solid melts into air."[14]

ADDING THINGS UP, OR THINGS ADD UP

Concurrent with the Industrial Revolution and mass production, such poets of the nineteenth century as Baudelaire were already writing about the complicated feeling of the individual caught in the web of consumption. According to Buck-Morss, "The devaluation of the old nature that found expression in Christian allegory is experienced *sui generis* by Baudelaire in the marketplace, where the 'meaning' of commodities is not their act of creation, but their extrinsic and arbitrary price."[15] In analyzing Benjamin's discussion of Baudelaire as an allegorist, the theorist Max Pensky cites this notable account by Benjamin: "Relation of commodity and allegory: 'value' as natural magnifying glass outdoes 'meaning.'"[16] With industrially produced goods, personal meaning is overturned by a more prescriptive meaning that one simply assumes but does not really take part in. There is a distancing between the merchandise and its history, signaled most clearly by Adorno's definition of a commodity as "a consumer item in which there is no longer anything that is supposed to remind us how it came into being."[17]

The newfound freedom of access to so many products and the variety contained within the arcade also created an anxiety about choice and made one deeply aware of what is not known about the things we buy. And while the profusion of so many goods in one site glorified the progress of industry, it also made one acutely, physically sensitive to how much there is to have, and what one doesn't have. Perhaps hoarding, an affliction of modernity, could be viewed as a response to the new "gaze" first developed in the arcade and now multiplied in virtual space; the hoarder desires to turn the home into the store and to fill it to the visual register of having everything. Pensky hints at this condition in his further investigation of the souvenir, describing it as

> saved, but saved as dead: The souvenir is the complement of the *Erlebnis* [life experience]. In it the increasing self-alienation of the person who inventories his past as dead possession is distilled. . . . [I]t is the graphic depiction of the death of experience, of life reduced to the null point of significance, as static object or hollow fragment.[18]

Shopping seems to be a particularly good place to pinpoint these ambiguous feelings in the midst of global capitalism. Shoppers are part of a forward-moving machine, which they cannot stop: they have infinite choice but no choice to stop the choices.

SHOPPING IN THE AGE OF MECHANICAL REPRODUCTION

While the arcade helps consumers move toward the capitalistic, consumer utopia of the world at their fingertips, it also distances them from understanding how or where things are made and how they came to be available for appraisal. Today, as commodities become flattened pictures (representations), coupled with a price and gridded to be scanned, the object is devalued. Laid out on a flat illuminated screen, a product has value only through its "extrinsic and arbitrary price," linked only to supply and demand rather than to any real purpose or connection with the thing one is buying (buying into?). There is the pleasure of shopping, which implies the power of selecting, but also the anxiety that comes with selection, meaning something is also lost or left. Slowly the pleasure of selecting becomes supplanted by a sense of being part of a machine that devalues independent appraisal of the qualities of things toward a dehumanized, collective determination of cultural value. One is implicated in a system whose workings are not visible and that seems to run with no one person at the wheel, unable to be steered. The system has taken on a life of its own. Shopping on the Internet brings access to goods on a scale never before realized, and yet shoppers know so little about the goods, the laborers who made them, and the environment in which they were made. Now things simply arrive at our doors in boxes.

In another seminal essay published in 1936, "The Work of Art in the Age of Mechanical Reproduction," Benjamin states, "To an ever greater degree the work of art reproduced becomes the work of art designed for reproducibility."[19] What insight does this statement provide concerning virtual shopping today? From the development of merchandise to be selected as image over other qualities, to the determinates of packaging and shipping (first developed by the big box stores, most brilliantly by Ikea, where all things needed to break down to fit in the trunk of a vehicle), new ways of shopping are once more changing the relationship between the consumer and products to be consumed. If the arcades created the ideal space for the development of the flaneur, what have the virtual spaces of shopping online done for how goods are valued and selected? What is the body's role in online shopping (touching the finger pad as opposed to walking a turtle)? How are objects of consumption presented? The space of the screen compacts the walls of the arcades even farther and demands new ways of making information and goods available to the consumer.

While commercial sites on the web may seem organized in a neutral way, they are not; the tabs, forms of scrolling, and other elements hide a subtle belief system. As the arcades hinted at nearly two centuries earlier, when one organizes things vertically they become compared and contrasted; they become "read" more than considered as individual objects, and that organization affects the way we understand things. In the end, *The Arcades Project* was not really about the arcades *per se*, though Benjamin does deconstruct their materials and forms of display. The architecture is really just a starting place for understanding how we are organized, how our thinking might be structured, by the material world we inhabit.

THE REVELATIONS OF RUINS

Benjamin was able to read a certain history into the architecture of the arcades in decay. Because they were physical objects, they were able to hold that history, becoming a literal record of their change and with the help of photography and writing, a record of culturally changing attitudes about the city, society, and consumption. Benjamin's investigation provides a useful framework for considering the way that we shop now, nearly a century later. While we are not stuck between two world wars, we have, in 2014, endured a decade of wars and are only slowing emerging from a widespread economic crisis. In the United States the collapse of the housing bubble and the increasing divide between the wealthy and the poor have led to questions concerning the efficacy of an economic system that might go unquestioned when much of the population has enough to be comfortable. Entire countries are in jeopardy in Europe as bubbles continue to burst, revealing a system that was conceived, as Pensky phrases it, in "the phantasmagoria of capitalist 'eternal progress.'"[20] Unfinished building projects, the large empty spaces of unused shopping centers, and such bankrupt, shrinking cities as Detroit, constructed on the dream of industrial progress, alongside the immense development and popularity of increasingly virtual and mobile forms of technology, make us question our economic assumptions and recalibrate our thinking.

Friedberg reminds us in *Window Shopping* that "[t]he nineteenth-century passage was readable to Benjamin while in its decline. Perhaps, equally, the contemporary shopping mall now emerges as a comprehensible cultural space as it is threatened with its own obsolescence."[21] A 2012 article in *The New York Times* gives insight into what ruins can reveal:

> Cleveland's Galleria at Erieview, like many malls across the country, is suffering. Closed on weekends because there are so few visitors, it is down to eight retail stores, eight food-court vendors and a couple of businesses like the local bar association.
>
> So part of the glass-covered mall is being converted into a vegetable garden.
>
> "I look at it as space, I don't look at it as retail," said Vicky Poole, a Galleria executive. "You can't anymore."[22]

SHOPPING VIRTUALLY

The malls, like the glass-ceilinged arcades, are being repurposed from consumer paradise to a mix of uses, including greenhouses, schools, churches, and pop-up holiday stores. These monuments to consumption, increasingly empty, are too expensive to tear down. The utopic world of shopping first created in the arcades led to malls, but where it is finally and most accurately realized is in the online shopping experience. Online shopping promises a new arcadia, a wilderness of unbounded, fresh possibilities. On the screen, space has been truly flattened. Where the arcades provided respite from the elements, the Internet provides the means to shop without leaving one's home. In the hyperlinks of the Internet, the intertexuality that had developed in the sign systems of the narrow passage extends into an infinite passage through virtual space.

In virtual space, our distance from the products we purchase has been increased to a degree that Benjamin could not have imagined. On a lit, flat screen, photographs of the products (often with many views) are stacked to be scrolled through, and reorganized with a click to suit an individual browsing customer: price (high to low or low to high), most popular, and so on. The grid is easily scanned, nothing is behind anything else, nothing is hidden, and prices can vary wildly. But it is hard to know the reality of these products: weight, construction, surface, even color (where the same palette varies from screen to screen). We know what they look like, what they cost, how much it costs to ship them to our door, whether it is worth it to pay for shipping. Often, it is, because physical spaces can be messy and require travel; things are not organized according to our direct need; a store runs out of product, or we cannot find what we are looking for; and large chains, after having made it difficult for small businesses to survive, have shut down themselves in the face of online competition, creating a vacuum in our neighborhoods for certain goods

It may be too soon to look dialectically at how shopping behaviors are determined by new technologies, especially the Internet and such portable devices as pads, pods, and smartphones that can connect to it. But it is interesting to look at the megastores that such technologies both encouraged, in their creation of near immediate gratification, and are now coming to displace. One significant example is the large chain bookstore. These megastores arose out of public demand to have an ever-greater availability of physical titles. They incorporated economies of scale to solve some of the problems that local bookstores faced: making an educated guess about what the public would want, purchasing those books in hopes of selling them at profit, paying for the shipping of small numbers of weighty books from a variety of locations, and pulping what did not sell. The stores tended to be housed in massive, library-like spaces to hold large numbers of books that could be delivered in a single shipment from the publisher. Books could be easily shifted to differing markets and their local demands, and a national/international network could be established to cut down on the cost for moving the hefty physical objects.

The mega bookstore developed alongside, and to some degree because of, Internet models for the distribution of books. But they were bound to lose. Internet-based sellers, chief among them Amazon.com, didn't have to guess what the public wanted; they could print books on demand. Without the limits of physical space, they could expand their model of selling to any number of other industrially produced goods beyond books. To compete, the mega bookstores needed to carry music, videos, toys, and other products. Perhaps the one thing the megastore could provide that the virtual store could not was coffee, and thus part of their massive space was set aside for cafés. Less space was available to dedicate to the physical books they had been designed around, and they began to look more like general stores.

As Benjamin's "dialects at a standstill" predicted, the very desire the new bookstores helped to develop could be better filled by a new technology. The mega bookstore helped create the demand for immediate gratification that the electronic tablet currently fulfills par excellence. The last remaining chain mega bookstore has dedicated a great deal of its space to the selling of digital reading pads, which presumably, when enough are sold, will render the physical building unnecessary.

The closing of the original US mega bookstore, Borders, seemed ripe with allegorical implications as it went bankrupt and slowly closed. My local Borders started its decline with the obvious move of putting merchandise on sale. As items were sold, the remaining goods were brought forward from the carefully categorized sections in the back of the store. The massive space was shuttered in stages, back to front. With further price drops, only the front eighth of the store was occupied. Goods were simply piled together, no longer organized, just a mass of items to be sold. I remember looking back at the rest of the space, now dimly lit to avoid attracting attention, its rows of industrial-spec bookshelves, the hallmark of the bookstore, now empty, bare. The shelves had become awkward objects that not unlike the cost-efficient architecture of the megastore itself, served no purpose, being too large to be useful in a house and no longer required for a commodity that could be better warehoused and sold in another way (Figure 4.3).

The last time I entered the former Borders it was being used as "The Halloween Store." The dialectic seemed tangible as I took my daughter in to complete her costume. The temporary holiday store was something Michel Foucault would describe as a "heterotopic space": a fluid space that houses the temporal flow of goods, specific to a particular time or season. Here were the cheaply manufactured "souvenirs" of Halloween, all under one roof. For a short time, the store became a new kind of town hall for the consumer class, where every holiday is commodified to sell goods. Because even the abundant costumes could not fill the space, it was divided in half by a temporary curtain wall. Searching briefly for an Alice in Wonderland costume for my tall eleven-year-old daughter, I was

Figure 4.3. The empty bookshelves of a now-closed Borders bookstore. Such shelves are no longer needed as books become digitized. *Source: Used by permission of Mary K. Swanson.*

finally sent to the adult section, which offered only "sexy" versions of the standard Halloween characters—the cute, gruesome, and erotic comingling happily under the vaulted, though in this case, not-glass ceiling.

THE FUTURE OF SHOPPING

One can only guess at the ramifications of whatever technology comes next after the tactile electronic pads that scroll through the world of goods at the swipe of a finger. The most recent techno-utopic discussion is about home 3-D printers. With such technology, the place of production and the store are now the consumer's home; a printer there makes a wide variety of objects from digital models. The most newsworthy use is the printing of operational guns out of plastic undetectable by metal detectors; another early use is personalized sex toys. Both remind us, as in the passages of Paris, about the intricate way that progress is entangled with human desires and their fulfillment. As technology advances, something may be gained and some things may be lost. And this is why shopping can be a fraught and complex activity. Benjamin understood the complexity of feeling that comes with the immense freedom of choice that the arcades hinted at in the nineteenth century and that Internet shopping offers us today, coupled with awareness that our forms of shopping are subtly affecting how we think about the world.

Shopping on the Internet brings a nearly infinite array of goods. Sites like Shopzilla have forgone tabs altogether, instead opting for the Google-like single window that accesses all of virtual space. Embedded in the portal is the phrase "what are you shopping for," as Shopzilla searches other shopping sites. Not a "store" of its own, it digests the huge number of stores available in virtual space and organizes them for specific personal needs. Shopzilla is a virtual world of consumption, laid out, mapped, and organized for efficiency. It is the dream of networks and the hope of community as it works from grassroots manufacturing to massive distribution.

As you enter ever-narrower search terms, the number system alone (pages 1–10 and a button for "next") makes the selection seem never ending. You cannot be sure about what you might be missing. You are encapsulated in an ambiguous relationship to global capitalism as you try to find uniqueness in the realm of mass production; you become a selector, not an inventor. The layout of the screen reminds you that you are subject to someone else's assumptions about goods and with so much seeming control, still caught in a system that is not of your own making. Even though it may seem the obvious choice for display, the scrolling grid is not "natural," but constructed.

THE NATURE OF PASSAGES

In a well-known segment from his "Theses on the Philosophy of History," Benjamin describes a painting by Paul Klee, "Angelus Novus," which

> shows an angel looking as though he is about to move away from something he is fixedly contemplating. His eyes are staring, his mouth is open, his wings are spread. This is how one pictures the angel of history. His face is turned toward the past. Where we perceive a chain of events, he sees one single catastrophe which keeps piling wreckage upon wreckage and hurls it in front of his feet. The angel would like to stay, awaken the dead, and make whole what has been smashed. But a storm is blowing in from Paradise; it has got caught in his wings with such violence that the angel can no longer close them. The storm irre-

> sistibly propels him into the future to which his back is turned, while the pile of debris before him grows skyward. This storm is what we call progress.[23]

We, too, are being propelled into the future at such speed that we may not be able to witness the wreckage. Our arcades today are not material but virtual, showing decay in ways we might not have imagined. The empty big box stores sit as physical reminders of one dream of mass consumption and the easy availability of goods, now temporary spaces for holiday merchandise. Before virtual space began to overcome them, these stores were the models for bringing the world of goods to us. It is hard to feel sympathy for the rectangular husks of these big box stores, and yet we know so little about their replacement: the small rectangular box that we now hold in our hands. The efficiently constructed big box stores could at least be walked into, with the goods really there, in their somewhat bloated quantity. The small rectangular box of the smartphone shows so little of how it functions. The screen links endlessly to other screens, yet we know almost nothing of how we got *there*. Imagine Klee's angel being replaced by the smartphone, its back toward the future, recording what it has left in its wake. But the phone looks both ways; it has a lens in its back, eyes in the back of the proverbial head, so that one can face time while scanning an item to find the best cost.

This scenario, almost science fiction, has become such a common reality that we do not even consider it. The liminal yet expansive space of the screen, if a space, is the new dream of the world coming to you, perhaps another incidence of "dialectics at a standstill." Benjamin's description of mechanical reproduction enabling "the original to meet the beholder halfway, be it in the form of a photograph or a phonograph record,"[24] seems both prescient and quaint against the realities that we have developed. The world, or at the least the universe of products and entertainment, is quite literally at our fingertips through a touch screen. We can compare and contrast in a flash: no bartering, no messy interactions with other people. Goods delivered to our door. This is the environment that we now inhabit and if Benjamin's insights hold, embeds within it the next spaces and structures for shopping in a postmodern world.

NOTES

1. Translated by Bruce D. Bromley and quoted in *Making Figures: Reimagining Body, Sound and Image in a World That Is Not for Us* (Champaign, IL: Dalkey Archive Press, 2014).
2. Anne Friedberg, *Window Shopping: Cinema and the Postmodern* (Berkeley: University of California Press, 1994), 49.
3. Rolf Tiedemann, "Dialectics at a Standstill: Approaches to the *Passagen-Werk*," as cited in Christopher Rollason, "The Passageways of Paris: Walter Benjamin's Arcades Project and Contemporary Cultural Debate in the West," accessed online January 3, 2014, http://www.wbenjamin.org/passageways.html.

4. Rollason.

5. Susan Buck-Morss, *The Dialectics of Seeing: Walter Benjamin and the Arcades Project* (Cambridge: MIT Press, 1991), 245.

6. Friedberg, 57.

7. Walter Benjamin, *The Arcades Project* (Cambridge: The Belknap Press of Harvard University Press, 1999), 120.

8. Rollason.

9. Rollason.

10. Sandy Isenstadt, Chapter 1 of this volume.

11. Friedberg, 37.

12. Guy Debord, *The Society of the Spectacle,* trans. Donald Nicholson-Smith (New York: Zone Books, 1995), 12.

13. Friedberg, 49.

14. Marshall Berman, *All That Is Solid Melts Into Air: The Experience of Modernity* (New York: Simon & Schuster, 1982), 15.

15. Buck-Morss, 239.

16. Max Pensky, *Melancholy Dialectics: Walter Benjamin and the Play of Mourning* (Amherst: The University of Massachusetts Press, 1993), 168.

17. Rollason.

18. Pensky, 181.

19. Walter Benjamin, "The Work of Art in the Age of Mechanical Reproduction," in *Illuminations: Essays and Reflections,* ed. Hannah Arendt, trans. Harry Zohn (New York: Schocken, 1969), 224.

20. Pensky, 168.

21. Friedberg, 109.

22. Stephanie Clifford, "How About Gardening or Golfing at the Mall?" *The New York Times,* February 6, 2012, A1.

23. Benjamin, "Theses on the Philosophy of History," *Illuminations,* 257.

24. Benjamin, "The Work of Art in the Age of Mechanical Reproduction," 220.

FIVE

The Shop Around the Corner

Change, Continuity, and the Independent Neighborhood Grocer

Anne Krulikowski

Corner grocery stores have been critical retail institutions in the development and functioning of the modern city. Along with churches and schools, grocery stores make up the triad of institutions that have traditionally defined urban neighborhoods. Despite both their historical significance and their ongoing importance, the role of small neighborhood grocery stores in the life of the American city is easy to overlook. Chain supermarkets and downtown department stores have been more visible. Their distinctive purpose-built design has made them landmarks of our lives, while their corporate archives provide ample scope for historians of almost every specialty. Small, usually family-owned neighborhood businesses, such as groceries, most often operated out of physical spaces designed as family dwellings and have left few records behind to document their often brief existence.[1]

While it might be difficult to study one grocery store in detail, abundant textual and visual sources (e.g., advice manuals, trade publications, photographs, advertisements, and oral interviews) provide rich evidence to document the evolution of this important urban institution. This chapter traces that evolution with a focus on the Philadelphia region.

EARLY FOOD MARKETS AND THE FIRST GROCERY STORES

Neighborhood grocery stores were a practical development amid a chaotic system of urban food distribution. Since early colonial times, outdoor street markets (which still exist in many cities) located near the waterfront provided fresh meat, fish, and produce. Public markets continued to be the primary location for town and city dwellers to purchase most food items until well into the nineteenth century. Sometimes a public market was not a specific building but simply a space: a convenient and centrally located place where farmers and other food producers brought meats, fish, vegetables, and other foods at specified times and/or days. These areas would be noisy and congested as farmers with horses and wagons and scores of customers with market baskets tried to do business. Larger towns and cities often had public markets several days of the week, even every weekday.[2]

To reduce the chaos and move congestion away from other urban activities, city fathers began designating spaces for food markets on the fringes of built-up areas. After the invention of the railroad, food markets would be sited near railroad depots. Official markets were shed-type buildings under a roof but open on several sides to accommodate horses, carts, and people. These market houses rented stalls to butchers, hucksters (sellers of fruits and vegetables), and farmers, who brought dairy products and eggs. Stall retailers competed with the many street vendors, who moved around the city or operated small carts in city streets. Regulating cleanliness and preventing congestion of city streets remained a challenge for municipal governments.[3]

In the decades just before the Civil War, an increasing number of grocery, produce, and butcher shops located in urban neighborhoods began attracting the urban customer away from the central open markets, which began to serve mainly as wholesalers. As early industrialization and immigration spurred the growth of the urban population, some families moved even farther from the old colonial centers into newly developing residential districts. Before electricity and refrigeration, families had to purchase many food items almost daily. To serve them, conveniently located small general stores carried some food items along with necessary staples, but the selection was limited.

Entrepreneurs soon recognized the opportunity to open specialized grocery stores in these districts. Stores specializing in food items had first appeared in American cities in the eighteenth century as the colonial economy prospered. These early stores often offered expensive "fancy goods": sugar, chocolate, bulk cheese, oatmeal, coffee, tea, olive oil, wine, molasses, rice, and fruit. Gradually such stores offered more mundane foods as well, and the number of food stores multiplied in the early nineteenth century. Historian Edward Spann quotes one New Yorker of 1850 who noted, "[I]t has become so fashionable to have a meat-shop on almost every corner and fruits and vegetables in almost every grocery, and fish and oysters well nigh swimming through the streets that our large markets are to some extent foresaken." This New Yorker described a time when shopping for food still required visits to several stores: meat and fish were generally carried in specialized stores, but clearly general groceries were becoming common and were known to carry produce as part of their specialized and expanding inventories.[4]

THE PROFESSIONAL GROCER

While neighborhood groceries proliferated in the decades following the Civil War, even in the 1860s such stores were numerous enough to warrant a professional manual. In 1869, Samuel H. Terry published his *Retailer's Manual*, possibly the first professional manual for small shopkeepers. Terry drew on his own thirty years' experience to offer guidance to retailers, much of which was directed to the grocery trade. His goal was to provide practical advice, which, he drily noted, was always cheaper for the student than was experience.[5]

Terry's manual reflects a period of change when small, specialized retail businesses, which were not predominantly high-end shops, were becoming more common. Such stores were so new that there was even some confusion over vocabulary. Terry pointed out that the word "store" was considered an Americanism and noted that the English used the word "shop" to denote a place where goods were offered for sale. Americans used the word "shop" in the sense of a workshop, a place of manual labor. To avoid confusing his readers, Terry adopted the word "store" to denote the type of business for which he was proffering advice.[6]

Terry focused mainly on accounting and legal matters, but he also discussed topics such as relationships with employees and how to deal with customers of various national origins, perhaps the most surprising topic for today's readers. The greatest challenge for early grocers and food vendors, though, concerned matters of inventory. Before the advent of canned and boxed foods, grocers often misjudged the quantities of food they could sell before items went bad. Overstocking resulted in financial loss for the grocer. Terry noted that inexperience in judging inventory quantities was the main reason for the high failure rate of food stores, which he believed went out of business more frequently than other types of retail businesses.

Another sign that Terry wrote his manual before packaged foods is the absence of visual elements in the manual itself. Artfully arranging items for sale was not a concern for Terry or contemporary grocers. No diagrams, drawings, or any other type of illustrations were necessary to suggest effective displays. There was little possibility of artistic display when bulk foods were sold out of open containers and baskets placed on the floor for easy access. Cleanliness and order were the most that could be achieved. Terry did suggest that grocers try to get sunlight into the store and choose a clean-looking paint color for the interior, but these were practical rather than primarily aesthetic matters.

THE GOLDEN AGE OF THE NEIGHBORHOOD GROCERY

The great proliferation of specialized grocery stores after 1870 reflected the increasingly complicated and extensive regional, national, and global networks of producers, wholesalers, retailers, and transportation routes, bringing food to larger populations in expanding industrial cities. To the urban resident, the neighborhood grocer became the most visible link in this developing global network, bringing food items from many continents to the family dinner table. Chain grocery stores first appeared in the 1890s, but the number of small independent groceries continued to increase for the next several decades, at least into the 1920s. One contemporary expert estimated that in 1913 there were approximately 8,700 grocery stores in the city of Philadelphia. Of these, about 82 percent were "independent grocers," while about 10 percent were small grocers who belonged to the Retail Grocers' Association; only about 7 percent were chain stores at that time. In all, there was an average of one grocer for every two blocks in the city. This same writer estimated that New York City held more than 11,000 independent groceries and another 4,000 chain groceries and Association member grocers.[7]

The familiar image of the corner store captures reality. Corner sites in urban residential neighborhoods were the most common locations for grocery stores (Figure 5.1). Often, row-house blocks were framed on each end by slightly larger dwellings than those in the middle. Thus, the end dwellings offered somewhat more space for business purposes. Corners provided more visibility to potential customers. Corner locations also offered access to more sidewalk space to display both inventory and advertising signs, expanding the relatively limited space of most urban row-house interiors.

Whether sited on the stereotypical corner at the end of a long uniform row of houses or located in a neighborhood characterized by detached or semidetached dwellings, most independent neighborhood grocery stores (and some chain stores in their early years) operated in a structure designed to be a family house. Grocery stores were, in effect, extensions of domestic family space. Outside the South, where grocery stores were not considered acceptable female spaces, women and children were the main customers. Women might run in and out every day, even several times in a day as they planned and prepared meals. Women also found the stores to be informal sites for conversation and the exchange of gossip. Before

Figure 5.1. Typical corner grocery store, Fitzwater Street near Twentieth Street, Philadelphia, early twentieth century. The visible corner location in the midst of this residential neighborhood also allows the grocer to take advantage of sidewalk space. *Source: Image courtesy of Gus Spector.*

the playground movement, many urban children had nowhere to play but in neighborhood streets. Numerous surviving nineteenth- and early twentieth-century photographs of neighborhood groceries include gaggles of children lined up to have their picture taken. Such charming scenes emphasize the domestic nature of the corner grocery store.[8]

THE PROGRESSIVE GROCER

As economic and social institutions, neighborhood grocery stores reflected the larger evolving trends in the American and global economies to which they were linked. The political and social agendas of residents, reformers, and the new urban planners and engineers and the consequent drive for legislation to establish a variety of new standards meant that small neighborhood grocers had to keep up with new trends. The process of modernizing and professionalizing retail practices, display, and the use of physical space was much more uneven than in the corporate and chain-store world but just as evident in the stores of independent grocers.

Trade journals and textbooks offer information about the concerns of the small grocer and trace the physical changes in inventory, display, and the arrangement of the store interiors. As the number of small grocery stores increased so, too, did the advice literature. In the same year that Samuel Terry published his *Retailer's Manual, The American Grocer* also began publication. Within a few years, editors were proud to claim that

The American Grocer was the "best grocery trade paper on earth." Philadelphia and Camden, New Jersey, grocers, butchers, and produce vendors could also subscribe to the *Philadelphia Cash Grocer* and the *Brooklyn Market Journal,* which circulated through the mid-Atlantic. In the late nineteenth century, many regional and state grocery journals were published. In the quickly growing state of California, for instance, *California Grocer* and *Retail Grocers' Advocate* of San Francisco were a few of the trade publications that provided advice and guidance for both novice and experienced grocers in that region.

As every issue in the 1890s made clear, the editors of *The American Grocer* saw that food production and distribution had become a matter of global connections. The global perspective of this publication was also indicated in subscription rates: in 1910, American grocers and food wholesalers paid $3.00 to receive this weekly publication for the year; those in Britain, European nations, China, and Japan paid $4.56 that year to read the latest worldwide grocery-related news. The reiterated theme was that proprietors of even the smallest neighborhood groceries had to be cognizant of worldwide events. Grocers had to know when droughts or hurricanes had wiped out a crop or when labor issues on Hawaiian pineapple plantations or a planned railway strike on the West Coast might affect the availability or price of items. Such information was crucial to planning inventories and budgets. Facts would also help the grocer explain shortages or increasing prices to customers and maintain good relations with them. Writers constantly reminded grocers that after mortgage or rent, food was the most expensive item in the family budget. Most advice writers expressed the belief that grocers had an ethical responsibility to understand and honestly explain increases in food prices to their customers.[9]

Trade publications continued to emphasize cleanliness and efficiency as Samuel Terry had in 1869 but added a new element: visual aesthetics. Food in cans, boxes, jars, and bottles could be displayed on wall shelving and countertops. Many foods formerly displayed in sacks (apples, potatoes) moved from the floor to bins. Sealed food containers stored along the walls and in appropriate bins and glassed-in counters underscored new standards of hygiene. The sensory experience of buying and selling food changed from touch and smell (no longer possible when foods were prepackaged) to one that was mainly visual. Packaged foods introduced colorful, well-designed boxes, cans and jars that lent themselves to eye-catching and sometimes very complicated displays to attract customers.[10]

Trade journals and textbooks themselves reflected this new visual emphasis in the buying and selling of food. Photographs, diagrams, and other illustrations became important tools in teaching the modern grocer his business. Trade publications routinely offered detailed figures, diagrams, and floor plans that demonstrated how to make the most efficient use of limited retail space while providing room for customers to circulate comfortably around the store, viewing all that the grocer had on offer (Figure 5.2).

This so-called march of improvement cost money. Professional advice writers and, not surprisingly, the manufacturers who advertised display cases and shelving units suggested that each type of food item have its own appropriate display unit. The grocer who kept up with the times and remained competitive, manufacturers and advice writers implied, would eventually profit from the significant expenditure necessary to acquire all kinds of new shelf units, bins, and glassed-in display cases. Writers emphasized that the expanded inventories and obvious cleanliness made possible by these new display methods would draw in more customers and soon offset the cost of remodeling the store interior.

Moving inventory from the floor to the walls and increasing the amount of stock in the store at any given time meant that tracking and readily accessing goods became more complicated. Trade publications offered diagrams of carefully considered item placement on shelves. The guiding principle was efficiency: the most quickly moving items should be stocked near the register and slower-moving items, toward the rear of the store. Grocers were instructed to track their footprints for a period of time to see which goods they most frequently took off the shelves. With that knowledge, grocers could organize inventories more efficiently. Because trade writers provided an array of possible arrangements that considered store size, quantity of stock, and likely customer desires, it is possible that many grocers gained help that was relatively specific to their own particular business.

Some of the diagrams and arrangements at first glance might seem too complicated for the typical small independent grocery store, but this advice *was* probably very helpful. Lone grocers who left the counter to run around the store retrieving items slowed down sales and forced customers to wait for longer periods of time to make their purchases. Turning away from a customer standing near the cash drawer presented other risks as well. These new techniques of organizing the inventory would have greatly helped the independent neighborhood grocer, who most frequently worked alone in the store.

THE PLATE GLASS STOREFRONT WINDOW AND "TRANSPARENCY"

Accenting the new visual emphasis of the grocery business, professional advice writers agreed that large glass display windows were a necessary exterior feature. Once plate glass became available and affordable, the most common exterior photograph of neighborhood grocery stores shows the grocer (and perhaps family members) posed outside the store in front of the window, usually with a display of packaged foods visible

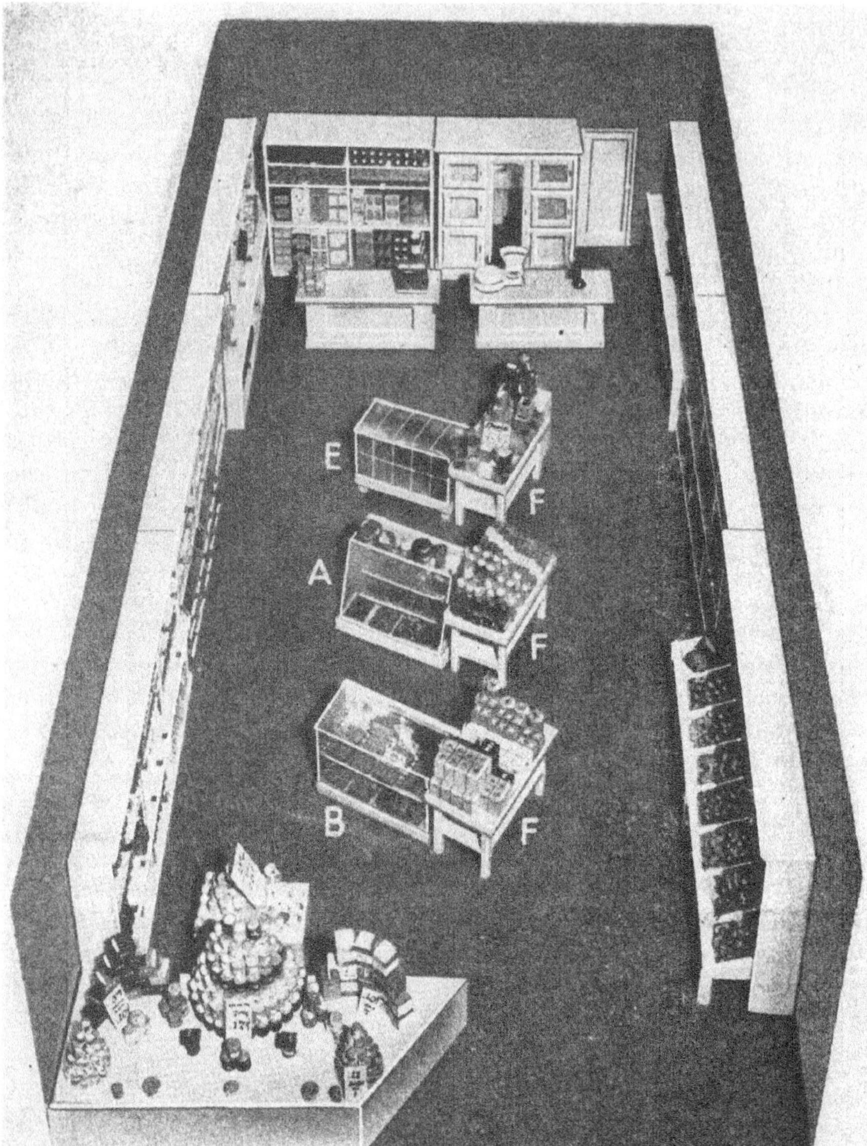

Figure 5.2. Textbook plan for a narrow neighborhood grocery store. The plan demonstrated to grocers the increase in inventory made possible with packaged foods placed on wall shelves and in glass display cases. *Source: From* The Progressive Grocer, Better Grocery Stores *(New York: The Butterick Publishing Company, 1928). Image Courtesy of Stagnito Media.*

behind the family. Large plate glass windows linked the passerby on the sidewalk to the interior of the store and the inventory on offer. The transparency of such display windows signaled a modern, progressive grocer who kept pace with new standards of cleanliness; in addition, passersby could see that he sold hygienic packaged foods and openly displayed them for the customers' information.

As urban food distribution became more complicated, problems with contaminated milk, water, and food were egregious in many cities. Reformers and urban planners identified many reasons for contaminated food; such muckraking journalists as Ida Tarbell frequently cited grocers as the source. The Progressive drive for federal legislation to curb such problems developed in the 1880s and strengthened until 1906, when Congress passed the Pure Food and Drug Act. Reformers documented conditions and reported on proposed legislation in academic journals (e.g., the *Annual of the American Academy of Political and Social Scientists*), newspapers, and widely circulated magazines such as *Harper's*. Writers in grocery trade publications followed the struggle and responded to the attacks levied by muckrakers. They advised what today would be called "transparency." Trade journals favored publishing the names of those grocers found guilty of adulterating food or weighting scales to demonstrate the commitment of the great majority of grocers to honest business practices.[11]

Even after 1906, as states and municipalities oversaw inspection and enforcement, reformers kept these issues—and the "problem" of the neighborhood grocer—before the public. Journalists provided the details of legislation and suggested that all customers become unofficial inspectors of their local grocery stores. School biology textbooks of the period (themselves an outgrowth of the Progressive drive for cleanliness and hygiene) devoted considerable attention to teaching American children to judge the practices of their own neighborhood grocers. One textbook author suggested that teachers require students "by personal inspection" to find which neighborhood grocers and bakers, as well as meat, fish, and produce dealers, best met the pure food regulations. He not only provided a list of questions to guide their observation, he also suggested the course of action to be taken toward grocers who did not meet new standards:

> Does the grocer with whom you deal have a clean and well-ventilated shop? Are the receptacles containing flour, sugar, etc., always kept covered? Are vegetables and fruits exposed so that people may handle them and flies and other vermin touch them? If so, you should not patronize the place.

With Americans being taught as schoolchildren to become inspectors of the food trades, grocers had to be careful to "measure up" to new standards or risk losing customers.[12]

THE ART OF WINDOW DRESSING FOR GROCERS

Plate glass window storefronts, then, can be seen as part of the Progressive drive to improve standards of cleanliness and hygiene as well as to provide information to the public. In addition, these windows offered spaces to attractively display a variety of canned and boxed foods to entice customers into the store. Like the big city department stores, smaller grocers, too, were informed that "window dressing as a branch of business building is now recognized as one of utmost importance and is being developed to a high point of perfection." Albert Bauer explained this new marketing tool in *The Art of Window Dressing for Grocers*, a small textbook he wrote to offer step-by-step guidance to untrained grocers for composing elaborate displays of cans, bottles, and boxes.[13]

Bauer equated window design and display with theater. He counseled grocers to acquire a range of props to create attractive, attention-getting displays: baskets in different sizes and shapes, a few barrels, fabrics in different colors for swags, some green plants, even a palm tree or two to display certain produce with appropriate atmosphere. Displays of packaged goods could be quite complicated (Figure 5.3). Trade publications offered careful row-by-row instructions, which in their level of detail often resembled knitting instructions.

Bauer particularly emphasized the use of mannequins in his window displays to simulate the presence and activities of actual customers. He believed that lifelike tableaus encouraged passersby to imitate the mannequin's own interest in the goods displayed and would thus increase sales. Some of the most amusing window arrangements are those that included body parts. For instance, in one illustration of a model window display, two trousered legs sticking up from a barrel—indicating that a man had fallen into the barrel—implied a tumble or drop in prices. Presumably, small grocers were expected to keep several whole mannequins on hand, as well as a supply of limbs, to convey various messages to potential customers passing by on the sidewalk. In fact, the illustrations in Bauer's book suggest that grocers have on hand a fairly large range of props to enable frequent changes in their displays.

Whatever props and mannequin parts were included in window displays, the main focus was on the packaged foods—and not so much on the food but on the packages and labels. By the 1890s, experts considered brand names and brand labels to be the most effective items for display and advertising; brands and labels were even more emphasized after the passage of the Pure Food and Drug Act. By that time, professional trade writers considered ads painted on buildings and signs propped up on the sidewalk to be old fashioned. To many, these lingering practices signaled the uninformed neighborhood grocer who did not take the trouble to learn about and adopt modern methods. Although advice books of the time, such as *The Art of Window Dressing for Grocers,* lacked color illustra-

Figure 5.3. Window display of packaged foods. Although pictured in black and white, this display was clearly planned around the patterns of brand labels and contrasting colors for its eye-catching appeal. *Source: Albert G. Bauer,* The Art of Window Dressing for Grocers *(Chicago: Sprague, Warner & Company, 1902).*

tions, many of the most complicated arrangements of cans and boxes were obviously designed around the artful use of brand labels and their color patterns and contrasts (Figure 5.3). The progressive grocer, however, really did not need to construct the windmills, lighthouses, wishing wells, and mannequin tableaus advocated by trade journals and textbooks. Photographs of actual stores demonstrate that most grocers found the simple pyramid sufficient to display the brands they carried and thus inform customers primed by crusading journalists to follow such brands.

NEIGHBORHOOD GROCERY OR QUAINT LITTLE SHOPPE

While even small neighborhood shops began installing display windows in the early years of the twentieth century, and others later on, such modifications were not enough to satisfy many Progressive reformers and urban planners. The growing number of zoning advocates especially found mixed residential and commercial neighborhoods to be undesirable holdovers of the unregulated industrial city. They worked to separate urban land uses. Their success in creating zoned districts did not end the neighborhood grocery but did to a large degree change cultural perceptions of what modern and professionally run grocery stores *should* look like and where they *should* be located.

City planning and zoning agendas created work for architects, who began paying attention to the design of small stores (groceries, bakeries, bicycle shops) as zoned retail districts became more prevalent. In the 1910s and during the building boom of the 1920s, such commissions became a more significant part of the work of some architectural firms. In 1925, the *Architectural Forum* featured a two-part series examining current designs for small shops. Significantly, most of the projects described and illustrated represented shops that were designed as part of zoned retail districts, not individual neighborhood stores. They signal the success of urban planners and zoning advocates in reallocating (i.e., segregating) uses of urban space.[14]

The title of the first part of this series—"Design Derived From Period Precedent"—suggests the appearance of these groups of shops. A few illustrations, particularly by architect Aymar Embury II, featured simple colonial and federal styles. Most examples depicted, though, were in more fanciful styles, such as the Tudor Revival, a popular suburban style at the time. Another page carried a photograph of an old French shop front in the collection of the Metropolitan Museum of Art side by side with a newly designed shop front "in French style" in Providence, Rhode Island. Such fanciful designs were charming but out of reach for most grocers—and would have looked quite out of place in most urban neighborhoods. But it is easy to see that once such shops began appearing on the streets of retail districts, neighborhood stores operating out of houses could seem somehow less professional—relics of the dirty industrial city.

Once again, the independent neighborhood grocer became the target of those who saw themselves as championing progress. The *Forum* writer here noted that if architects had not been as involved in designing small stores in the past, that was largely because the small storekeeper was "often so devoid of imagination that he cannot appreciate until he has it the commercial worth of architectural beauty." Undoubtedly, most small storeowners were limited by budget rather than lack of imagination. Undoubtedly, the Dutch, Tudor, and French designs illustrated in this series were much too expensive and too impractical for the finances and locations of most neighborhood grocers.

Architects were perhaps a little hard on some of these small storeowners because small shopkeepers who had some money to modernize more frequently hired the architect's arch-competitor: the local contractor. Modernizing the storefront right in the neighborhood was more affordable and practical for neighborhood grocers. The Detroit Show Case Company (DESCO) offered advice to local builders and contractors about how to convince small retailers to install modern storefronts and provided them with technical construction information on completing the work. The examples illustrating this trade publication, though, appear to be retail spaces on the first floor of larger office buildings rather than small neighborhood shops. Thus, even DESCO understood that by the

1920s, most small shopkeepers could not even afford remodeling projects. Like architects, they, too, sought the more lucrative contracts to be had from larger projects downtown and in new retail districts.[15]

The federal government also lent financial and thus cultural support to zoned commercial districts rather than to small neighborhood shops. In the 1930s, New Deal programs provided millions of dollars, mainly through the Modernization Credit Plan, to update stores. This program was a Main Street or commercial district program, not one that would assist independent grocers in neighborhood corner stores. Thus, New Deal programs funded more "modern" environments and participated in reshaping cultural perceptions and expectations about grocery stores and small retail shops in general. All the forces for modernization favored not just zoned commercial districts but purpose-built establishments, not businesses operating out of dwellings. After World War II, many neighborhood groceries—along with their neighborhoods—were swept away in large-scale urban redevelopment programs as part of the process of removing "blighted" districts from cities.[16]

MODERNITY AND TRADITION MEET IN THE NEIGHBORHOOD GROCERY STORE

Unlike chain supermarkets and the new commercial districts, neighborhood groceries blended the old and the new. The "modernization" and "professionalization" of the neighborhood grocery store was a very uneven process, differing from region to region and perhaps even more from grocer to grocer within the same city. By the end of the nineteenth century, even in small towns many grocers carried packaged foods that they displayed on the walls and in storefront windows. Yet, in both small towns and large cities independent grocery stores combined a range of new and traditional practices. Perhaps this mix obscured the ways in which many small grocers *had* adapted new practices. Critical reformers and urban planners might also not have realized that old practices actually met the needs of many residents in American towns and cities.[17]

The town of Millersburg, Pennsylvania, located in Dauphin County just a few miles from the state capital of Harrisburg (and just about one hundred miles from Philadelphia), provides evidence that Progressive Era professionalization had reached grocers even in small towns by the early years of the twentieth century. Advertisements and photographs of retailers included in Millersburg's 1907 centennial souvenir book indicate that some grocers were well aware of new professional standards. Ads and illustrations also indicate that some of the same grocers also maintained some traditional retailing practices. Only two grocers described themselves as "exclusive" grocery stores; the fact that both used this term indicates both proprietors saw specialized food stores as something new or better.[18]

Other advertisements indicate that even in 1907 food shopping in Millersburg remained a complicated, time-consuming process that required errands to a number of stores, as it had been earlier in large cities. Many types of stores carried food items. All ten dry good stores advertised carried some groceries. There were also bakeries, dairy stores, and soft drink stores; several of the dairy stores also advertised local fresh produce. The two feed and coal stores sold sacks of flour and potatoes. Steever's Drug Store, with its reputation for cleanliness, sold not only "pure drugs" and patent medicines; it also carried "pure spices of all kinds, whole and ground." This was one year after the Food and Drug Act. Details gleaned from these advertisements remind us that the development of specialized grocery stores affected the traditional retail practices of other types of stores as well.

The full-page advertisement for Snyder & Shetron, grocers who offered "staple, fancy and green groceries," shows in a photograph that this small grocery blended the new and the old (Figure 5.4). In their modern display window, they arranged their packaged goods in simple pyramids that were easily visible to passersby. But they still made more traditional use of the sidewalk space around their corner location. At first glance, bulk produce displayed outside might characterize this establishment as an old-fashioned country store. But outdoor displays were a practical way to show goods to passersby. The only reason many grocers in more complex urban areas stopped the practice was that reformers banned it. Practicality was also an issue: grocers in large cities probably had to haul such displays inside every evening and set them up every morning. Perhaps in a smaller town such as Millersburg outdoor displays could be safely left out overnight.

All, or at least several, family members pose proudly beside the store and their inventory; very likely, all the family members depicted worked in the store, even the little boy. More unusual, a customer is included in the photograph, in the midst of choosing an item and paying for it. Even if the proprietors had not read some of the professional trade advice suggesting the use of mannequins, Snyder & Shetron understood the psychology of incorporating a satisfied customer in the display: in this case, not a mannequin but a real person.

Most important, they emphasized their connection to the global economy by noting they carried both "Foreign and Domestic Fruits." The Snyder & Shetron advertisement testifies to the mix of change and continuity that could exist side by side in one small grocery business. This particular example is from a small town, but numerous such examples were common in large cities as well.

Even in large cities, neighborhood grocers who stocked modern packaged foods and adopted new methods of display and advertising contin-

Figure 5.4. Full-page advertisement for Snyder & Shetron General Grocery Store, Millersburg, Pennsylvania. Both the image and the text of this advertisement indicate the intermixing of change and continuity in the independent grocery business. *Source:* Souvenir Book: Millersburg Centennial Celebration, *published by the Committee on Printing and Advertising, 1907. From the author's collection.*

ued to offer some bulk goods as a convenience to customers, as well as specialty ethnic and "homemade" foods. In many urban neighborhoods such traditional offerings were not viewed as old fashioned but were prized by customers. Stocking traditional foods provided one way for immigrants to bring some of their inherited culture with them to America.

The small neighborhood grocery indeed offered immigrants one path to success in America. Philadelphia city directories and census information reveal that by 1900 perhaps the majority of small grocers were immigrants or the children of immigrants. One early twentieth-century Italian language pamphlet, today housed in the Historical Society of Pennsylvania, features photographs of Gennaro Pinto and his South Philadelphia grocery store. Pinto's grocery was a typical corner store in a three-story brick dwelling with a shed roof extending over the sidewalk, where a great quantity of goods was displayed. The writer described Pinto's successful store to suggest the grocery business was one of the opportunities America offered to other Italians. Pinto's store was located in the midst of a large Italian section of the city. Newly arrived Italians who did not know English had no trouble communicating with an Italian grocer. This was one business in which an immigrant could have an advantage over a native-born grocer. The success of the Pinto family illustrated the writer's point that operating grocery stores was one of the most practical livelihoods for new immigrants in America.[19]

First- and second-generation Americans who had inherited ethnic traditions and food ways from a parent often took pride in running modern stores, as many photographs of Philadelphia region grocery stores illustrated. They also took pride in preparing and offering to their customers homemade (quite literally) foods. Frank Agent was a Lithuanian immigrant who opened his first meat market shortly after arriving in the United States in the early twentieth century. Around World War I, he moved into the Clearview neighborhood in Southwest Philadelphia. Agent was an enterprising businessman; his store was in a semidetached dwelling, which he expanded in the back to include several rental apartments on the first and second floors, while the family lived nearby. The sons took over in the early 1930s and began to modernize the shop, installing wall shelving and glass display cases (Figure 5.5). To commemorate their renovations, the Agent brothers proudly posed beside their new meat case for this photo. The Agent store was a general grocery, but the brothers carried meat, which was unusual, so they advertised their store as the only meat market in the neighborhood.[20]

Two other grocery stores were within a few blocks of the Agent Market. Sam Jaspers advertised his grocery store as a "dairy store" because he was the only one of the three who sold ice cream. None of these three grocery stores carried any produce before World War II because pushcart vendors came to the neighborhood every morning.

George Doppler owned the third grocery store in the little Clearview neighborhood (Figure 5.6). Doppler's father had migrated from Germany in the 1880s and opened a butcher shop near the Fels Naptha plant in Southwest Philadelphia. George Jr. learned the butcher trade from his father, although he eventually owned and operated a general grocery store. His own store was a small one-story, detached frame building, not

Figure 5.5. Agent Grocery Meat Market, Clearview, Southwest Philadelphia, early 1930s. The Agent brothers proudly stand by their modern glass meat counter in their newly remodeled store interior. The vase of cut flowers added a celebratory touch. *Source: Image courtesy of Frank Agent, Jr.*

literally a corner store but within a residential neighborhood and convenient to passing foot traffic on Buist Avenue. Doppler took advantage of his location across the street from the Read School and stocked a variety of penny candy. Former neighborhood residents and family members remember that Doppler's store was the hangout for children.[21]

Doppler was proud to offer to his customers—many of whom were native born and not of German descent—the special German meats he learned to make from his father. Doppler constructed a smokehouse beside his garage; at Easter, his smoked hams attracted customers from many neighborhoods. He tried raising turkeys, kept his own hens and sold the eggs, kept bees to make and sell honey, and for years made his own wine.

Thursday was Doppler's day for making scrapple. He built a special kitchen in the basement of his house for this purpose. Doppler started the ingredients cooking by 6:00 a.m. and then went off to open the store. He came home at lunchtime to start the cooling process. Then he went back to the store until it closed, coming home to work past midnight to finish the scrapple. Customers knew freshly made scrapple awaited them on

Figure 5.6. George Doppler's Grocery Store in Southwest Philadelphia, c. 1940. Doppler's simple frame neighborhood grocery store had large storefront windows and prominently advertised brand names. *Source: Image courtesy of Isabel Doppler Foster.*

Friday. Doppler's daughter Isabel remembered that her father also made "mush, dried beef, bacon, and sometimes franks and special German lunch meats. But his specialty was smoked turkey, which no one else around had ever seen or heard of at that time. . . . It killed him to take a day off and he hardly ever did."[22]

Grocers like the Agent brothers and George Doppler carried the popular brand names that customers expected but also took pride in making traditional homemade foods that their customers also savored. Thus, they adopted modern practices but knowingly blended these with tradition.

CHANGE AND CONTINUITY

The 1920s seem to have been a turning point in the history of the independent grocery store. Prosperity benefited neighborhood grocers but also increased chain-store competition. Social reformers and zoning advocates worked to separate residential and commercial zones, particularly where food was concerned. Legal restrictions reduced the number of immigrants, who had accounted for the majority of independent grocers. The ongoing decline of the industrial economy and suburbanization throughout the twentieth century drew people away from the city. Finally, midcentury planners swept away many older neighborhoods and their grocery stores, which had deteriorated during the Depression and World War II.

But such stores persist today as they adapt to changing products and practices. Individual grocery stores such as the Agent Brothers or George Doppler's store combined a mix of new and old practices. Compared to chain stores and stores located in commercial districts, such stores might appear to be old fashioned. But characterizing lingering practices as out of date is misguided. Bulk nonpackaged foods provided affordable quantities for families on strict budgets; homemade foods continue to be sought after by many customers. It might very well be that despite longstanding attempts to regulate and limit their businesses, traditional characteristics, such as convenient neighborhood location, familiar ethnic foods, and the possibilities of purchasing a half dozen eggs or one "stick" of butter, explain their ongoing importance to urban neighborhoods today.

NOTES

1. Of course, many independent grocery stores have been family operated for three, four, and even more generations.

2. Carl Bridenbaugh, *Cities in the Wilderness: The First Century of Urban Life in America, 1625-1742* (New York: Ronald Press, 1938); *Cities in Revolt: Urban Life in America, 1743-1776* (New York: Alfred A. Knopf, 1955); Gerald Carson, *The Old Country Store* (New York: Oxford University Press, 1954).

3. Thomas F. DeVoe, *The Market Book: Containing a Historical Account of the Public Markets in the Cities of New York, Boston, Philadelphia, and Brooklyn With a Brief Description of every Article of Human Food sold therein.* Two volumes. (New York: The Author, 1862). A recent and comprehensive history of the physical spaces of food retailing in the United States is James M. Mayo, *The American Grocery Store: The Business Evolution of an Architectural Space* (Westport, CT: Greenwood Press, 1993). A brief but fascinating account of the activities that took place during the night to provision urban populations can be found in Peter C. Baldwin, in the section titled "Early Phased Work: Food," in the *Watches of the Night: Life in the Nocturnal City, 1820-1930* (Chicago: University of Chicago Press, 2012), 108–14.

4. Edward K. Spann, *The New Metropolis: New York City, 1840-1857* (New York: Columbia University Press, 1981), 127.

5. Samuel H. Terry, *The Retailer's Manual: Embodying the Conclusions of Thirty Years' Experience in Merchandizing* (Newark, NJ: The Author, 1869), 13.

6. Terry, *The Retailer's Manual*, 19.

7. Clyde Lyndon King, "Can the Cost of Distributing Food Products Be Reduced?" Special Issue, "The Cost of Living," *Annals of the American Academy of Political and Social Science*, XLVIII (July 1913): 210. Estimates of the numbers of food stores in every city vary; the number is difficult to determine accurately because many types of stores (delicatessens, butchers, meat and fish markets, restaurants, variety, and even dry goods stores often offered a few food items as a sideline. Obviously, these sideline activities presented competition to independent grocers just as chain stores did.

8. Lisa C. Tolbert, "The Aristocracy of the Market Basket," *Food Chains: From Farmyard to Shopping Cart*, ed. Warren Belasco and Roger Horowitz (Philadelphia: University of Pennsylvania Press, 2009): 180–95.

9. Such advice provides a counterpoint to the attacks of many social reformers concerned with rising food prices and family budgets. These writers frequently de-

picted the independent neighborhood grocer as the main enemy of the American family's economic security. See the articles in the Special Issue, "The Cost of Living," *Annals of the American Academy of Political and Social Sciences*, XLVIII (July 1913).

10. Quite likely, just as the display of goods was considered from a visually aesthetic viewpoint, the absence of certain odors might have been considered an aesthetic improvement as well.

11. Ida Tarbell, "The Cost of Living and Household Management," Special Issue: The Cost of Living, *Annals of the American Academy of Political and Social Science*, XLVIII (July 1913): 127–30. For the intricate problems of regulating food production, transportation, distribution, and sale, see G. T. Ferris, "How a Great City Is Fed," *Harper's Weekly*, March 22, 1890, 229–32.

12. George W. Hunter, *A Civic Biology: Presented in Problems* (New York: American Book Company, 1914); George W. Hunter and Walter G. Whitman, *Civic Science in the Community* (New York: American Book Company, 1922): 181.

13. Alfred G. Bauer, *The Art of Window Dressing for Grocers* (Chicago: Sprague, Warner & Company, 1902): III. Sprague, Warner & Company had a vested interest in encouraging both window displays and inventories of canned and boxed foods. They began in the 1860s as a small neighborhood grocery store in Chicago. By the early twentieth century, Sprague, Warner was a large corporate manufacturer of "Fancy Groceries," including Richelieu jams and preserves. Mason Warner, *Sprague, Warner & Company, 1862-1912* (Chicago: Sprague, Warner & Company, 1912). http://www.archive.org/details/spraguewarnercom00warn, accessed January 28, 2013.

14. "The Architecture of the Small Shop. Part I: Design Derived From Period Precedent," *Architectural Forum* XLII (February 1925): 97–120. An editor's note indicated that the second part of the series, to appear in the August issue, would focus on arcaded commercial spaces, emphasizing the growing number of zoned retailed spaces.

15. Detroit Show Case Company. *Store Fronts: Remodeling Store Fronts Is One of the Most Profitable Branches of the Contracting Business* (Detroit: Detroit Show Case Company, 1922). http://www.archive.org/details/StoreFrontsRemodelingStoreFrontsIsOneOfTheMostProfitableBranches, accessed January 31, 2013.

16. Gabrielle Esperdy, *Modernizing Main Street: Architecture and Consumer Culture in the New Deal* (Chicago: University of Chicago Press, 2008). Main Street nostalgia represents the success of zoning advocates at the expense of the neighborhood grocer. Several recent books examine both Main Street and Main Street nostalgia. See, for instance, Miles Orvell, *The Death and Life of Main Street: Small Towns in American Memory, Space, and Community* (Chapel Hill: University of North Carolina Press, 2012); Ryan Poll, *Main Street and Empire: The Fictional Small Town in the Age of Globalization* (New Brunswick, NJ: Rutgers University Press, 2012); and Richard V. Francaviglia, *Main Street Revisited* (Iowa City: University of Iowa Press, 1996).

17. New packaged foods presented a hardship for some families. Grocers and street cart vendors sold single eggs, even egg yolks, or flour by the cup. Women could purchase the exact ingredient quantities they needed. Grocers who continued to offer bulk goods along with packaged goods often did so because they understood the needs of their customers, not necessarily because they were unaware of new standards of hygiene. For more on pushcart vendors, see Daniel Bluestone, "The Pushcart Evil," in *The Landscape of Modernity: New York City, 1900-1940*, ed. David Ward and Olivier Zunz (New York: The Russell Sage Foundation, 1992).

18. *Souvenir Book: Millersburg Centennial Celebration*, published by the Committee on Printing and Advertising, 1907.

19. Giuseppe Brocato, *La Colonia Italiana de Filadelfia*, 1906. Historical Society of Pennsylvania, Books and Pamphlets Collection (oversize F158.9.I8 C6x). Operating small grocery stores in neighborhood dwellings offered a path to success for many individuals. In 1900, city directories indicate that black Philadelphians, about 7 percent of the city's population, operated about one hundred grocery stores. About 10 percent of Philadelphia's grocers were women. Studying California, Jessica Ellen Sewell found that women generally accounted for 10–12 percent of a city's grocers,

although in Los Angeles they accounted for about 30 percent of all grocers. See Sewell, *Women in the Everyday City: Public Spaces in San Francisco, 1890-1915* (Minneapolis: University of Minnesota Press, 2011), 54–55. Constance Cooper, curator, Historical Society of Delaware, is researching female grocers in Wilmington, Delaware, and has found higher than average numbers of female grocers in that city as well.

20. Frank Agent, Jr., taped oral interview with author, November 8, 1999.

21. Isabel Doppler Foster and Nancy Melnick, taped oral interview with author, October 27, 1999. George Doppler Jr. "Roots of the Laughlin/Robinson/Russell/Doppler Families." Copy of typed manuscript generously lent to author by Isabel Doppler Foster.

22. Isabel Doppler Foster and Nancy Melnick, taped oral interview with author, October 27, 1999.

SIX

Farmers' Markets, Food, and the Architecture of Control

J. Ritchie Garrison

In the fall, the Newark, Delaware, Farmers' Market is not much to look at. Open on Sundays in a parking lot in front of the Newark Natural Foods Co-op, it emphasizes flexibility over order. Vendors bring tables and, usually, folding four-post metal frames with fabric tops that shade vendors from sun or rain. They command the edges of the lot facing inward to form a courtyard, where customers congregate and circulate. Nearby parking intended for the retail and medical offices in the area provides free spaces that are usually congested the rest of the week. Many customers walk but most drive, park for a few minutes, make their purchases, load them into their vehicles, and are off for the afternoon game or Sunday dinner. Whether we start with the parking lot, the Co-op, the food, or the "farm" trucks that carry the merchandise, objects link people in complicated ways.[1]

The Newark Farmers' Market embodies behaviors that have deep historical and biological roots. Because the world's food supplies depend on varying environments, humans have developed ecological, economic, and political coping strategies to try to flatten supply variations, improve health, and measure and manage results. Thus, the Newark Farmers' Market is never just about ethically and regionally sourced food (Figure 6.1). In any given week, there are local farmers who sell the things they raise or process. But if buyers spend time outside the circle of customers and study what happens in the rear areas of the parking lot, they will also find panel vans with open back doors. Inside are the cardboard boxes of vegetables or fruit, purchased wholesale in the Philadelphia market and shipped in from California's Central Valley. These boxes remain out of casual sight. To preserve the impression of local farming, only unpacked produce makes it to the plastic tables under the temporary pavilions. It is easy to dismiss the produce boxes as a cynical form of deception, but behaviors are rarely that simple. Everyone at the site—the farmers and the would-be farmers who are really retailers—is hoping to do business, make a profit, or have some fun. People are well behaved. There are no bar codes, unit pricing, or checkout registers. It is cash and carry; whether any of the day's profits will get reported to the IRS is impossible to determine. Everything will be gone that evening, with little more than some crushed beet greens to show some parking lots lead second lives.[2]

The farmers' market challenges scholars to interpret appearances. Supplying our bodies with food is so basic to human biology that it is easy to forget how complicated the process is and, consequently, how entangled people are with objects, political economies, and nature. The case studies presented in this chapter—big agriculture in the Central Valley of California, market landscapes in colonial Boston and Philadelphia, and the Newark Co-op and Newark Farmers' Market—are deliberately limited and impressionistic. The tight focus on differing spaces and time periods reminds readers that changes to our food ways have always been messy, that what many people think of as new problems have long histories, and that change is branching rather than linear. These flexible yet

Figure 6.1. Newark Farmers' Market, October 2010. ***Source: Image courtesy of the author.***

structured relationships were designed for strategic diversity in a world of uncertain supply. The conclusion emphasizes concepts derived from the case studies. As humans try to make decisions based on complex causal relationships, actions and outcomes often depend on trade-offs between small things easily overlooked or oversimplified; in turn, the variables that change or remain the same always reference the constants embedded in human existence. At the most basic level it comes down to "what's for dinner?"

THE CENTRAL VALLEY

Whatever the original intent may have been, the Newark Farmers' Market pulses to the initiatives of small local businesses that grow their own produce *and* long chains of commercial agriculture and wholesale distributor's commodity exchanges. The latter are not just large well-capitalized corporations but also family farmers who are subsidized in various ways by regulated water systems, the Extension Service, university experiment stations, transportation infrastructure, migrant laborers (some of them "illegal" or "undocumented" immigrants), and tax payers. We choose to overlook the injustices and ecological liabilities of this system because it produces cheap, high-quality food in quantities that the rest of the world envies. To gain an impression of how the material and political are intertwined, it is instructive to take a field trip to the Central Valley of California, one of the most valuable agricultural regions in the world.[3]

In May the valley landscape around Fresno, California, projects an image of lush bounty that is deceptive. By June, temperatures climb into the high 90s and low 100s. The heat reminds visitors that aridity is the land's natural condition. The soils and crops are cultural artifacts. Irrigation transformed California and much of the Southwest. In many years, the Central Valley is frost free, setting up conditions in which famers can grow marketable products for most of the year. Consequently, people in the area manage water, topography, crops, and animals to reduce inefficiencies and undesirable variation. Beginning in the 1880s, private companies in the Fresno area have diverted water from local rivers, a process that has grown only more complex over time with overlapping private and public jurisdictions.[4]

We can see the long-term effects of these changes on the Enns Ranch near Reedley. Begun in 1899 on forty acres, the family-owned and operated ranch now raises stone fruits, mostly peaches and plums, on sixty acres and another 350 leased acres. By state standards it is a small ranch that produces about 200,000 boxes of fruit a year and processes fruit for several neighboring ranches. To set that output in perspective, Paul Groth and others have pointed out that the big corporate operations produce tens of millions of boxes of fruit on multiple farms located in various parts of the world.[5]

Although privately owned, the Enns Ranch, like many others in the Valley, depends on government experiment stations and private researchers. In a good year, California peaches start ripening in mid-May, when the "Earlitreat" varieties come in. Thereafter, new varieties arrive in sequence about every two weeks until late October, when workers pick the "Last Chances." The long season extends work opportunities for field labor and helps stabilize cash flow. It also has depended to a considerable extent on low fees for tree varieties charged by the Kearney Agricultural Station of the University of California and the USDA's Research Station for the San Joaquin Valley. Private companies have begun to compete with publicly funded institutions by developing patented varieties with significant market demand and charging per-tree or per-box fees. It turns out that fruit, like so many other things in American material culture, goes out of fashion. Consumers, not just horticultural scientists or farmers, shape trees and economic decisions. Suppliers track consumer purchases to predict future demand.

Walking the farm lane behind the Enns Ranch's offices and sheds brings visitors to the irrigation canal that sustains operations (Figure 6.2). It's 10–12 feet wide and about four feet deep, with sloping earthen sides. Although state officials are working to get more of them covered to reduce evaporation, most of these canals, including the one that supplies the Enns Ranch, are still open to the sky. When water is admitted to the main trunk lines at certain times of the day, it flows out to the ditches that supply the trees in the field. It is not as efficient as drip irrigation, but the ditches are cheap to build, maintain, and adapt as new sections are planted or removed.

Valley farmers are not sentimental about their trees. They divide the ranch's orchards into sections by varieties that are designed to produce fruit in predictable windows of time, in dry conditions, and with as little variation in size and weight as the science can deliver. Moving pickers from one section to the next reduces labor costs. Defective trees get no quarter. Workers cut down trees past their prime and replant or graft new scions to older tissue. A short walk reveals the relentless calculus of the market. Some sections have mature trees; others are newly planted or grafted with a variety that the family hopes will sell well. The business carries significant risk because new stock takes time to mature and the owners need to balance producing stock with trees that are still too young to produce much fruit (Figure 6.3). Pickers harvest ripe fruit by hand, placing it in round buckets or plastic totes. Most of the trees are low to the ground because setting up ladders to pick fruit high up wastes time and puts workers' safety at risk.

Speed counts in this hot, arid climate; workers have to wash, inspect, cull, and get the fruit into cold rooms as soon as feasible to preserve its

Figure 6.2. Irrigation canal, Enns Ranch, Reedley vicinity, California, May 2008.
Source: Image courtesy of the author.

freshness. Rotten or bruised fruit earns nothing. Machines wash the fruit. Humans inspect it, placing culls onto a conveyor that takes the rejects out of the processing shed. Workers recycle the culls as fertilizer, as they have no recoverable market value. Fruit that passes inspection goes through

Figure 6.3. Newly planted orchard, Enns Ranch, Reedley vicinity, California, May 2008. ***Source: Image courtesy of the author.***

computer-managed machines that optically weigh, size, and tag the fruit with "PLU" (price look-up) stickers. The machine then sends the fruit to the proper packing station for that weight, where workers, mostly women, cull rejects and pack marketable fruit into cartons (Figure 6.4). These cartons may consist of loose fruit in boxes (the cheaper fruit most in evidence at the Newark Farmers' Market) or plastic trays, into which packers place individual fruit before they go into the cartons.

Thus food is an aesthetic, not just nutritional, problem in supply-and-demand economics. Scientists can with time develop cultivars that resist bruising and rot, but consumers will not buy them unless the fruit tastes and looks good. Up to a point, marketers can try to mitigate problems via advertising, display techniques, and pricing, but most shoppers judge food by feel, smell, sight, and experience. They also judge by means of gossip and tactical thinking. Some value price over taste; others prefer consistency, freshness, or cleanliness. Retailers try to quantify consumer preferences to hedge their bets when buying, but the probabilities are hard to predict because there are so many variables.

Bad weather, low water, poor market prices, technological changes, and government regulations put pressure on profits and alter assumptions and the landscape. The Enns Ranch has two large sheds that shelter its operations and fruit from the intense sun. Ken Enns put up the "old" shed in three phases between 1981 and 2000. The new shed went up in

Figure 6.4. Optical sizer machine, Enns Ranch, Reedley vicinity, California, May 2008. *Source: Image courtesy of the author.*

1999, when the US government required a PLU sticker on every piece of fruit sold in American grocery stores. These stickers help track the fruit if public health problems occur and facilitate inventory control at the retail end of the supply chain. Small family operations either had to adopt the expensive new machinery used to grade and sticker the fruit, pay someone else to do it, or sell the ranch to a larger outfit. The Ennses acquired the new $250,000 machinery and built a shed to house it. In it, they process their own fruit and collaborate with some of their neighbors.

On the wall next to the office in the new shed, where the optical sizer automatically sorts fruit, hang a series of old fashioned stamps used with an ink pad. The stamps identify the neighboring ranches that process their fruit in the Enns's shed. These layers of old and new reflect the complicated continuities and changes that are a part of American agriculture. A regulator's decision in 1999 on the other side of the country profoundly altered the lives of the Valley's farm families and the landscapes they live in. Fruit became a commodity in a digital age, but the old-fashioned rubber stamps and the social ties they represent continue to organize relationships the optical scanners cannot sort.[6]

If we set out to identify the ways in which Americans have regulated, measured, commodified, and specialized food, it is easy enough (and accurate) to render the Central Valley as a product of capitalist superstructures and power relationships. But the ability to raise food and sell it to others implicates us all in health and safety and in our expectations about the common welfare of others. Governments intervene in the marketplace to make food affordable to the poor, or to provide for safe food, or to favor constituents' wishes. Particularly in urban locations where people depend upon markets rather than neighbors to acquire their daily bread, governments have long regulated weights and measures and manipulated the market logic of distribution, warehousing, and preparation.

COLONIAL AND EARLY NATIONAL FOOD MARKETS

Exploring colonial and early national food markets is a way to think about persistence and change in the constant of hunger. In British America, Boston authorities imposed market restrictions around the morality of a "just price," a belief that a person could make a reasonable profit but not at the expense of his or her neighbors. This notion was shaped by Boston's topography, for the town had little arable land or firewood and had to import basic necessities even in the 1630s. By the end of the century, town selectmen regulated the assize on bread, using the prevailing market price on wheat to gauge how large a loaf of bread must be. When the price of wheat went up, the size of a loaf of bread decreased; if the price on wheat went down, then the size of a loaf had to increase. In effect the town's bakers received a guaranteed price and therefore a profit for their bread, but they could not raise their prices in a time of shortage or keep their loaves small when wheat prices went down. Other cities in colonial America, including New York and Philadelphia, also followed this system. For bakers, the law imposed tough standards of accountability. Being off by as little as an ounce could expose retail bakers to fines or allow authorities to confiscate their wares for cheating their customers.[7]

As it was, organizing food supplies in the seventeenth and eighteenth centuries was a troublesome form of administration with significant differences of opinion about effective policy. Many towns prohibited engrossing, the process by which retailers intercepted incoming produce to monopolize supplies and control market prices, or rebating, the related process by which retailers aggrandized market share by paying a supplier a rebate under the table in exchange for exclusive access to supplies. Both practices concentrated control of supplies in the hands of the few and reduced competition. The desirable outcome from the perspective of Boston's selectmen was a centralized marketplace, initially open on prescribed days but eventually on every day except Sunday, to which the region's farmers would bring supplies in sufficient quantities to hold down prices so the poor could afford to eat. That was the theory. Authorities implemented the theory by imposing laws and enforcing them with fines, social opprobrium, and if necessary, jail time. They also used public funds and Peter Faneuil's legacy to the town to create a central market that would physically concentrate supplies and increase competitive pricing.[8]

Located more or less in the center of Boston's population during the eighteenth century (where the current Faneuil Hall is located) for easy access by hungry consumers, the new market was a mixed success. Regulations prohibited peddlers who did not have to charge as much for their supplies because they had lower capital costs and did not pay property taxes. The rule pleased the grocers and merchants who rented stalls in the market or maintained shops and warehouses in its vicinity. Consumers now had to come to them instead of buying from peddlers. But many consumers liked the convenience of buying from peddlers, who sold them items at their door, saving them time and a trip to the market.

Scholars like to find patterns in the structures of economics and politics, but so much of human decision making, now and in the past, depends upon the prosaic and practical. Could a parent leave children home while fetching supplies or did they have to come along? People in trades lost productivity if they had to go food shopping. Farmers from the countryside grumbled at lower prices if the markets were glutted and they had the cost of freighting their wares to town for little or no profit. In short, scholars' ability to discern patterns in documented regulations challenges them to explain what such patterns mean.[9]

There was always more to colonial markets than provisioning. The market was a center of sociability and entertainment. It concentrated retail traffic and stabilized the exchange of information via oral communication. The importance of these functions was articulated by the amount of space devoted to the market and the permanent architecture that sheltered market activities. By the beginning of the nineteenth century, all of America's most important cities and quite a few smaller ones had market facilities. In the largest cities, such as Philadelphia, these included a head house with office and meeting spaces and the "shambles," long wooden-roofed sheds supported by masonry or wooden piers that were open at the sides. The sheds accommodated the needs of farmers who brought their produce to the market in season. Grocers, butchers, bakers, tavern keepers, coffee houses, and liquor retailers clustered nearby to serve customers when winter weather would have frozen liquids or ruined produce kept in the open sheds. Many of these food services were lodged in basements to prevent things from freezing or to take advantage of cooler temperatures in hot summer months, but it is important to understand that permanent, indoor, retail establishments always complemented the more fluid activities of the farmers' markets in the shambles.

Of the early market houses, the ones in Philadelphia are best documented, largely because William Birch and his son drew a series of views of Philadelphia and had them engraved, printed, and bound. A smaller market, south of the one on present-day Market Street—the New Market—has survived and was restored in the 1960s (Figure 6.5). A number of the plates in Birch's book show the city's early market house and shambles, which stretched westward down the middle of what was then High Street from Second Street and eventually to Sixth Street. It was a common arrangement with parallels in London, Southwark, Bristol, and Norwich in the United Kingdom and in New Orleans, Louisiana; Charleston, South Carolina; Annapolis and Baltimore, Maryland; New Castle, Delaware; Lancaster, Pennsylvania; New York City; Providence, Rhode Island; and Boston, Massachusetts. Some were linear like those in Philadelphia; others were rectangular or conformed to the spaces available. Many, such as the one in Schafferstown, Pennsylvania, simply had open yards in which vendors could congregate. Some of the shambles like those in Charleston or Philadelphia have survived and are still in use. The Birch views and a series of sketches made by John Lewis Krimmel allow us to populate the architecture with life as these delineators selectively depicted it.[10]

Visual sources and travel narratives suggest that markets were filled with varying forms of exchange and unchoreographed street theater. Men and women, young and old, black and white, Native Americans and newly arrived immigrants, populated the streets of early American cities. John Lewis Krimmel, a German artist who sketched and painted scenes in southeast Pennsylvania, was fascinated by Philadelphia's market. He depicted several scenes of street vendors that suggested the diversity of the city's consumers (Figure 6.6). A young African American worker sells Pepper-Pot stew to her white customers in a scene that Krimmel fabricated using preliminary studies, but it registers as an accurate depiction of what he must have experienced.[11]

Bounding the street in Philadelphia were two- and three-story brick buildings. The basements and the bottom floors of these structures often provided retail shops close to the action. Higher up were rental spaces or owner-occupied rooms that could house domestic space or workshops at varying price points depending on condition and access. The street itself was paved and served as a stage for the work of the market since the slow pace of horse-driven vehicles allowed people time to get out of the way of oncoming traffic. It was a liminal zone, literally betwixt and between the politer rhythms on either side of the street. Both Krimmel and Birch depicted peddlers, butchers, and wood merchants selling their wares in the street (Figure 6.7). In one view showing the corner of Market and Third streets, a butcher with a bloody apron cuts off a roast from a carcass set on top of a butcher's wooden horse. The butcher conducted his visceral business directly outside one of Philadelphia's most posh retail buildings, a structure filled with large windows and innovative design but doomed as a commercial enterprise because the sensory world of the market was ill suited to the kind of rational distancing politeness sought. Many of Philadelphia's most fashionable retail stores were on

Figure 6.5. New Market head house and shambles, 1804 (restored 1994), Philadelphia, Pennsylvania. *Source: Image courtesy of the author.*

Walnut and Chestnut streets, farther south and away from the unruliness and smells connoted by the term "shambles."

The shambles shielded shoppers from sun and precipitation, but they were open at the sides to allow easy access, reduce costs of construction,

Figure 6.6. John Lewis Krimmel, *Pepper Pot: A Scene in the Philadelphia Market, 1811*, oil on canvas; 19½ × 15½ in. *Source: Image courtesy of Sumpter Priddy III.*

and provide flexibility for different sorts of vendors. Basic amenities were already in place. Inside the shambles were iron hooks driven into the beams, which ran horizontally between the brick piers. Vendors could tie their wares to the beams or hang them from the hooks until they were wanted. Some brought portable tables with attached bench seats that

Figure 6.7. William Birch and Thomas Birch, Southeast Corner of Third and Market Streets, Philadelphia, from *The City of Philadelphia, in the State of Pennsylvania, North America as It Appeared in the Year 1800.* [Philadelphia]: W. Birch, Springland Cot, near Neshaminy Bridge on the Bristol Road, Pa., 1800, RBR NA735 P54b PF. *Source: Image courtesy of The Winterthur Library, Printed Book and Periodical Collection.*

they could assemble and serve from. The Winterthur Museum has a surviving market table that represents one type of portable furniture that vendors could break down and store—the antecedent to the portable pavilions and fold-up tables modern vendors bring to the Newark Farmers' Market. Probably used for serving food, it reminds us that the market not only existed to sell food that people would carry home to prepare but also had food that customers would consume on site (Figure 6.8).

Despite the small visual cues in the Birch views that seem to individualize identity via dress and deportment in the swirl of commerce, this was a landscape of negotiation. Customers strolled through the shambles and outside on the streets in varying degrees of finery. If they had means, they could hire a cartman to deliver their purchases; if they did not or did not wish to pay for help, they had to carry things for themselves in baskets or bags. Prices were not posted. Sellers sized up the customer's ability to pay and asked what they hoped they might get; buyers evaluated the goods, asked about prices, and if the parties agreed, the deal was closed. Thus, it took experience to shop efficiently and effectively. The freshest and best produce was likely to be gone if buyers did not get to the market early; the bargains might come late in the day when the sellers

Figure 6.8. Peddler's bench and storage trunk, maker unknown, northeast United States, 1800–1850, pine, maple, paint. ***Source: Image courtesy of The Winterthur Museum, bequest of Henry Francis Du Pont, 1959.1671.***

would rather unload their stock at a discount than return home with it unsold or leave it to rot. If all the vendors showed up with turnips to sell and the market was glutted, the price collapsed. If consumers wanted parsnips instead but there were none, they changed dinner plans. It was a world in which freshness and abundance were still defined by the season and lack of refrigeration. City residents had to participate in the market to understand its patterns and pricing; outcomes often depended on flexibility and patience.

There are some critical differences between these early markets and behaviors still visible in the Newark Farmers' Market. Over time, most markets moved indoors; supply chains changed in response to faster transportation, wholesaling, and the development of commodities markets; and science and technology reoriented regulatory standards to mitigate problems with disease, food preservation, and nutrition. Colonial shoppers were more aware of these issues in the pre-germ theory era than many nonspecialists realize; they might not understand the relationships between bacteria and food poisoning, but they were good judges of food that was rotten or spoiled.

COOPERATIVES AND SUPERMARKETS

As food sales moved indoors, they became easier for authorities to regulate, but the risks of buying tainted food in farmer's markets or highly regulated commodity chains remain. People still like buying unregulated food if it seems locally sourced and fresh. They also know from experience that regulations, scientifically grounded or not, cannot stamp out all risks. Science is not a neutral bundle of methods and objective practitioners. Scientific methods also cannot adjudicate many ethical problems that people and societies must argue out and decide. The founding of food cooperatives and farmers' markets in the 1960s not only reflected continuity with past forms of commerce but also a counterculture movement against big corporate systems and government regulation.

The Newark Natural Foods Co-op is located behind the parking lot where the Newark Farmers' Market convenes. Founded in 1967 as a food buying club to acquire and sell organic and unrefined food, the Co-op incorporated in 1975 to serve the needs of its membership. Like many similar organizations established during the height of the counterculture movement in the 1960s, incorporation stabilized operations after its "Founding Mothers" got too busy to continue as a volunteers. The Co-op's mission is grounded in overlapping social, ideological, and political principles: it runs for the benefit of its members rather than investors or owners, it sells goods and services that ecological and fair trade practices shape, and it promotes an ethic of cooperation rather than competition. It looks like a small neighborhood grocery store without most of the processed foods laden with salt and sugar that show up in regular retail chains, and with a range of bulk foods and holistic supplements that its members like. The lawyers have vetted the language of the bylaws to clarify that items sold to members and the public are in compliance with the "Articles of Incorporation and to the fullest extent permitted by statute." The membership wants to make the world a better place via individual action, but opinions clearly vary on how to do that.[12]

The competition is nearby in the form of supermarkets and the big box chains, Costco and BJ's. These stores descend from the early supermarkets that developed toward the end of the 1920s and expanded rapidly in the 1930s. Those first supermarkets were large by the standards of their place and time; most of them responded to the rapid growth in automobility and suburbs. They served the needs of families far from downtown markets and benefited from the lower capital costs of rural and suburban land. Supermarkets offered parking and an extensive stock of produce, meats, and canned goods, much of it presented on accessible shelving. By contrast with the urban groceries (which are still with us) that prided themselves on attentive customer service, the new supermarkets reduced much of the clerical staff and let the customer fend for him- or herself in return for lower prices. Once through the checkout, customers could load up their automobiles. In that sense, the automobile had become a kind of market basket that allowed busy adults to make fewer trips to the market and carry more when they did go because they did not have to negotiate multiple trolley cars, buses, or subway lines.[13]

The Newark Co-op has survived for more than fifty years by adapting. It runs with modern computers and business practices because it cannot survive if it does not make enough of a profit to pay the fixed costs of staying in business. Despite its not-for-profit status, its prices are not necessarily cheaper than those of the ferociously competitive retail chains that increasingly stock organic and non-GMO (genetically modified organism) foods. Health regulations for both establishments impose standards of refrigeration, hygiene, packaging, pest management, energy use, and record keeping. Co-op members are not just buying food; they are making a statement about a set of ethical principles that they value.

FIVE MAJOR CHANGES IN THE ARCHITECTURE OF FOOD

Neither the continuities with the past nor explicit political critiques of for-profit agriculture and multinational food distributors can hide the profound changes in America's food markets over the nation's history. If readers consider the meta themes that emerge from these case studies—large-scale commercial agriculture in the Central Valley of California, market landscapes in colonial Boston and early nineteenth-century Philadelphia, and the modern Newark Co-op—they can see the effects of five major changes in the architecture of America's food system.

The first change involves sustained efforts to flatten variations in supply. Most Americans now expect that they can get all kinds of food, including fresh fruits and vegetables, without regard to the seasons. The only way to accomplish this was to chill fresh foods to retard rot and move produce quickly through global supply chains. It is a stunning achievement. In the colonial era and for millennia before, people salted, smoked, dried, pickled, and sugared foods to retard spoilage. In the nineteenth century, they began to take advantage of canning, refrigeration using ice, and railroads to speed food to markets. In the twentieth century, Americans adopted mechanical refrigeration as the electrical grid expanded, began flash freezing foods, and accelerated transportation by air freighting perishables or via container shipping. We have fresh foods constantly available because the supply chains are now global.

The second change is a focus on public health and the importance of protecting food and therefore people from contagious disease or contamination. Scientists have a clearer understanding of the causes of disease; they also have a more sophisticated body of knowledge about the interconnections of environment, physiology, and nutrition. On the one hand, scientifically based health policy has dramatically improved the supply of healthy food. On the other, it has raised concerns about managing variables humans previously did not understand or worry about. As our knowledge of microbiology grows, it has become apparent that humans vary in their resistance to or absorption of certain chemicals or nutritional compounds. Developing sound public policy about regulation and safety, about the definitions of words (such as "organic"), about legal liability for undercooked meats, about acceptable levels of salt, or about the effects of sugars or food additives is inherently contested and political. Is the caffeine in coffee good or bad for health? Is corn syrup a major cause of the nation's obesity crisis or just another sugar partially subsidized by the government via direct and indirect price supports for corn? If corn syrup *is* safe, do the quantities people consume matter? And who has the responsibility for supersize sodas, the seller or the buyer?

The third change is the development of better statistical measures—signified by the PLU stickers that the Enns Ranch must affix to produce. Scholars, businessmen, and bureaucrats like to measure and quantify things so that they can see patterns, reduce bias in decision making, and predict outcomes. The effect of rigorous scientific method has served Americans well in the effort to advance safety, productivity, profits, and prices. The downsides are that quantification always involves a form of translation from things or behaviors to numbers. Something is always lost in the translation. We may see accurately what we measure, but we do not always measure what we need to see; sometimes what we need to see is not measureable, predictable, or subject to simplification.[14]

The fourth change is an expanding conversation about the moral rights and responsibilities of humans in an increasingly connected world. In the relentless pursuit of profits, efficiency, and personal interest, what are our duties to other human beings? How do we feed people who are poor? Do we have the right to buy up most of the quinoa from South America—a key source of nutrition for indigenous people—just because we like its taste, value it as a "super food," and can afford to? Is the crowding of chickens into cramped quarters acceptable because it yields high-quality protein at low prices? Are we stealing freshwater from Mexico to grow lettuce in the desert? Do we need to mitigate the consequences of the power money gives us, and if so, are we wise enough to know how?

The fifth change is the increasingly diverse *and* entangled relationships of people and their things. The Newark Farmers' Market serves a purpose in the community. It continues a pattern of face-to-face exchange that goes far back in time. Nearby are the climate-controlled big box supermarkets that sell an astonishing array of items, which inventory scanners track via bar code so that managers will know what is selling and what inventory needs replenishing from places like the Enns Ranch. It is a system that seems powerful and manipulative and closed, but an outbreak of *E. coli* bacteria, a winter blizzard that knocks out the power, or an inconvenient parking lot can break it.[15]

Most of us live lives filled with small disruptions. The great humanistic insight is that we can cope with them because we have more creativity and resilience than we sometimes realize. Back at home from shopping at the Farmers' Market, I slice up the chicken I got at a supermarket and some potatoes that might actually have come from Delaware. We put them and some vegetables in the crock pot and turn it on. It will be done in six hours, just in time for the arrival of our two sons and their French bulldog, Guinevere. About six o'clock, we will set the table and sit down for a meal to replenish our bodies and spirits: we and our things are inseparable, and powerful together.

NOTES

1. Fieldwork for the Newark Farmers' Market occurred in the fall of 2010.

2. For more information on the world of supermarkets, see Andrew Seth and Geoffrey Randall, *Supermarket Wars: The Future of Global Food Retailing* (New York and London: Palgrave Macmillan, 2005); Barbara E. Kahn and Leigh M. McAllister, *Grocery Revolution: The New Focus on the Consumer* (New York: Prentice Hall, 1997). For a perspective on British grocery chains and their international connections, see Geoffrey Randall and Andrew Seth, *The Grocers: The Rise and Rise of the Supermarket Chains* (London: Kogan Page, 3rd. ed. 2011, orig. ed. 1999).

3. For insights on the development of big agriculture in California's Central Valley, see Donald Worster, *Rivers of Empire: Water, Aridity, and the Growth of the American West* (New York: Oxford University Press, 1985). For a perspective on the development of the supermarket in California, see Richard Longstreth, *The Drive-In, the Supermarket, and the Transformation of Commercial Space in Los Angeles, 1914-1941* (Cambridge: MIT Press, 2000).

4. This essay was shaped in part by fieldwork in the region around Fresno, California, in May 2008 and by the field guide (hereafter *Field Guide*) produced for the Vernacular Architecture Forum's annual meeting in 2008: *In the Garden of the Sun: California's San Joaquin Valley*, ed. Karana Hattersley-Drayton (Fresno, CA: Planning and Development Department, City of Fresno, April 2008). Paul Groth wrote the section titled "Farms, Farm Workers, and Packing Plants: People and Process in Recent San Joaquin Agribusiness Landscapes," 19–31. In 2008, for example, the Alta Irrigation District near Reedley, California, irrigated 173 square miles—about 111,000 acres of crops raised on carefully flattened land.

5. *Field Guide*, 22–28.

6. *Field Guide*, 26.

7. For a discussion of the doctrine of "Just Price," see Bernard Bailyn, *The New England Merchants in the Seventeenth Century* (Cambridge: Harvard University Press, 1955), 21. For the most complete discussion of the bread assize see Karen J. Friedmann, "Victualling Colonial Boston," *Agricultural History* 47, no. 3 (July 1973): 189–205. For a discussion of the bread assize's effects on New York City's bakers, see Howard B.

Rock, *Artisans of the New Republic: Tradesmen of New York City in the Age of Jefferson* (New York: New York University Press, 1979).

8. Nancy S. Seasholes, *Gaining Ground: A History of Landmaking in Boston* (Cambridge: MIT Press, 2003), 34–35.

9. Friedmann, "Victualling."

10. William Birch and Thomas Birch, *The City of Philadelphia, in the State of Pennsylvania, North America as It Appeared in the Year 1800* (Philadelphia, 1800).

11. Anneliese Harding, *John Lewis Krimmel: Genre Artist of the Early Republic* (Winterthur, DE: A Winterthur Book, The Henry Francis du Pont Winterthur Museum, Inc., 1994), 17.

12. http://www.newarknaturalfoods.com/co-op/, accessed May 4, 2013.

13. Longstreth, *The Drive-In.*

14. Alfred W. Crosby, *The Measure of Reality: Quantification and Western Society, 1250-1600* (New York: Cambridge University Press, 1997).

15. Ian Hodder, *Entangled: An Archaeology of the Relationships between Humans and Things* (Malden, MA: Wiley-Blackwell, 2012).

SEVEN

Living in a Bubble in the 1950s

The Material Culture of Effervescence

Jay Gitlin

Plop plop, fizz, fizz. Snap, crackle, pop. They are sounds that capture a most elusive aspect of the 1950s: cultural objects that are literally superficial, more surface than solid, that incorporate gas or hot air, that self-destruct. Mission Impossible? How do we define a subject that, by design, keeps floating away from us?

We think of the 1950s as a square decade—but there in the heart of it all, roundness everywhere—polka dots, red balloons, trial balloons, tiny bubbles. This is about the fifties I grew up in—a decade of great fancy and imagination, a decade of high hopes that produced baby boomers who, even in the face of serious issues, had a psychedelic streak. This essay will try to pin down the effervescent strain of our material culture in the postwar era, from the fizz of Alka-Seltzer and champagne music to the frothiness of bubble bath, an era that commoditized and incorporated the lightness of new materials from our floating soaps to our picture windows and translucent buildings. What connects these various objects? Is it the transience of bubble gum and bubbles? We were nurtured on dreams of flying, from astronauts to Mary Poppins. I think, above all, it is the opposite of gravitas and its cognate, aggravation. Born in our parents' dreams of creating new lives—ours—that might be spared the human sorrows of war and horrors of the Holocaust, our lives were shaped by the designed bubbles of suburbia. Up, up, and away we floated in our beautiful balloons. Nurtured on "populuxe"[1] and perpetual playfulness, we entered the sixties with great idealism, surrounded by a thin candy shell.

What follows, then, is an attempt to carry moonbeams home in a jar, to be serious—for just a moment—about our very lack of seriousness, to recapture our childhood of toys designed to defy gravity, from yo-yos to hula hoops, to weigh that almost weightless strand of our material culture.

A HAPPY CONVERGENCE

The end of World War II, much like the end of World War I, unleashed a powerful desire to "return to normalcy."[2] However, "normalcy," that is, the way things were before the war, is rarely achieved—not in the 1920s nor in the 1950s. Returning veterans rushed to embrace loved ones, and to no one's surprise, the result in both cases was a baby boom.[3] The boom that occurred roughly between 1946 and 1964, and especially in the United States, Canada, Australia, and New Zealand, was unprecedented. Marriage and birth rates soared.[4] Having survived a depression and a war, the parents of the baby boomers "were more likely to marry, married earlier, divorced more rarely, and had more unabashed pride of ownership than their parents or children."[5] Many a soldier in the midst of battle might have said, "If I can just get home, I'll be alright."[6]

And so my boomer generation has constituted what we might describe as a demographic blip—or for the purposes of this essay, a bubble—drawing the focus of analysts, historians, and manufacturers at every phase of our noisy lives. As historian Landon Jones put it, we have resembled "the pig in the python."[7] Our power as young consumers was recognized from the start. A children's song, "Rudolph the Red-Nosed Reindeer," written by Johnny Marks and recorded by Gene Autry, reached the top of the *Billboard* charts during Christmas week in 1949. It sold 2.5 million copies in its first year. Many of us grew up in newly constructed suburban communities. Suburbs grew 8.5 times faster than central cities did from 1945 to the late sixties. By the 1970s, we had become a suburban nation.[8] Driven by many factors, including a postwar housing shortage, new construction techniques, and federal policies designed to aid returning veterans, new communities rose like mushrooms on the peripheries of older urban centers. This new world did not resemble the prewar landscape. Though our Little Golden Books pictured prewar small towns with pedestrian-oriented Main Streets, our suburban developments were linked internally by yellow school buses. Televisions and consumer culture connected us to the world beyond our homes.[9] At the heart of our communities were schools, many of them built quickly to address the sudden demand. It was a new world, described by some social scientists as "filiocentric."[10] History began anew in 1946.

And into this perceived tabula rasa came stuff, stuff galore. Everything an empty home could need—once the consumer industrial complex retooled—was for sale, with advertisements blazing an image of the ideal suburban home that like a Norman Rockwell Thanksgiving dinner, had all the trimmings: refrigerators, washing machines, ovens, televisions, and lots of toys for good girls and boys. And there were jobs with good wages to buy all this stuff. Families with incomes in the $4,000–$7,000 range, the middle class as defined by *Fortune* magazine in 1953, accounted for 35 percent of the nation's population and earned 43 percent of the national income. The number of families in the lowest income class declined, and the share of national income earned by families in the higher bracket (above $7,500 annually) declined. According to Thomas Hine, "America was materially more democratic than it had been at any time in its history."[11] To use another Thomas Hine word, more Americans than ever before had entered the "buyosphere."[12]

There was a third element after suburban baby boomers and a flourishing buyosphere in our trilogy of preconditions that converged to produce the material culture of effervescence. It was the chemical industry and its ability to produce a variety of new materials, many of them pioneered in the 1930s, displayed at the New York World's Fair in 1939–1940, and developed during World War II. "Chemists Make a New World," an article in *National Geographic* proclaimed in November 1939.[13] They were right. We grew up in the fifties with materials as synthetic as their names: melamine, polyethylene, Styron, and Dacron. Disposable products accompanied disposable income. Yes, we had old-fashioned toys—dolls, bicycles, and my personal favorite—a clunky old metal dump truck. But we also had new and wondrous items—hula hoops and beach balls—as colorful as they were superfluous. Thanks to DuPont's "Wonderful World of Chemistry," we had things that were barely things. With that, we go back in time and begin with bubbles.

BUBBLES

Bubbles, being a natural phenomenon, have always been with us. What exactly is a bubble? Water molecules cohere. In a drop of water, molecules on the surface are attracted to the center, which gives a drop of water its round shape—a spherical shape providing the least possible surface area. If you stretch the surface, say by introducing air, you reduce the surface tension, but those water molecules keep wanting to stay together and create a bubble. Soap complicates things further. Soap molecules, long chains of carbon and hydrogen atoms, have two ends—one (hydrophilic) that is attracted to water molecules and the other (hydrophobic) that finds water repulsive. So if you add soap to water and blow air into the mixture, you produce a circular membrane or skin with soap molecules facing the air on either side with water molecules in between. In short, according to Dr. Gruner (online at the Cornell Center for Materials Research), "[T]he reason soap, water and air makes bubbles is because air and water molecules don't like to stick together but will stick to different ends of soap molecules."[14] Therefore, the new filmy membrane, with the greasy (hydrophobic) end of the soap molecule sticking out from the surface of the bubble, prolongs the life of the bubble—though not by much—because it delays the process of evaporation.[15]

Seen without the science, soap bubbles are spherical, fragile, and colorful. They are fascinating, and they are ephemeral. They're not lighter than air, but they are so light that a breeze can toss them around, and so they tend to lift our spirits. Bubble blowing in Europe seems to have become a more noticeable children's activity in the eighteenth century. This may have been the result of the intersection of two habits: smoking tobacco—introduced into Europe from North America in the mid-sixteenth century—and a more consistent use of soap. Children would blow bubbles with leftover washing soap through clay pipes used otherwise for tobacco. French artist Jean-Baptiste-Siméon Chardin captured such a scene in his painting *Soap Bubbles* in 1733 (Figure 7.1).

Around this same time, bubbles acquired an additional cultural connotation when John Law, a Scottish pioneer of financial capitalism, proposed a scheme to refinance French public debt by converting it into publicly traded shares in a company—the *Compagnie des Indes*—whose intent it was to exploit the resources of France's new colony on the Mississippi River: Louisiana. The company, formed in 1717 and granted a monopoly on trading rights with other French colonies, became part of the scheme in 1719. As the demand for shares rose, the Banque Royale increased the amount of paper currency in circulation. Inflation, and ultimately a run on the bank in May 1720, caused the "bubble" to burst. A similar plan was launched in England in 1720—involving some of the same actors—with the South Sea Company (formed originally in 1711) serving as the instrument by which Great Britain refinanced its public debt. That bubble burst later in the year. Both the South Sea Bubble and the Mississippi Bubble came to represent the dangers of irrational speculation, though a recent history suggests that the stock market, at least in Great Britain, soon became a relatively stable source of government credit.[16] But this financial sense of "bubbles" entered the culture signifying a risky or unsound investment, having the appearance of a good deal (that outside membrane) with nothing inside but air. Such investments might bring profits, even luxury, in the short term, but in the end, like soap bubbles, they proved ephemeral. A related word, "inflation" (to blow air or fill with wind), came to have an economic meaning as well in the 1830s, referring to an increase in the amount of money in circulation and later, a general rise in prices.

Figure 7.1. Jean-Baptiste-Siméon Chardin (French, Paris, 1699–1779), *Soap Bubbles.* Date: c. 1733–1734. Medium: oil on canvas. Dimensions: 24 × 24 7/8 in. (61 × 63.2 cm)Metropolitan Museum of Art, New York City. Wentworth Fund, 1949: Accession Number: 49.24 *Source:* Image © The Metropolitan Museum of Art.

Bubbles, then, both economic and the soapy variety, came to signify the ephemeral, with a lingering association with delusions of luxury or dreams of rising higher. Children might dream; adults who pursued "get-rich-quick" schemes were deluded. And so bubbles were increasingly associated with children or childishness. When Pears soap acquired an 1886 painting (*A Child's World,* later known simply as *Bubbles*) by Sir John Everett Millais and used it to sell soap for many decades, the image of a child looking up, somewhat anxiously, at a bubble he has just blown, reinforced the double-edged nature of the activity: the upward trajectory of the bubble is countered by the anticipation of ephemerality—of the bubble, of childhood, and even of life itself (Figure 7.2).

An American hit song, "I'm Forever Blowing Bubbles," published in 1919, provides a useful transition from our Victorian British bubbles. The lyrics begin with echoes of past bubble encounters: "I'm dreaming dreams, I'm scheming schemes, I'm building castles high. They're born anew, their days are few, just like a sweet butterfly." But the key difference is the illustration of the cover of the sheet music. A pretty, young red-haired woman surrounded by bubbles links the activity not so much to the expectation of failure but to the beauty and romance of dreaming—perhaps an activity best indulged in by women and children. In the United States, optimism is a way of life.

POSTWAR BUBBLES

A plethora of bubbles burst onto the American scene not only right after World War II but even during the war. There were bubbles for adults—soapy bubbles, champagne, and ginger ale—and bubbles for kids—bubble gum and new bubble-blowing toys.

Early in the American century, bubble baths became known as a woman's activity. There are three distinct ways to produce a bubbly bath: mechanical aeration (as in a Jacuzzi); the use of carbonated products to produce gas in the water; and the use of soap products, especially those enhanced with chemical surfactants such as alkyl sulfate. Carbonated products, known variously as bath fizzies or bath salts, became popular early in the century, but the use of surfactants was given a boost by the appearance in 1933 of Dreft, produced by Procter & Gamble and one of the earliest synthetic detergents. Foam baths soon became a noted phenomenon, and it was Hollywood that led the way. An article in *The Milwaukee Journal* on December 31, 1940, proclaimed: "Bubble Bath New Fad in Filmdom."[17] It did not take long for film directors to realize the titillating potential of foamy suds—Gloria DeHaven appeared in a bubble bath in the movie *Step Lively* with Frank Sinatra in 1944. On June 7, 1946, *The Pittsburgh Press* observed: "Bubble Bath a Great Boom for Film Girls—and Censors." The article went on to say: "Even Studio Plumbers Hail This Epic Advance in the Art of Movie-Making." The cover of *Life* magazine for August 21, 1950, featured three lovely "Bubble Bath Girls," young actresses with charmingly bare shoulders and perfect complexions in a vat of bubble bath. The cover story revealed that a new Broadway musical produced by Michael Todd[18] (later married to Elizabeth Taylor) and titled, appropriately, *Peep Show*, featured as its climax number thirty girls in a gigantic foamy bubble bath. The article described the show as a "leg opera" and reported that the final extravaganza cost $36,000 and employed a consultant from Procter & Gamble, flown in from company headquarters in Cincinnati.[19]

Figure 7.2. Sir John Everett Millais (English, 1829–1896) *A Child's World* (later retitled *Bubbles*) painting, acquired by A. & F. Pears and used as print advertisement for Pears soap. Date (original painting): 1886. Lady Lever Art Gallery, National Museums Liverpool, UK *Source: Reproduced with kind permission of Unilever from an original in Unilever Archives.*

It did not take long for a Hollywood fad to find a mass market in the populuxe postwar decade. An article in *The Pittsburgh Press* in 1945 suggested that every woman should pamper herself—and there were practical considerations in addition:

> And don't underestimate the value of seemingly frivolous bath aids. Nothing is frivolous that gives your morale a lift and helps you lick devitalizing weather. Bubbles which wrap you in clouds of foam can change your mood and give more solid benefits than a bath. The solid virtue hidden under the froth is a softening agent that releases tension of water and gives you better action than from soap.[20]

Connecticut resident Arlene Shea reminisced that a bubble bath in the early 1950s was considered an affordable luxury reserved for Saturday night. Overtones of its Hollywood origins could be found in her father's remark when she emerged from the bathroom in her robe: "Lefty [her nickname], who do you think you are, a movie star?"[21] Various brands emerged in the 1940s, including Colgate's Swerl, which announced that it was not only good for "greaseless dishwashing" but also would provide a "refreshing, cleansing, *deodorizing* 'Hollywood Bubble Bath' at trifling cost."[22] Door-to-door sales agents from Avon and the Fuller Brush Company spread the word, with one salesman from the latter, Don Bergen, reporting that in 1955 he "had convinced a lady that Fuller's bubble bath solution was so wonderful that, even though she didn't have a bathtub, she should go over to her friends' house next door and use their tub. She bought a case of bubble bath." He felt so guilty that he resigned soon thereafter.[23]

After a nice soapy bubble bath, adults in the 1950s might settle in for a bubbly evening of fun and dancing with the Lawrence Welk Show and his "Champagne Music." The show aired on Saturday nights on ABC, beginning in 1955. A "bubble machine" sent large bubbles across the bandstand to complete the effervescent atmosphere of a night on the town that could be enjoyed in the comfort of your own home. Add some balloons and a real bottle of champagne, the very essence of lightheartedness and lightheadedness in the fifties, and it was New Year's Eve (Figure 7.3). Hawaiian musician Don Ho closed the circle with his pop hit of 1966, "Tiny Bubbles." The intoxicating mix of bubbles and romance made Hawaii a popular honeymoon destination, especially after Hawaiian statehood in 1959 and the introduction of jet travel to the islands the following year.

Not surprisingly, as champagne became a more popular luxury item in the 1950s, a new vessel for drinking the intoxicating brew also emerged. According to design historian John Stuart Gordon, the champagne coupe, with its wide bowl, had been fashionable in the 1930s, but in the postwar period, "the flute became the glass of choice for champagne. The narrow bowl results in a smaller surface area, so carbonation

Figure 7.3. "Champagne" (1961). Postcard image, adapted from a painting by Walter Nichols, with recipe on the back for champagne cocktail. The bubbles in the image emanate from the bottle of champagne and get bigger as they rise and envelop the bikini-clad woman, conjuring both balloons and bubble bath. The three types of bubbles set us up for a New Year's Eve celebration. *Source: From the author's collection.*

is retained, and the almost vertical sides make for dramatic nucleation (the visible bubbles and lines of bubbles)."[24] The more bubbles, the better.

For those who might have imbibed a bit too much bubbly, a fizzy remedy existed. Alka-Seltzer, introduced by the Miles Medicine Company in 1931, became a hugely successful product in the postwar period, taken for minor aches and pains, headaches, heartburn, and hangovers.[25] Its trademark character, Speedy (originally named "Sparky"), was introduced in 1951 and used in over two hundred commercials between 1954 and 1964. The literal embodiment of fizz, Speedy's body and hat consisted of tablets. The effervescence, "produced by the baking soda (sodium bicarbonate) and citric acid reacting to form sodium citrate and carbon dioxide gas," ensured quick action.[26] Whatever discomfort effervescence might cause after the fun had evaporated, a different form of effervescence could cure.

Kids had plenty of bubbles for themselves—for bathing, playing, drinking, and chewing. Indeed, bubble bath products for kids may have eclipsed the popularity of similar products for their moms by 1961, the year the Gold Seal Company introduced Mr. Bubble. Crazy Foam, manufactured by the Aerosol Corporation of America in Massachusetts in the 1960s, featured cartoon character and superhero faces. No kid wanted for entertainment in the tub. You could use your floating Ivory Soap as a battleship and make a mess of the tub walls with your Crazy Foam, all while lounging in a sea of Mr. Bubble bubble bath.

Kids might also run around outside and blow bubbles. New chemically enhanced bubble solutions were marketed by Chemtoy (an ominous name to be sure—they also sold cleaning supplies) in the early 1940s. Tootsietoy acquired the smaller company and put bubble solution into mass production in the late 1940s. The small plastic bottles that came with a plastic wand or a pipe were a kid favorite and remain so to this day.[27]

And, of course, like their parents, kids could drink their bubbles. If various colas and ginger ales were not enough—and who can forget the 1950s Schweppes ads featuring "schweppervescence"—you could make your own carbonated soft drinks using Fizzies, "the TABLET that makes an INSTANT SPARKLING DRINK."[28] There was more to this, of course, than bubbles and cavities. Fizzies and such noncarbonated drinks as Tang, Kool-Aid, and Ovaltine showed baby boomers that the various states of matter were mutable. Through the magic of effervescence, we began to understand that things were not necessarily what they seemed. As children, we became accustomed to altered states of being.

But no bubble product enveloped kids in the postwar decade as much as bubble gum. A bit of background is in order. Humans have been chewing a variety of materials since, as they say, time immemorial, mostly different kinds of gum, resin, and latex from a variety of trees and shrubs. Mastic is one such resin that has been popular in the Mediterranean since ancient times and from which we get, through the Greek, the English word "masticate."[29] The most popular natural gum base has been composed primarily of chicle, a latex from the sapodilla tree of Central and South America.[30] A handful of American entrepreneurs, including Thomas Adams and William J. White, popularized the chewing gum habit in the last few decades of the nineteenth century and formed the American Chicle combine in 1899. In the meantime, William Wrigley Jr., gum's greatest salesman, had turned the United States into a gum-chewing nation with a variety of promotional techniques, including his famous electric sign in Times Square. (Wrigley's first brand name was "Vassar." Women apparently chewed more gum than men did in the 1890s.) By 1910, Wrigley's Spearmint had outpaced all its competitors. During World War I, millions of packs of chewing gum, said to calm the nerves, were sent to soldiers abroad. (World War I had a similar impact on the habit of eating candy bars.) In short, chewing gum was a deeply entrenched American activity by the 1920s, and in that decade (August 1928 to be precise), an employee of the Frank H. Fleer Company, Walter Diemer, invented bubble gum.

Diemer had been experimenting with various formulas, trying to produce a gum with more elasticity to produce larger bubbles that wouldn't stick to the face when they popped. For the record, Diemer, when interviewed, noted that "pink food coloring was the only one I had on hand, and that's the reason ever since, all over the world, that bubble gum has been predominantly pink."[31] As for the elasticity, gum historian Robert Hendrickson tells us that a "harmless rubberlike tree latex—similar to the one used for making girdles—was the ingredient that gave the first bubble gum its elasticity, though synthetics such as vinyl resins and microcrystalline waxes are used today."[32] Fleer's Dubble Bubble was an instant hit. Prewar sales of Dubble Bubble and its competitors, such as Bowman's Blony, reached over $4 million a year.[33]

World War II, however, brought shortages and rationing. Manufacturers continued to produce gum for soldiers, but domestic supplies dried up and at war's end, bubble gum producers couldn't keep up with the pent-up demand. Hendrickson quotes Robert McShane, a salesman looking back on his youth during the war years: "I remember four people best from World War II: Hitler, Mussolini, Tojo and Cynthia Bolo. When I lived out in Far Rockaway, Cynthia Bolo used to sell me bubble gum at *one dollar* a piece!"[34] John Hendsey, a bookseller whom I asked about this, corroborated the "pink market" tale. A third-grade student in Hartford in 1946, John said kids were so desperate for bubble gum that year that some of them would walk to a distant store to buy penny bubble gum pieces and sell them in school for a nickel each.[35] According to Hendrickson, "[T]he postwar years brought a bubble gum boom never equaled by any plaything anywhere." The *Milwaukee Journal* reported in 1946 that a

Republican seeking election to the state assembly was accused of tampering with the electorate by distributing bubble gum to children.[36] Bubble gum–blowing contests were the rage, and "bubble-gum" became an adjective applied to various forms of kid's consumer culture.

What can we make of all this? Bubble gum is a food product that isn't food. If we disaggregate the act of food consumption, chewing is the only part of that complex act that applies to bubble gum. Bubble gum, as a food product, represents the ultimate in empty calories. You can blow better bubbles once you dissolve and digest the sugars—and when you do that, you lose the flavor and need more gum. A Lonnie Donegan song released in the United Kingdom in 1959 asked "Does Your Chewing Gum Lose Its Flavour (On the Bedpost Overnight?)." The song hit number five on the charts in the United States in 1961. The answer, of course, is yes.[37]

What bubble bath, bubble soap, and bubble gum all have in common is air, which costs nothing. Cheap sources of small pleasures, bubbles were also a marketplace phenomenon. Philip Wrigley, son of William, observed that his father raised him "to have a five-cent point of view."[38] A New York candy store owner said, "I don't make much on one piece of Bazooka, but 3,000 pieces a week!"[39] Hendrickson, in his 1976 book on the subject, observed that "Topps sells more than a billion and a half pieces of Bazooka annually."[40] Although how to dispose of your used-up bubble gum was, in fact, a problem for parents, theater owners, and school teachers everywhere, the disposability and ephemeral nature of these various bubbly products set a new standard for our consumer culture in the postwar decade. They represented a triumph of marketing over matter, and the profits were substantial.

MAKING BUBBLES LAST: THE PLASTIC AGE

Soap and gum bubbles were far from being the only ubiquitous, air-filled concoctions in the fifties. Balloons, for example, first cousins to bubbles, also abounded. Balloons have also existed for a long time. Once made from animal bladders, the first modern rubber balloons were made by scientist Michael Faraday in 1824, according to most references. Only a year later, Englishman Thomas Hancock introduced a form of toy balloon, and by 1847, vulcanized toy balloons were being manufactured by J. G. Ingram of London. Credit for creating the first modern latex toy balloons apparently goes to Neil Tillotson in 1931, who capitalized on the more pliable rubber product. (The Tillotson Company also produced latex medical gloves and silver mylar balloons.) Natural and synthetic rubbers are elastic—that is, their long polymer chains reconfigure themselves to distribute an applied stress and will return to their original shape when the stress is removed—you know, balloons![41] The advantage of mylar, or foil, balloons, first made for the New York City Ballet in the late 1970s and produced from polyethylene, nylon, and aluminum, is that they will hold helium gas for a longer period of time.

Much like bubble gum and bubble bath, modern latex balloons predate the fifties. They attracted few headlines after the war. But like those other products, they seem to have been everywhere in the postwar decade. Perhaps it was all those baby boomer birthday parties or maybe it was simply their use to attract families with young kids out searching for appliances and cars in our "shopping spree" decade. Beach balls, another air-filled concoction, hit the scene after the war, though their invention is attributed to a California man, Jonathan DeLonge, in 1938. Lightweight vinyl panels made possible the creation of this somewhat permanent bubble. Large, but light, the beach ball represents the ultimate in frivolity. When the baseball game drags in the middle innings, beach balls provide a kind of extra entertainment at the entertainment venue for those who need constant fun. At the beach, they provide a diversion from the more "serious" work of constructing sand castles.

DEFYING GRAVITAS AND GRAVITY: CHILDREN'S FLIGHTS OF FANCY

Even if we go back to the *Bubbles* painting of Millais in the late nineteenth century, it is clear that one characteristic of and attraction to bubbles and balloons is their lightness, their ability to float on air, however temporary that ability may be. Should we attribute their ubiquity in the postwar period simply to being a by-product of the intersection of young, easily amused baby boomers and new plastic polymers? The fifties also witnessed a new focus on flying and space. Even before Pan Am became the first airline to use a jet for passenger travel in 1958, ads for families in flight surrounded us. American Airlines in 1950 proclaimed: "There's no such thing as a DISTANT relative." A Pan Am ad from 1955 pictured a mom and dad and six kids on a mobile airstair, and a Delta Air Lines ad that same year beckoned families to a Miami Beach vacation.[42] Dreams of flying were becoming a reality for middle-class Americans. No doubt the space program also factored into all of this. It was no coincidence that Arthur "Spud" Melin and his partner Richard Knerr of the Wham-O Manufacturing Company came out with two gravity-defying novelty toys, the hula hoop and the Frisbee, in 1957–1958, perfectly timed with the launch of Sputnick, the first successful artificial earth satellite and the official beginning of the space age. Plastic played its role. According to plastics historian Stephen Fenichell, a "brand-new high-density, extremely lightweight polyethylene"—perfect for the hula hoop—had recently hit the market and "become available in a wide range of bright colors."[43] The Frisbee had a longer history, beginning—as the story goes—in the 1870s when Yale students took to "sailing discarded pie tins" from the

William Russell Frisbie bakery in Bridgeport, Connecticut. A California inventor named Walter Morrison "plasticized the pie tin" and "enhanced its aerodynamic potential" by adding the "curled-up lip." Wham-O bought the rights to Morrison's "Pluto Platter" and renamed it the "Frisbee," apparently after hearing that college students in Connecticut were still using that name.[44]

Fenichell notes that each hula hoop cost Wham-O about fifty cents to produce. They sold for $1.98 each, and "by the spring of '58 . . . hoop sales topped fifteen million."[45] Plastic and instant profits aside, there is something interesting and perhaps ironic about this convergence of material culture at its pop, future-garage-sale-item peak and the somewhat ethereal nature of the objects themselves. Although one can grant the Frisbee more staying power—indeed, it has become the basis of a whole new sport—it was, at the time, along with the hula hoop, a fad. Both objects might be said to be doubly ephemeral. Objects of limited temporal interest, they were also objects of very limited material worth—in short, cheap plastic crap. Their value as products derived from ingenuity, marketing, and their potential for playfulness. And yet, both objects—and we might throw the Duncan yo-yo into this mix—derived their value as playthings from their potential to either glide or work against the downward pull of gravity.

Flying was in the air in the 1950s. The Disney studios released its adaptation of J. M. Barrie's 1904 stage play, *Peter Pan, or The Boy Who Wouldn't Grow Up*, in 1953. Though Peter Pan teaches the Darling children to fly ("look at me, way up high, suddenly, here am I—I'm flying") and their father—a practical man of his times—softens by the end of the movie, the plot remains true to the values of Edwardian London. We remember the flying, but the Lost Boys—who, after all, are lost—return to Never Land, and the Darling children return to their beds, one presumes, to grow up, unlike Peter Pan.

A short film with, I think, a different message and one more appropriate to the bubbles and balloons of the 1950s was *The Red Balloon* (*Le ballon rouge*). Directed by French filmmaker Albert Lamorisse, the movie premiered in France on October 15, 1956, and was released in the United States in March 1957. A book tie-in was first published in the United States by Doubleday in 1957 and became a children's classic. The plot of the movie, which has almost no dialogue, is simple. A young boy, Pascal, encounters a red, helium-filled balloon on his way to school. The balloon, Pascal discovers, has a mind of its own—it becomes not only a toy but a companion that follows him everywhere. Ultimately, a gang of bullies destroys the balloon. But other balloons from all over Paris rush to Pascal, and as he clutches them and holds on tightly, they take him for a ride high over the city, to a "magical world where children and balloons can be friends forever"[46]

Having recently viewed it again, I thought—yes, that's what all these bubbles and balloons in the fifties are about. Unlike the Millais painting and Peter Pan, there are no overtones of ultimate decay or the adult world of gravitas and aggravation, to which we must return. This movie begins and ends with a child, his innocence and dreams intact. The movie takes place in post–Occupation France, a country—as one critic wrote—"happy to forget the blood and death of Hitler's war a decade earlier."[47] The film is set in the decaying Belleville area of Paris, which would soon become a site for urban renewal.[48] For all its magical elements, the movie evokes a sense of documentary realism. The balloons provide a dash of color against the somewhat somber black-and-white grittiness of the city. Here is a postwar statement about the importance of children, their effervescence, and their uplifting playthings. Leaving the old city behind—and below—we might create a new place to live, where the sounds of children playing filled the air, much as air filled their bubbles and balloons.

LIVING IN A BUBBLE: THE BUBBLE AS METAPHOR AND ENVIRONMENT

Looking back on it now, I should have realized why I was attracted to the idea of writing about bubbles, about effervescence—but I didn't see it then. Our neighborhood in North Massapequa, a suburban town on the South Shore of Long Island, had all the right characteristics. Our street was a semicircular cul-de-sac. We lived right in the middle of it. We had a picture window that looked out on the street. My parents later added a dining room with a picture window that had a nice view of the woods in the back.[49] I see it now—the circularity, the transparency: we lived in a bubble.[50]

Bubbles, seen this way, have several additional key characteristics. They are visibly enclosed. We see that they embody, in however fragile a fashion, a neat, little world. We had that, and it was not simply a perception or illusion. Our neighborhoods were easy for children to navigate—by foot or for longer adventures—with bicycles.[51] Neighbors kept an eye on us—as did our parents, looking out their picture windows. We played in the streets—stickball and football. The only cars that came and went were driven by our parents and neighbors. It was not the city.[52] It didn't need to be a gated community. We felt safe, and we were. The bubble contained a filiocentric environment.

Bubbles are also transparent. As architectural historian Sandy Isenstadt has noted, summing up the pro-window orientation of Le Corbusier and Mies van der Rohe, "Transparency was . . . the foundation of glass's moral effect: it revealed truths of structure and lives spent within."[53] We were proud of our humble houses. The "lives spent within" were the priority. And the transparency signaled a shared sense of values. There were critics. Some argued that most suburbanites, looking out their picture windows, could see only their neighbors, looking out their picture windows. More fortunate suburbanites might see deer and trees. An advertisement in *House Beautiful* in 1950 asked: "Is there a Picture in your Picture Window? Misuse of a very good idea is turning American houses into fish bowls and unwittingly robbing people of privacy."[54] True enough—but it was equally important to keep an eye on the kids, and privacy was easily obtained. You simply closed the curtain. Wrote Hilaire Belloc in 1902: "Never ridicule windows. . . . By windows love often enters. . . . I will keep up the high worship of windows till I come to the windowless grave."[55]

But our suburban neighborhoods were not only spatial bubbles; they were temporal ones as well. William Upski Wimsatt, in his book, *Bomb the Suburbs*, argues that suburbs, among other things, "erode the sense of history."[56] Restoring a sense of contingency to his observation, I would argue that the suburban places we grew up in, seen historically, were unique in that they were new and shaped by the needs of a postwar generation. We watched our homes and neighborhoods being built (Figure 7.4). They were built for us. We experienced the construction of a little world built on—literally—new foundations. Historians Rosalyn Baxandall and Elizabeth Ewen quote one baby boomer, David Beers, on this very point:

> [It] was a new empty space . . . in their brand new subdivision. . . . Nowadays when suburbia is disparaged as a "crisis of place" cluttered with needless junk and diminished lives, it is worth considering that it was not suburbia's stuff that drew people like my parents to such land in the first place, but the emptiness. A removed emptiness, made safe and ordered and affordable. An up-to-date emptiness made precisely for us.[57]

We had a sense that history started with us—a sense I think that our parents, given that their past included the Depression and the death and destruction of World War II, welcomed. Why not start over? Plastics reinforced that sense. As Fenichell observes, "In the good new days, all man-made materials worth their salt sported popular brand names: Dacron and Orlon, Saran and Naugahyde, Tupperware and Wham-O, Silly Putty, Plexiglas, Velcro, Formica."[58] New stuff, new names: everything was new. The people were new to each other—no old neighborhoods, no extended families, no old churches, only strangers. As one woman observed, "[I]n the suburbs you made friends through your children."[59]

It might be argued, persuasively, that the spatial and temporal bubble we lived in had a strong element of escapism. No question about that: it did. Escaping from the past, from so-called urban blight. White flight was also a factor. But as Lynn Spigel cleverly observes in her book, *Welcome to*

Figure 7.4. Photograph of the author and his mother watching their home being built (c. 1953, North Massapequa, Long Island, NY). ***Source: Image courtesy of the author.***

the Dreamhouse, "'white flight' might also refer to *The Jetsons* and *Lost in Space*.[60] Searching for an image of a "suburban bubble" online, I came across a Ford advertisement from 1946.[61] There it is: postwar suburbia in a bubble, with a caption that reads, "Lots of Room . . . C'mon along." It took some time for me to realize that the ad copy below reads, "There's a Ford in your future." What I perceived as a bubble was actually meant to be a crystal ball—though in all honesty, it looks more like a bubble (Figure 7.5). But they work together nicely: we were pointed in the direction of the future.

And we were also surrounded by images (and toys) taken from the dreams and realities of the space program. Astronauts wore space helmets made, apparently, of clear, impact-resistant, polycarbonate plastic.[62] They looked like bubbles (Figure 7.6). A 1956 advertisement for Puffin Biscuits shows a small boy, head in a bubble, and an even smaller girl, with braids and a ribbon, gazing lovingly at biscuits circling overhead. The caption read: "So light they almost fly."[63] The Piccards, father and son, set a record in 1953 by descending to a depth of over 10,000 feet under water. In their helmets, their rockets, and their bathyscaphes, explorers were using bubbles to live in outer space and the deep sea. Discovery and escapism went hand in hand. Gaining a new perspective on

Figure 7.5. Ford advertisement from 1946. *Source: Image courtesy of the collection of Sally Edelstein, www.envisioningtheamericandream.wordpress.com.*

our world and finally visualizing the significance of Columbus, we observed that the earth really is round. It is, we might say, a metabubble.

THE DARK SIDE OF EFFERVESCENCE

With the assassination of John Fitzgerald Kennedy on November 22, 1963, a day remembered by all baby boomers, our childish bubbles burst. The following year, British author Roald Dahl published his third and, perhaps, most famous children's book, *Charlie and the Chocolate Factory* (made into the film *Willy Wonka & the Chocolate Factory* in 1971).[64] Dahl's stories are, of course, wonderfully imaginative. They also tend to have a dark side, and in *Charlie and the Chocolate Factory,* Dahl may have provided a literary counterpoint to our positive notions of effervescence. Dahl poked not-so-gentle fun at the consumerist tendencies of children in his characters: Augustus Gloop is described as "a greedy boy"; Veruca Salt is "a girl who is spoiled by her parents"; Violet Beauregarde is "a girl who chews gum all day long"; and Mike Teavee is "a boy who does nothing but watch television."[65] The fifth child, and the book's hero, is Charlie Bucket, a kindhearted soul who lives in poverty with his parents and grandparents. In the movie, Charlie and Grandpa Joe are tempted by and almost fall victim to one of Wonka's inventions—but in the book, a description of that invention is sufficiently foreboding:

> FIZZY LIFTING DRINKS, it said on the next door. "Oh, those are fabulous!" cried Mr. Wonka. "They fill you with bubbles, and the bubbles

Figure 7.6. "Sunset on the Earth," Topps Space Cards, 1957 (#28). ***Source: Topps trading cards used courtesy of The Topps Company, Inc.***

> are full of a special kind of gas, and this gas is so terrifically *lifting* that it lifts you right off the ground just like a balloon, and up you go until your head hits the ceiling—and there you stay." "But how do you come down again?" asked little Charlie. "You do a burp, of course," said Mr. Wonka. "You do a great big long rude burp, and *up* comes the gas and *down* comes you![66]

And so, in one fell swoop, Dahl dismantles it all: the fizzy bubbles, the balloons, the silly consumerism, even the aspirations of defying gravity. Back to Earth we fall with a long and rude burp. Dahl's dark side matched the growing seriousness of adolescent baby boomers approaching their college years with a more critical stance.

The material culture of effervescence—from bubbles and balloons to hula hoops and polka-dotted bikinis—encouraged baby boomers to be at once the best-trained consumers, taking our cues from kids' shows on television, and the most self-conscious critics of that same consumer culture as we reached our twenties.[67] As Sharon Zukin observed in her book *Point of Purchase,* student activists, environmental groups, and Nader-inspired consumer advocates in the sixties and seventies challenged our childhood shopping impulses and "revived old ideals of ethical consumption."[68] Yet Thomas Frank—the author of *The Conquest of Cool: Business Culture, Counterculture, and the Rise of Hip Consumerism*—has suggested that we, as a generation, quickly succumbed to niche marketing and marketing pitches that would appeal to our values of individuality and nonconformity, rebellion, and authenticity. According to Frank, we became hip consumers and consumers of hip.[69] Ironically, our street cred as consumers of cheap, faddish, child-oriented populuxe items constructed from sugars and plastics, from Fizzies to vinyl 45s, included an evolving consciousness of the limits of materiality. Much as we learned to see behind the small screen, to understand, as taught by Marshall McLuhan, that the medium was the message, we also learned that something might, indeed, be created from nothing. This was a harbinger of "things" to come. Our own children understand this. They are deeply aware of the role that design, branding, and advertising play in the shaping of commodities and their decision making as consumers. Of course, that awareness hardly renders them impervious to the charms of goods or any less desirous of seeking elusive authenticities.[70]

BUYING BUBBLES: CONVENIENCE STORES

Having discussed the intrinsic qualities of effervescent things and, to some degree, their social contexts and qualities as commodities, it remains—before we conclude—to discuss how and where our various items were sold in the postwar, or populuxe, era. Commodities are shaped by how they are bought and sold. Likewise, the spaces of shopping are very much shaped by the things sold within those spaces. Picture, for example, the appropriate differences, inside and out, between a supermarket and a used bookstore. It is especially important to discuss the stores in which most kids bought such items as bubble toys, balloons, and hula hoops, as this genre of retail stores is rarely discussed.

Having turned up very little in the literature, I conferred with a substantial number of generational mates, and we all agreed that hula hoops, soap bubbles, and the like were not usually purchased in well-established, old-fashioned department stores or specialty shops, with their stodgy and weighty stock of goods. Though bubble gum, at least on the East Coast, could be found in neighborhood "candy stores," newspaper stands, or pharmacies, even in suburban areas, many of the other items were likely found in convenience stores—known in Québec as *dépanneurs*, or "deps"—such as 7-Eleven and discount stores such as E. J. Korvette and Times Square Stores, the forerunners of today's Walmarts and the like.

The 7-Eleven chain, the largest group of convenience stores today and the pioneer in the field, began as a group of ice plants and retail ice docks or ice stations in Texas in 1927. Given the necessity of ice in that part of the country and at that time when iceboxes were still commonplace, these early convenience stores kept long hours and were even open on Sundays. Slowly adding a variety of items, such as milk, bread, cigarettes, and chilled watermelons, the Southland Ice Company grew. The stores became known as Tote'm stores and, after World War II, as 7-Elevens, reflecting their hours of operation (Figure 7.7). The point for us is that this invasive species of retail stores was exactly the kind of place young consumers found these items of effervescence. Their own corporate history observes: "In the '50s, selling everything from 'soup to nuts,' 7-Eleven had added TV tubes, money orders, magazines, sunglasses . . . hula hoops, and keys 'made while you wait.'" Emphasizing their "adaptation to shifting customer desires," 7-Elevens and other such convenience stores were based on a diverse stock of goods, quick turnover, and low overhead. The idea of selling goods, even small toys, with a limited shelf life may have come from their origins as purveyors of melting ice. Possessing, as they say, "a unique personality quite different from its big brother—the supermarket . . . kids seemed to feel more at home in a 7-Eleven because it was close to their own size. . . . [T]he candy rack was handy and in easy sight of even the smallest youngster."[71]

Like weeds growing in a newly developed field of suburban communities, convenience stores and discount stores became the everyday shopping places of our generation, supplementing the more episodic trips to department stores located either back in older downtowns or in newer malls. Despite the efforts of such department stores to compete in new suburban markets (Dayton's, for example, built the Southdale Center in suburban Minneapolis in 1956), the new trends of convenience and dis-

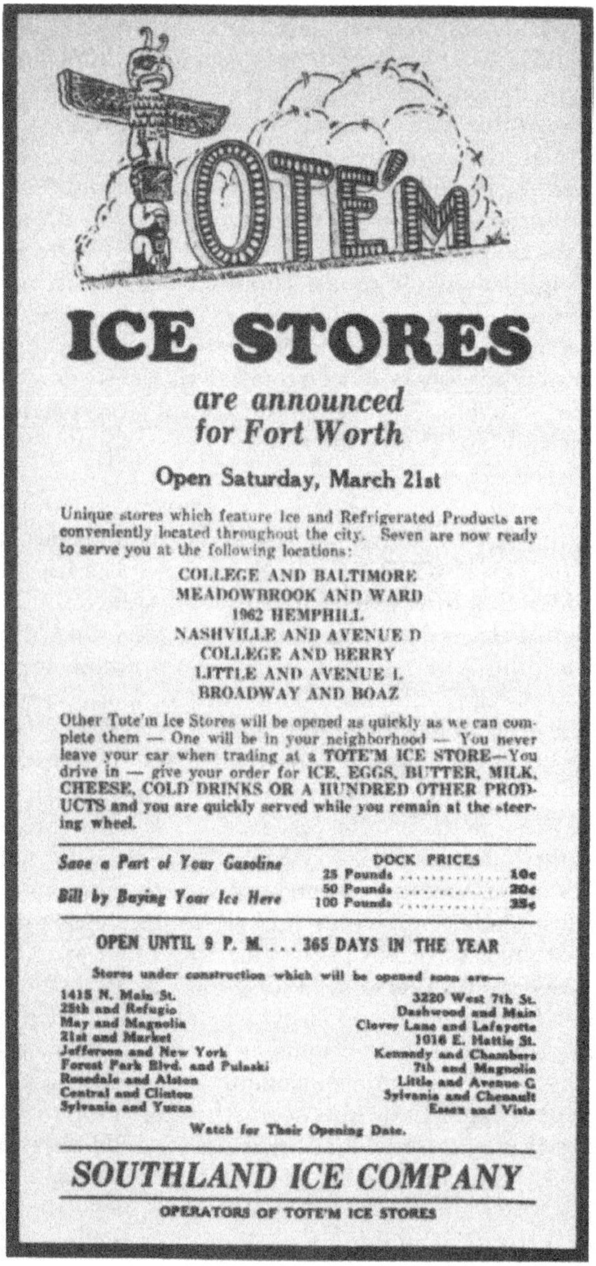

Figure 7.7. Tote'm Store (pre–World War II name of the 7-Eleven convenience store chain). This 1931 advertisement appeared in the *Fort Worth Star-Telegram*. Taken from Allen Liles, *Oh Thank Heaven! The Story of the Southland Corporation* (Dallas: The Southland Corporation, 1977), 38. *Source: Used by permission of 7-Eleven, Inc.*

counting had turned the tide by 1962, the year Walmart was founded in Arkansas and older stores such as Kresge's and Dayton's opened their first Kmart and Target, respectively.[72] Capitalizing on cheap goods within easy reach of both suburban homes and youthful allowances, the new retailers became fixtures on the landscape.

FLIGHTS OF FANCY

But only to consider the material and even business consequences of such kiddie purchases would be to miss an important part of this story. Though one might find many other themes in an examination of the postwar years—the Cold War, nuclear anxieties, the struggle for civil rights, even the toy guns we played with and mock battles we fought—the bubbles and balloons were real. They, too, had their place. We cherished our flights of fancy as our parents cherished us. With the character of Mary Poppins, the Disney filmmakers in 1964 once again urged children of all ages to go fly a kite and be transformed by our imaginations and our kinder natures. The Beatles beckoned us to get aboard a yellow submarine—or was that the yellow school bus of our suburban youth? As late as 1967, The 5th Dimension, singing Jimmy Webb's song, "Up, Up and Away," urged us to ride in their beautiful balloon.

Our parents, emerging from years of death and deprivation, sought, above all, to protect us. Perhaps the greatest gift from the "Greatest Generation" was to create an environment of relative safety and prosperity, where so many of us could laugh and play and hold on tightly to that balloon. We yearn to do the same. In the end, effervescence is a bubbly state of mind, a sense of innocence, wonder, and enthusiasm. I keep that feeling with me always and hope that all children, everywhere, can have it as well. Bubbles cost so little, but mean so much.

NOTES

1. A word coined by historian Thomas Hine in his book of the same name, *Populuxe* (New York: Knopf, 1986). Populuxe describes the material culture of America in the decade from 1954 to 1964, "one of history's great shopping sprees" (p. 3). More a feeling of available abundance than a look or single style, populuxe is "an expression of outright, thoroughly vulgar joy in being able to live so well" (p. 4).
2. The campaign slogan of Warren G. Harding in 1920.
3. Baby boomers tend to think of themselves as belonging to a unique generation—and that may well be true; however, their parents also belonged to a boom generation, born between 1918 and the later 1920s. That boom was also driven by the postponed desire to start families and the prosperity of the twenties. See Douglas Owram, *Born at the Right Time: A History of the Baby-Boom Generation* (Toronto: University of Toronto Press, 1996), 17.
4. The birthrate rose from 2.2 births per woman in the 1930s to 3.51 by the end of the 1950s. See Clifford E. Clark Jr., *The American Family Home, 1800-1960* (Chapel Hill: University of North Carolina Press, 1986), 205–206.

5. Owram, 6.

6. A quote from a song, "Grandpa Wright," written by my wife, Ginny Bales, in honor of her ancestor who fought in the Civil War.

7. Landon Jones, *Great Expectations: America and the Baby Boom Generation* (New York: Coward, McCann and Geoghegan, 1980), 3.

8. Owram, 55–56. See also, Clark, *The American Family Home*; Kenneth T. Jackson, *Crabgrass Frontier: The Suburbanization of the United States* (New York: Oxford University Press, 1985); Barbara M. Kelly, *Expanding the American Dream: Building and Rebuilding Levittown* (Albany: State University of New York Press, 1993).

9. For a brilliant look at the role of television, see Lynn Spigel, *Welcome to the Dreamhouse: Popular Media and Postwar Suburbs* (Durham: Duke University Press, 2001).

10. Owram, 60.

11. Hine, *Populuxe*, 16–17.

12. Thomas Hine, *I Want That! How We All Became Shoppers* (New York: HarperCollins, 2002), 65.

13. Robert Freidel, "Scarcity and Promise: Materials and American Domestic Culture during World War II," in *World War II and the American Dream*, ed. Donald Albrecht (Cambridge: The MIT Press, 1995), 46.

14. http://www.ccmr.cornell.edu/education/ask/?quid=1044

15. For more about bubble chemistry, see, for example, www.tnopportunity programs.org/Bubbleology.doc?

16. Larry Neal, *"I Am Not Master of Events": The Speculations of John Law and Lord Londonderry in the Mississippi and South Sea Bubbles* (New Haven: Yale University Press, 2012).

17. The various newspaper articles were accessed through Google newspapers.

18. Todd also produced the movie *Around the World in 80 Days* in 1956, which won the Academy Award for Best Picture and featured a ride in another form of bubble, a hot-air balloon. Earlier in his career, Todd had achieved some notoriety for producing an attraction for the 1933–1934 Century of Progress Exposition in Chicago called the "Flame Dance." "In this number, gas jets were designed to burn part of a dancer's costume off, leaving her naked in appearance." See Art Cohn, *The Nine Lives of Michael Todd* (New York: Random House, 1958).

19. "Slips, Slurps and Suds: This is how Broadway creates a big bubble bath," *Life* magazine, August 21, 1950, 63–67.

20. "Bubble Bath Cools You: 'Has It All Over' Chilly Shower," *The Pittsburgh Press*, August 17, 1945, 24 (accessed through Google newspapers).

21. Arlene Shea, telephone interview with the author, January 11, 2013.

22. Advertisement, *Life* magazine, July 19, 1948, 59.

23. http://www.reminisce.com/2011/08/working-at-fuller-brush-co/

24. John Stuart Gordon, e-mail to author, January 16, 2013. Gordon is the Benjamin Attmore Hewitt Associate Curator of American Decorative Arts at the Yale University Art Gallery.

25. Alka-Seltzer is now owned and marketed by Bayer.

26. http://en.wikipedia.org/wiki/Alka-Seltzer

27. http://bubbles.org/html/history/toyhistory.htm

28. Johann Jacob Schweppe (1740–1821) became the first successful commercial producer of carbonated drinks in the late eighteenth century. English scientist Joseph Priestley discovered a reliable method of infusing water with carbon dioxide in 1767. Yale professor Benjamin Silliman, who had met Priestley and much admired his work, introduced Americans to artificial mineral waters, or "soda waters," in New Haven in 1806. See Chandos Michael Brown, *Benjamin Silliman: A Life in the Young Republic* (Princeton: Princeton University Press, 1989), chapters 4 and 6, and http://mrfizzys.com/Fizz-tory.html). Fizzies were first introduced by the Emerson Drug Company, makers of Bromo-Seltzer, in 1957. When the Warner Lambert Company acquired Emerson, Fizzies became a national sensation. They achieved iconic status in the mo-

vie *Animal House* when the members of Delta House dumped a truckload of Fizzies into a swimming pool (http://en.wikipedia.org/wiki/Fizzies).

29. For this and all other information relating to the history, production, and lore of chewing gum, see Robert Hendrickson, *The Great American Chewing Gum Book* (New York: Stein and Day, 1976), 23. See also, Hendrickson, "Since 1928 it's been boom and bust with bubble gum," *Smithsonian* 21, no. 4 (July 1990).

30. Hendrickson, *Chewing Gum*, 21. "Chicle" comes from the Nahuatl word *tziktli*, meaning "sticky stuff." For a more scholarly history of chicle, the product, and the *chicleros* who extract and collect it, see Jennifer P. Mathews, *Chicle: The Chewing Gum of the Americas, From the Ancient Maya to William Wrigley* (Tucson: University of Arizona Press, 2009).

31. Ibid., 144.

32. Ibid.

33. Hendrickson, *Chewing Gum*, 146.

34. Hendrickson, "Since 1928," 5 (online version) and *Chewing Gum*, 147.

35. John Hendsey, conversation with author in Hartford, January 6, 2013. John added the following in an e-mail to the author on January 18, 2013: "Everyone wanted it, but it was very hard to find. . . . We used to go from one to another of the mom-and-pop stores throughout our Frog Hollow neighborhood in search of bubble gum. It was usually sold out from the time we received the information from someone blowing bubbles to the time it took to get to the store that had sold it. My ship came in one day when I discovered bubble gum in the corner store (Ward and Lawrence streets) across from my school. I bought two pieces with all the money I had—2 cents, and sold one for 5 cents. . . . I don't remember how long the bubble gum craze lasted, but I think its time was short. Soon the stores were flooded with it. The black market collapsed."

36. "Bubble Gum Count Bursts in Court Test," *The Milwaukee Journal*, October 16, 1946, 46.

37. Arlene Shea, in a fax to the author (January 22, 2013), recollected her childhood experience with bubble gum in the 1950s in Hartford: "When I blew a bubble, it was about the size of a grapefruit. . . . I couldn't make bigger bubbles until one day I mixed one Fleers Chiclet with my Double [sic] Bubble gum. I could blow a bubble as big as my head. . . . I remember trying mixtures. . . . [W]hen I made a good batch I would save it and put it on my bed rail when I went to bed at night."

38. Hendrickson, *Chewing Gum*, 127.

39. Ibid., 158.

40. Ibid.

41. See http://www.answers.com/topic/tillotson-corp, http://en.wikipedia.org/wiki/Balloons, and http://www.balloonhq.com/faq/history.html#rubber

42. Ads all taken from Jim Heimann, ed., *All-American Ads: 50s* (Köln: Taschen, 2003), no pagination.

43. Stephen Fenichell, *Plastic: The Making of a Synthetic Century* (New York: HarperCollins, 1996), 264.

44. Ibid., 266–67.

45. Fenichell, *Plastic*, 264–65.

46. http:/en.wikipedia.org/wiki/The_Red_Balloon

47. Ibid.

48. Ibid.

49. When I worked for the Suffolk County Planning Department in the summer of my sophomore year in college, I found out that the woods, which had a little stream, belonged to a protected wetlands area once owned by a Brooklyn water company and then sold to the Long Island Rail Road. I was horrified to find out that the planning maps had it projected as the site for an extension of the Bethpage State Parkway. I protested to the director. The road was never built, though I'm sure I was not the cause.

50. My wife grew up in an entirely different part of the country (Kingsport in East Tennessee) and had a remarkably similar experience. She also grew up on a cul-de-sac

in a newly developed neighborhood, Ridgefields. The house has a beautiful picture window looking out on Bays Mountain. The major difference between our two suburban "bubble" neighborhoods: hers had a country club; ours had a Good Humor truck.

51. A ten-minute bike ride brought us to a candy store on the main commercial street, Broadway. There, without having to cross the busy street, with constant traffic, we had a candy store with comics, baseball cards, and a soda fountain. One more block took us to Angie Scordato's grocery store, where we could feel important by picking up groceries for Mom and, perhaps, some penny candy.

52. On this, see D. J. Waldie, *Holy Land: A Suburban Memoir* (New York: W.W. Norton, 1996), 100.

53. Sandy Isenstadt, *The Modern American House: Spaciousness and Middle Class Identity* (New York: Cambridge University Press, 2006), 160.

54. Ibid., 213.

55. Ibid., 80. For more on the evolution of the glass industry and its use in evolving architectural styles, see Isenstadt, chapter 5. For more on the criticism of windows and the increasing use of glass, see Isenstadt, 77–83.

56. Quoted in Rosalyn Baxandall and Elizabeth Ewen, *Picture Windows: How the Suburbs Happened* (New York: Basic Books, 2000), xxi.

57. Ibid., 166. Needless to say, the description of a brand-new container filled with "emptiness" again conjures up the idea of a bubble.

58. Fenichell, *Plastic*, 270.

59. Baxandall and Ewen, *Picture Windows*, 162.

60. See Lynn Spigel, *Welcome to the Dreamhouse*, Part Two, for an intriguing discussion of the space program, science fiction on television, and race.

61. The image I found had been posted by Sally Edelstein on her wonderful website: www.envisioningtheamericandream.wordpress.com. Her prose is smart and informed and beautifully illustrated with period advertisements, editorial cartoons, and the like. My thanks to her for sending a high-resolution scan of this image from her own collection.

62. For other cards in the Topps series, including "Piccard Descends 2 Miles Under Sea" Topps Scoops, 1954 (#69), see http://www.cardboardconnection.com/1957-topps-space-cards

63. See http://www.plan59.com/av/av033.htm

64. It has been suggested that Dahl's student years at the Repton School in Derbyshire provided the inspiration for the book. The Cadbury chocolate company would periodically send "a plain cardboard box full of new types of chocolate" to each student for testing. This apparently prompted Dahl to fantasize about the creation of new chocolates and candy bars. See Jeremy Treglown, *Roald Dahl : A Biography* (New York: Farrar, Straus & Giroux, 1994), 23.

65. Roald Dahl, *Charlie and the Chocolate Factory* (New York: Alfred A. Knopf, 1964), vii. It is worth pointing out that Wonka's chocolate factory itself is a rather dangerous place, however magical.

66. Ibid., 112. My thanks to my son and fellow historian, Basie Bales Gitlin, for bringing this book and passage to my attention.

67. There is a prodigious literature on the impact of consumer culture, television, and advertising discourse on the baby boom generation. See, for example, Owram, *Born at the Right Time*, chapter 4; Hine, *Populuxe*; Samuel R. Lawrence, *Brought to You By: Postwar Television Advertising and the American Dream* (Austin: University of Texas Press, 2001); and Spigel, *Welcome to the Dreamhouse*.

68. Sharon Zukin, *Point of Purchase: How Shopping Changed American Culture* (New York: Routledge, 2004), 186. A book that certainly shaped our new awareness as consumers was Vance Packard, *The Hidden Persuaders* (New York: David McKay, 1957).

69. Thomas Frank, *The Conquest of Cool: Business Culture, Counterculture, and the Rise of Hip Consumerism* (Chicago: University of Chicago Press, 1997) is essential reading.

70. To cite just one excellent book on this subject, see Alissa Quart, *Branded: The Buying and Selling of Teenagers* ((New York: Basic Books, 2003).

71. Allen Liles, *Oh Thank Heaven! The Story of the Southland Corporation* (Dallas: The Southland Corporation, 1977), 15, 159.

72. For more on these trends, see Isadore Barmash, *More Than They Bargained For: The Rise and Fall of Korvettes* (New York: Lebhar-Friedman Books/Chain Store Publishing Corporation, 1981); Nelson Lichtenstein, ed., *Wal-Mart: The Face of Twenty-First Century Capitalism* (New York: The New Press, 2006); Sandra S. Vance and Roy V. Scott, *Wal-Mart: A History of Sam Walton's Retail Phenomenon* (New York: Twayne Publishers, 1994).

EIGHT

A Toxic Safari in a Big Box Store

McKay Jenkins

A few years ago, my wife Katherine and I decided to explore the provenance of the myriad toxins streaming into our lives. To follow the river, as it were, to its very source. Not to the wellspring, exactly—we weren't going undercover in any Chinese factories or looking inside the cauldrons of a chemical multi-national—but to the grand municipal reservoir, where these chemicals accumulate in unimaginable volume before being piped in a steady stream into our homes. Rather than run around from hardware store and pet shop to furniture outlets and clothing boutiques, we decided to shop where millions of Americans shop every week, for everything from mattresses and toys to cosmetics and even food. It would be a kind of safari, if you will, full of mysterious landscapes and more than a few hidden dangers. We would walk slowly and deliberately through a Big Box store. We would turn over a few rocks and see what we could see.

Let me begin by admitting that I have an intense, even neurotic, dislike of shopping. When I need something—a tube of toothpaste, a can of paint, a new pair of pants—I zip into a store, grab what I'm after, and zip out. I don't browse, or linger, or paw through the racks. If I see a couple of brands side by side, I'm very likely to pick the one that is cheaper, and I'm not likely to think very hard about why the price might be so low. I'm cheap that way.

Which, I suppose, makes me a pretty typical consumer in a typical Big Box store. And Big Box stores attract a lot of typical customers. In 2009, the top ten Big Box chains, led by Walmart, Costco, and Target, sold merchandise worth more than 1 trillion USD.[1]

And it's worth saying right up front that there's very little for sale in a Big Box store that you can't find in dozens of mom-and-pop stores. It's just that in many places, Big Box stores have put all this stuff under one roof (and in many cases have also put these other stores out of business). It's also worth remembering that Big Box stores, at least where I live, come in clumps. In a typical mall around Baltimore, you are likely to find a Walmart sharing one wall with a Target, another with a Michael's Arts and Crafts, and a third with a Toys "R" Us. Though their marketing strategies may vary, these stores share a great many products, which in turn share a great many toxic chemicals.

The trouble is, other than price tags, the products for sale in most of these places provide very little useful information. Although virtually everything is stamped "Made in China," there is almost nothing else to go on. Huge swaths of products, from plastic toys to upholstered furniture, report nothing about what went into making them—not the materials, not the circumstances under which they were made, not whether or not they were "inspected," nothing. For the products that do list a few ingredients—paints, for example, or caulks, or some laundry soaps—labels are typically inscrutable, Latinate, and printed in fonts that seem purposefully difficult to read. It's like the information was created to dissuade you from asking too many questions.

In this way, Big Box stores are not unlike fast food restaurants: you walk in looking for a very inexpensive product, and that is what you get. Where the thing was made, with what ingredients, is simply not part of the equation. It's not what you came looking for, and you're not going to find it.

Which doesn't mean that there's not more to know. Peel back the curtain on fast food, and you'll find a cheap hamburger whose provenance—the industrial food machine—has successfully hidden a full range of social, environmental, and public health costs. Look a little closer at the products in a Big Box store, and you'll find an equally full range of compromises: a huge petro-chemical industry; a shocking lack of government oversight; an endless conveyor belt of products moving into this country from factories somewhere in China. There is a lot to look for in a Big Box store. It's just really hard to know where to find it.

THE SAFARI BEGINS

After parking our car out in the vast acreage of our suburban Baltimore megamall, Katherine and I made our way through the automatic doors and were immediately struck—we were looking with new eyes, don't forget—at just how perfectly denatured the Big Box environment was. There were no windows, so once inside the doors we lost all sense of any life going on outside. There were no clocks, so we quickly lost track of time. The store was so big we couldn't even see its walls; wandering the aisles, I began to feel as though I was adrift in a borderless, rolling sea of merchandise. The space seemed disorienting by design.

And it wasn't just the visual stimulation that overwhelmed us. It was also the smell. The moment Katherine and I walked in the door, we were hit with a blast of fragrance. Or perhaps I should say "fragrance." At first, the place smelled vaguely familiar, like the doorway of a shopping mall candle store, or a gas station bathroom: there was a powerful bouquet of vanilla and apple cinnamon, coupled with faint notes of . . . lemon? At the back of the palate, I thought I could detect a few notes of burning rubber, with a subtle chlorine nose. But the finish? What was that? I knew I'd smelled it before, just not in such vivid concentration. What was that? Was that "lavender"?

Katherine and I looked at each other. Wow, she said. That's very strong. I wonder where it's coming from? We looked around. To our left was the wing of the store devoted to personal care products. Was that it? Was this olfactory cloud coming from a brigade of shampoo bottles? Or was it drifting in from the laundry detergents? Was it over there, to the right, in among the scented candles and potpourri?

The truth was, it was impossible to tell. Almost every single product in the store, from the paints and caulks to the cosmetics and the baby bottles, had been manufactured, one way or another, from a mix of synthetic chemicals. The smells were all so ambient, so pervasive, discovering their provenance was clearly going to take some work.

It was about this time that an image popped into my head, of a toxicologist, standing atop a giant crane, wrapping the Big Box store in an enormous plastic bag. For the rest of my visit, I couldn't shake the image of this bag, sealed for a month, and then opened like a giant Pandora's balloon.

HARDWARE

Katherine and I decided to look first in the aisles featuring products that had raised so many red flags in our basement. If such a sickly odor in our home had been caused by just a dozen cans of paint, we figured we ought to take a look—or a smell, if you will—at the Hardware department.

When it comes to toxic chemicals, the Hardware section in a Big Box store is a Red Zone. On shelf after shelf there were lacquers and paints, strippers and thinners, grease and stain removers—the same stuff with which we had fumigated our home from below. These products were, for the most part, canned or shrink-wrapped. But as I held them in my hands I couldn't help thinking about all the toxic genies waiting to be released from their bottles.

In the first aisle, Katherine and I waded into what I came to think of as The Pond of Caulk. This was a place I imagined spending some money; the grout in our bathroom had begun to chip and crack, and I needed to figure out a way to seal the fissures between the tiles. I picked up a tube and looked. It said it contained ethylene glycol, gamma-aminopropyltriethoxysilane, formaldehyde, ammonia, and acetaldehyde. Some of these things, the packaging said, "may cause kidney, cardiovascular and liver effects." I put it down, gently. Another label said the product contained "phthalate esters," which, to be honest, deserved some kind of award. Of the thousands of products in the store that contained phthalates, this was the only product in the entire store that actually acknowledged it.

Like so many other synthetic chemicals, phthalates are "endocrine disruptors," meaning they mimic or interfere with the human hormone system, leading to things like low sperm counts in boys or early-onset puberty in girls. The trouble is, phthalates are absolutely everywhere: they are added to shower curtains and baby pacifiers and crinkly drinking water bottles—most anything requiring soft plastic; they are also added to cosmetics, soaps, and shampoos—most anything containing "fragrances." Nearly five million metric tons are consumed by industry every year—for a world of consumers that sees convenience, disposability, and cheapness—rather than sustainability, durability, and health—as paramount virtues. "The fact of life is that phthalates are a remarkably useful product that . . . allow people without a lot of money to have a first-world lifestyle," Marian Stanley, manager of the Phthalate Esters Panel for the American Chemistry Council, has said.[2]

In state after state, phthalates show up in every person who gets tested for them. In a Maine body burden study, phthalates were found in all thirteen participants; three phthalates, including those used to make car interiors, shower curtains, and personal care products, were higher than in 75 percent of all Americans who have been tested for them. In a "Pollution in People" study done in Washington State, ten out of ten participants were contaminated with phthalates. In Oregon, the numbers were the same: ten out of ten people had three phthalates in their bodies. Seven people had six.[3]

So that's a problem. Elsewhere in the hardware section, there were sealants guaranteed (on the front) to last 50 years and warning (on the back) that the compound can be fatal if swallowed and "contains chemicals known to the state of California to cause cancer and birth defects or other reproductive harm." In microscopic print, there was an advisory about how to dispose of the chemical, along with this bit of news: "Reports have associated repeated and prolonged occupational exposure to solvents with permanent brain and nervous system damage."

A number of these products recommended that they be applied with rubber gloves and that masks be worn. I found myself thinking back on all the home repair projects I had done over the years: all the painting, floor sanding, and caulking; all the fiberglass I had installed in my attic and the sealants I had put on my porch floor. I thought about the epoxies and resins I had used to fiberglass three canoes I had built out of strips of Western Red Cedar; despite the warnings on the resins, I had painted them on with bare hands. And since I built them outside, I never wore a mask.

I'm sure there are some people who wear gloves when they recaulk their bathtubs. But I bet there are many more who, when they see a stray swab of white gunk, simply wipe it up with a bare finger. Ditto for parents painting their kid's bedroom, or staining a bookcase in the garage, or rolling out a pile of pink insulation in their attic. And then, of course, once the stuff has been applied, we all have to live with it as it breaks down, becomes dust, and begins filling our homes.

Katherine picked up a tube of silicone. This might be better than caulk, she said. Isn't this the stuff they put in breast implants? How bad can it be?

I don't claim to have the first idea about what goes into a breast implant. But finding out what was in this particular tube of silicone caulk was tricky. It came with a multi-page label, with the ingredients listed inside. When Katherine read it, she found that the caulk "may cause kidney, cardiovascular and respiratory problems." If she wanted more information, she was offered a phone number.

"Just the fact that you have to go through all these steps to figure out if something is safe makes me nuts," Katherine said. "And look at this." She showed me the label. "Manufacturer can't be held liable for damages in excess of purchase price," it said. What damages were we talking about, I wondered? Damages to your bathtub? Or damages to your body? And how much damage would $1.97 cover, anyway?

One thing that distinguished the Hardware section was the presence of warnings on most labels. Cans of thinners and strippers were marked with "may be fatal or cause blindness." There were deck strippers that cause "severe burns to eyes and mucous membranes" and that contain chemicals "known to the state of California to cause cancer." (This was the second time I had seen this warning. What was it about California? Did these products cause cancer in California and not in other states?) Again, it was hard to tell which chemicals they were talking about, though the package did list sodium hydroxide as a possible suspect.

The spray-on "popcorn texture" for ceilings—a kind of meringue apparently meant to liven up an otherwise flat surface—said it contained an ingredient (though it didn't say which one) known to cause cancer and birth defects or other reproductive harm (again, in California anyway). Other ingredients in this product, I was informed, may affect the brain or the nervous system.

The popcorn ceiling spray was, for me, a kind of (unsavory) Proustian madeleine: I immediately thought back fifteen years, to when Katherine and I had briefly found ourselves renting a house in suburban Pennsylvania. We had chosen the house for a reason: the owner had allowed us to live there with our two dogs. As we toured the house, the landlord had boasted about the popcorn (or, in his words, "Hollywood") ceilings, including one right above our bed. (He had also boasted about how he had outfitted much of the house with floor-to-ceiling mirrors, but that's another story.) So desperate were we to find a place that accepted dogs, Katherine and I took the place and lived there for a year. Now, standing there in the Hardware section, I wondered: how much of that Hollywood ceiling had ended up in my lungs? And once in there, what had it done?

The Hardware aisles were also full of every kind of aerosol spray, each with its attendant warnings about chemicals and their potential effects. Polyurethane (ketones, butane; brain and nervous system damage). Lacquer (acetates, ketones; ditto). Polycrylic finish (dimethylether, 2 butoxyethanol; ditto). Peekaboo Blue spray paint (acetone, toluene, alphatic hydrocarbons; ditto). Rustoleum (toluene, acetone, xylene; ditto).

The truth was, after a half hour spent wandering around this Big Box store, I was starting to get a nasty headache. Whether this was from chemicals leaking out of individual products, or from the cumulative "fragrances," or from straining to read all those microscopic labels, I can't say for sure. I will also not speculate on whether this headache qualified as "neurological distress." As I say, I'm not a particularly joyful shopper even on a good day.

We kept looking, pushing our cart to an aisle given over to what I came to think of as The Arsenal. Here, it seemed, you can buy weapons to eradicate every living organism smaller than your thumb. There were aerosol ant killers, roach and termite sprays, flea powders, atmospheric "foggers." "Kills on Contact," these products brag. "Once and Done!" "Kills 180+ types of insects." "Kills Bugs Inside and Out." These products are intended to be shaken or sprayed over the width and breadth of indoor carpeting and feature warnings that you wash your hands and clothes after use. They say nothing about the consequences of breathing these poisons for weeks or months; as is true for so many kinds of dust, indoor pesticides tend to linger in carpeting for a very long time without breaking down. Ditto for the aerosol flea "bombs," meant to be set up in a sealed room until the entire space is fogged with pesticides. Users were advised to call poison control if the stuff got swallowed, but there were no ingredients listed for 96 percent of the contents. Here's what was listed, the so-called "active ingredients": linalool, piperonyl, pyrethrins. The last of these represented some of the pesticides the Centers for Disease Control had recently discovered "in much of the U.S. population."[4]

These chemicals are designed to kill insects living outside the bodies of dogs and cats. But aerosolized chemicals also enter lungs. And once powders settle into carpeting, they end up on animal fur, adult feet, and infants' hands—whence, whether through skin absorption or inadvertent oral consumption, they also enter our bodies. These compounds included organophosphate and carbamate pesticides, chemicals designed to damage a bug's nervous system.

And in people? While some effects on human health—such as vomiting or tremors—may be immediately apparent, other impacts are more pernicious. Childhood exposure to pesticides—both in the womb and during the first years after birth—has been linked to an increased risk of cancer and to increased risks of injury to both the developing brain and the nervous system. Pound for pound, one study reports, children are at far greater risk than adults "because they live and play close to the floor, breathe close to the ground and constantly put their fingers into their mouths."[5]

And finally we came to paint. Now, there may be some people who wouldn't know a sealant from a caulk. I myself remain confused about the difference between lacquer and polyurethane. But everyone knows about paint. We coat our houses with it, inside and out. We spend a great deal of time thinking about texture (forget gloss or semi-gloss; now companies can set you up with paints that glow with reflected light, or shimmer like sprayed-on metal, or look for all the world like suede). We think about fashion (Sherwin-Williams now sells a paint called "Recycled Glass.") Most of all, we think about color. (Ralph Lauren boasts that it carries over 60 shades of white.)

What we don't think about, at least not too deeply, is what goes into the stuff we spread all over our walls and ceilings. Or what happens when we breathe it. Or when it breaks down and ends up in the dust in our rugs, which ends up, over time, in our skin, and our lungs, and our food. On the front of one can, I read: "Recommended for family rooms, children's rooms and hallways." On the back: Contains crystalline silica. Long term effects: abrading or sanding "may release crystalline silica which has been shown to cause lung damage and cancer."

Next to this was a can of interior semi-gloss paint that offered a block-lettered public health warning—not about itself, but about the old paint you might find yourself replacing: LEAD IS TOXIC. EXPOSURE TO LEAD DUST CAN CAUSE SERIOUS ILLNESS, SUCH AS BRAIN DAMAGE ESPECIALLY IN CHILDREN. Next to this, in smaller print: "This product contains chemicals known to the state of California to cause cancer, birth defects and other reproductive harm." It also noted that the paint contained "VOC <50 g/l." The VOC I guessed was for "volatile organic compounds," the stuff that people with Multiple Chemical Sensitivity find particularly onerous. These compounds are released into the air, or "volatilized," as paint is spread. But the number? Was that a good number or a bad number? And how was I supposed to know? (When I looked into it later, I found that a VOC level below 50 grams per liter was actually pretty good. Nonetheless, the EPA notes, during and immediately after the application of paints and lacquers and thinners, levels of

VOCs can be a thousand times stronger than background levels. Which is not so good.)[6]

COSMETICS AND PERSONAL CARE

So the Hardware section was plainly a major pipeline into our collective barrel of toxic chemicals. But at least most of the products made some effort to display their ingredients and to offer warnings, however unsettling and vague. The same could not be said of the next section Katherine and I visited, where we found many of the same ingredients we had seen in Hardware, but without the warning on the labels. And these products were not meant to be applied with rubber gloves. They were meant to be slathered directly on your skin.

Walking down a cosmetics aisle, if you pay close enough attention, you can actually notice the smells changing with virtually every step you take. As Katherine and I moved from the "fragrance" section to the "powders" section to the "lotions" section, I could sense the changes with my eyes closed; I am not speaking metaphorically here.

Not that your eyes are particularly useful. As I've mentioned, most labels are not exactly brimming with useful information. It was Katherine who noticed that the children's bubble baths were marked "Keep Out of the Reach of Children." This was a few steps down from a nail polish, boasting to be both "Hi Res" and "Hi Def," that was packaged in a glass container with an ingredient list so microscopic that neither Katherine nor I could read a single word of it—except the words "Caution: flammable."

When I showed Katherine lotions called "Velvet Tuberose" and "Decadent Amber," we agreed that people selling these things must have been thinking about sex toys or the names of their favorite strippers. Over and over, her eyebrows rose when she compared the marketing strategies of the skin care stuff targeted at women with that targeted at men. For women, it was all Satin Luxury; Glowing Touch; and Caress. For men: Snake Peel; Instinct; Dark Temptation; Phoenix; High Endurance. The ingredient lists were equally opaque; despite the long lists of contents, it was impossible to tell what any of this stuff was made of. But in an ironic twist on a safety warning, Axe products marketed to men featured a silhouette on the back label of a man showering with not one but two women. Warning, the label read, "The Axe Effect may result in, but is not limited to, unrelenting female attention and/or late nights."

Katherine chuckled as she read it. (Interestingly, she noted, the Axe "hair" products featured a label with a man with only one woman. Not sure why this would be. Perhaps monogamous men are more likely to wash their hair.)

At one point, Katherine pulled down a body lotion billed as containing "shea and cocoa butter"; the third ingredient, far ahead of shea and cocoa butter, was petroleum. She also found petroleum in the deodorants. She examined an "exfoliating body wash." The stuff claimed to be made with "microbeads," tiny bits of plastic that, along with a vigorous scrubbing, help slough off dead skin. When she turned the bottle over, she found the wash's second ingredient was petroleum. Was that what the microbeads were made of? Or were they made of the acrylonitrile/methacrylonitrile/methyl methacrylate copolymer? It was hard to tell. Either way—and regardless of the effect these bits of plastic might have on warm, damp skin—all I could think of were all those fish swimming around in the countless trillion microbeads that end up flowing down the shower drain into the so-called Pacific Gyre—a swath of garbage-filled ocean marine biologists compare to "a toilet that never flushes." And where these microbeads would end up, once those same fish ended up in someone's fishing net. What goes around comes around.

As for the lotions that make the hair fall off your legs so you don't have to shave, Katherine said she didn't even want to know. All she could tell from the label was that they were toxic enough to merit a warning about getting the stuff too near your eyes, your nipples, or your genitals.

The Cosmetics section was remarkable mostly for the radical shift in its marketing slogans. There were no "Unbeatable" price signs here. What there were instead were dozens upon dozens of photographs of beautiful, rich, toothy bronzed celebrities. There were countless claims about products being "natural" (or, in some cases *naturale*). Others boasted of their products' "science," its powers of "therapy," or "healing." This was as true for the colognes as it was for the shampoos and hair colorings and nail polishes. If you believed the signs, this would be the healthiest section in the whole store.

Which, of course, is just the way the cosmetics industry wants you to see their products, and their marketing is plainly working. The average American applies some form of "personal care product" (toothpaste, shampoo, moisturizer, lipstick, nail polish) a dozen or more times a day; many of these products contain such carcinogens as coal tar and 1,4-Dioxane; such neurotoxins as lead and mercury; and such hormone disruptors as parabens. Fully one-third of women over 18 in North America, Japan, and Europe (and 10 percent of men over 40) use some form of hair dye, which can contain formaldehyde. All told, the personal care industry sells some six billion products a year, for roughly $50 billion a year in revenue.[7]

For decades, the health effects of personal care products were of no concern. Newspaper and magazine advertisements in the 1950s urged women to buy Satura, a skin cream boasting that it contained hormones to "plump up skin," and "smooth tiny lines." In the 1980s, ads in *Essence* magazine urged African-American women to buy Le Kair hair treatment with "Hormones Plus Vitamins"—and "Hask Perm-Aid with Placenta."[8]

But in recent years, researchers have been finding striking evidence that chemicals found in all sorts of personal care products are altering hormones in both animals and humans. More confounding is the veil that surrounds the ingredients in these products. If the Hardware department is where you find the most explicit warnings about toxic chemicals, there is probably no section in a Big Box store with less information than Cosmetics, even though you can find some of the same chemicals at work. Nail hardeners can also contain formaldehyde (used as a resin and preservative) and toluene (a clear, colorless liquid that acts as a solvent and helps suspend colored pigments in nail polish). Like phthalates, which can be found in everything from soaps to baby lotions, toluene is a possible reproductive and developmental toxicant. And the growing use in cosmetics of so-called nanoparticles—chemicals that are a thousand times smaller than a human cell—is raising a new set of eyebrows. Researchers at the University of Delaware recently found that synthetic nanoparticles are readily taken up by plants (in this case, by pumpkins), can accumulate in their tissues, and can thus readily enter the food chain. Of particular concern seem to be zinc oxide and titanium oxide, used to make products such as sunscreen transparent.[9]

Research is building that breast growth is starting as much as two or three years earlier than in the past, and that menarche begins as much as a year earlier. There has been a big jump in the number of girls developing secondary sex characteristics by the age of eight, and environmental estrogens may be causing this change. Other studies have shown troubling signs of early-onset puberty in African-American girls, possibly from the use of hair products that contain estrogen or placenta, products that are left unregulated by the FDA. (African-American women are less likely than white women to get breast cancer, but at any age they are more likely to die from it.) In May 2009, CBS News reported on a girl in La Mirada, California, who underwent a mastectomy as part of her fight against breast cancer. She is 10 years old. "I feel like she's been robbed of her childhood," the girl's mother said. "It's beyond shocking. You know. She's 10. She has breast cancer. It's unheard of."

And these troubles can arise even at levels of exposure well below accepted norms. An independent panel convened by the NIEH and the National Toxicology Program in 2000 found evidence that some endocrine disruptors can affect animal body functions "well below the 'no effect' levels determined by normal testing."[10]

All of this, Theo Colburn writes, suggests that over the last 50 years, "synthetic chemicals have become so pervasive in the environment and in our bodies that it is no longer possible to define a normal, unaltered human physiology. There is no clean, uncontaminated place, nor any human being who hasn't acquired a considerable load of persistent hormone-disrupting chemicals. In this experiment, we are all guinea pigs."[11]

This notion of hormone-disrupting chemicals being inescapable felt truer in the Big Box store than anywhere I had ever been. They were not just in the products themselves; they were literally in the air we were breathing. Throughout our visit, Katherine and I had not just been astonished at what we found on the labels; our noses and our throats had been assaulted by the stuff. Especially that "lavender" smell. We needed to find out where it was coming from.

HOME

At first, we had been sure it was coming from the shampoo aisle, but that was more a symphony of mixed-berry, tropical fruit, and coconut. Then we figured it was coming from the home cleaning aisle, but that proved more a source of lemon mixed with chlorine. Finally—at this point I felt like a bloodhound, my nose in the air—we discovered the Lavender Epicenter, right near the intersection of three departments: Pets, Home, and Kitchen. It came in waves I could practically see. Lavender body washes. Lavender foot washes. Lavender potpourri, dried (to be placed in a bowl in a bathroom). Lavender potpourri, liquid (to be placed in a pot on the stove and simmered). Lavender laundry soap. And, most overwhelming of all, lavender-scented candles.

It was here that I almost vomited.

I was standing by a shelf of deodorizers, marveling at a fist-sized air freshener that comes equipped with a motion sensor—you attach the thing to a wall, and it squirts fragrance into the air whenever someone walks in the room. I was marveling at the product's list of warnings (call poison control if ingested; beware of electric shock) when Katherine snuck up behind me and asked me to take a whiff. She held up a glassed-in candle, and removed the lid under my nose. What came out was a blast of "peach cobbler" so overpowering that I gagged and almost lost it.

Katherine laughed. She showed me another product, this one an aerosol can of "home-made apple pie." No need to fill your house with "heaping barrels of brightly colored spices," the label said. "Just give it a spray or two!"

As I tried to collect myself, Katherine pondered the meaning of these smells. Selling a product that used a combination of chemicals to make people imagine a "peach cobbler" or a "home-made apple pie" was selling nostalgia to people too busy or too overwhelmed to get the smell the old-fashioned way: by baking a peach cobbler or an apple pie.

"It's pretty sad that you have to spray the smells that you crave," she said. "What do these smells represent? That grandma is home taking care of you. These things are marketed to overworked people. It's all so nostalgic—for cleaning, and cooking, and comfort and security. Why bake an apple pie when you can spray an apple pie?"

REST AREA

My near explosion in the air freshener aisle—and the headache that was not going away—made it pretty clear that I needed a break. I located a bathroom, found a water fountain, and took a long, deep drink. The bathroom itself was pretty nice, I have to admit. It had no exterior doors, which I have always taken to be a good public health measure—no doors means no door handles, which means no spreading of germs. It had "hands-free" faucets and soap dispensers, another good sign. But especially given the context of my journey, the place was—how else can I say this?—incredibly smelly. Or perhaps I should say it was incredibly "deodorized." Either way, the bathroom was overwhelmingly saturated with the smells of detergents, floor cleaners, and—I'm here to tell you—"lavender."

HOME, PART TWO

In a Big Box store, the kid's pajamas are arranged according to their tie-ins to movies and television shows. In the girl's section, you can choose from Dora the Explorer, a variety of Disney Princesses, and Winnie the Pooh. Boys are offered an even wider selection: Thomas the Tank Engine, Spiderman, SpongeBob, Buzz Lightyear, and any number of sporty-themed pajamas (though none with any professional team affiliation, since these are presumably protected by licensing agreements). So what does a parent see? A familiar face (Dora, Cinderella, SpongeBob); a cheap price; and a tag, typically in block letters, reading: "Flame Resistant Sleepwear: Sleepwear should be flame resistant or snug fitting to meet U.S. Consumer Product Safety Commission sleepwear requirements." The federal Consumer Product Safety Commission, it turns out, requires that fabrics used to make children's pajamas "must self-extinguish after exposure to a small open flame." Sounds pretty good, right?

You'll find similar tags in the home furnishings aisle, attached to the mattresses and cushions of the swivel chairs. Read the fine print of the pamphlet that comes with a new computer, or a new television, and you'll discover the same. Or you also may not. Even if products are made with flame-retardants, it's not always possible to tell. When my wife and I replaced an old mattress recently, I yanked the label off the old box spring (the one warning that it should not be removed "under penalty of law" by anyone except the consumer). The tag was stamped with almost illegibly small print; when I looked for an ingredient list, all I could find was that it was made of "100% SYN FIB PAD/UNKN KIND." This was not exactly helpful information.[12]

So what's the story with all these flame retardants? Were they beneficial?

When I was a kid, my youngest brother and I slept in a bunk bed on the second floor of our house. One night, asleep on the top bunk, I awoke to a noxious smell coming from below. I leaned over, and saw that my brother had fallen asleep with a reading light still burning hot under his blanket. Acrid black smoke rose from the cheap foam mattress. I leapt out of bed, jostled my brother awake, and—in a move that remains part of family lore—heaved the entire mattress out the second-story window. The next morning, my parents—who had slept through the whole ordeal—looked outside and saw the mattress, with a nasty black hole in the middle, out on the lawn. As designed, it had smoked, but did not burst into flame.

Did the flame retardants save our lives? Who can say? According to the National Academy of Sciences, each year about 90 people, most of them children, die in fires in upholstered furniture that were started with matches, cigarette lighters, or candles. Another 440 people are injured and property losses amount to $50 million annually. Some say that flame-retardant chemicals save lives; others say foam cushions are among the most toxic objects in a home.

Here's the problem: the chemical structure of these compounds closely resembles the structure of far more notorious compounds like dioxins and furans—the acutely toxic chemicals created during the incineration of plastics—and of PCBs, the fire-resistant fluids found in electrical transformers that were considered so toxic they were banned 30 years ago. They're also structurally similar to thyroxine, the growth-regulating hormone created by the thyroid gland; scientists believe that once they begin circulating in the body, flame retardants may block the movement of thyroid hormones. This, in turn, can affect both physical growth and energy levels and disrupt prenatal development. Thyroid hormones are responsible for regulating many essential metabolic functions and are extremely important in promoting normal brain development in infants. The disruption of thyroid-hormone regulation has frequently been associated with permanent behavior problems and brain damage. Rodents exposed to the chemicals showed an increased risk for liver and pancreatic tumors as well as for thyroid cancer.[13]

Since the compounds do not chemically bind to plastics, they are prone to "migrating," or leaching out, as dust. Wipe your fingers along the baseboard of your house and look at your fingers; you'll find PBDEs. Vacuum your carpets, and you'll find them in the dust. You'll also find them in the lint in your dryer. Researchers have found increased levels of flame retardants in the air of office buildings, especially during business hours. Once thrown away, cushions and computers and television sets will, eventually, begin to break down. But their chemical components, apparently, do not.[14]

The quantity of flame retardants detected in people and wildlife appears to have doubled in North America every four to five years since the 1970s, a pace unmatched by any other contaminant. The chemicals turn up in human blood, fatty tissue, and umbilical cord blood in every region where scientists have conducted studies. In many areas, concentrations in humans have been increasing exponentially. But it wasn't until flame retardants started showing up in breast milk that people started to pay attention.[15]

As public concern over these chemicals grew, the Swedish government (at least) reacted quickly, moving to prohibit the use of PBDEs in late 1999. Simultaneously, large Swedish companies like IKEA and Volvo moved to phase them out as well. The effects? A follow-up study found that from 1997 to 2000, PBDE levels in Swedish breast milk dropped 30 percent.[16]

Even if you feel confident that a single exposure to toxins in food will not cause you any problems, what do you say, walking through a Big Box store, when products containing these chemicals fill your shopping cart? How about a lifetime of shopping carts? And what happens when these chemicals, once inside you, get mixed up with the chemicals you get exposed to, say, in your paint? Or your cosmetics? Or, more directly, when they simply release their toxins straight into your children's mouths?

In the moment when we reach unthinkingly for a product, we suspend judgment, and even, at times, common sense. When we act unconsciously, we implicitly grant authority—and trust—to what manufacturers have told us, that a product is "safe." But the truth is, whether the product is an apple, a T-bone steak, a can of air freshener, or a mattress makes no difference: we have no idea what has gone into making the product, even if someone, somewhere, has assured us that the product is benign. In many, many cases, this is clearly no longer the case. And as the physical and psychological distance has grown between us and the products we consume, we have traded an intimate knowledge for a vague and anxious "trust," a feeling that is inevitably accompanied by its darker corollary, fear and a loss of control. This does not seem like a fair trade.

TOYS

Big Box stores are frequently criticized for serving as the endpoint of a Chinese assembly line, and no section reinforces this idea as vividly as the Toy department. But as Katherine and I made our way into the toy aisles, it occurred to me that this is not, in fact, the end of the story. All of this stuff—in Toys, in Home, in Hardware, everywhere—will one day pass through our homes, end up in landfills or in the air, and begin breaking down. At least some of the ingredients will turn into airborne dust, or particles filtering up through the food chain, or molecules of volatized aerosols, and will end up in our bodies. It's just a matter of time. But somehow, the link between plastic toys and toxic chemicals seems particularly insidious—and, in recent years, particularly common.

We've all spent time in these aisles: plastic toys from floor to ceiling. In the store we visited, virtually every duck, dinosaur, princess, and superhero was made out of plastic and had been manufactured in China. I'm not talking about a handful of toys in a small corner of the store. I'm talking about acres of toys. As in the pajama section, a sizeable majority of the products were movie or television tie-ins: Star Wars, Batman, Ultimate Fighting Action Figures, Thomas the Tank Engine trains. Others were slightly more original: during our visit, Katherine looked at a product called the Pink Princess Step Stool Potty, which claimed to play four "royal" tunes as a "reward." She looked bemused, but then the color in her eyes changed. Though we had never bought a musical toilet, we had offered our daughter rewards for learning to use the toilet. We had taken her to a store not unlike the one we were now in and encouraged her to pick out a small toy. She had chosen a play umbrella. Some weeks later, rewarded again, she had picked out a pair of play gardening gloves. Six months later, both toys were recalled because they had been coated with lead paint. So much for enlightened parenting.

Just two years before our Big Box safari, the United States experienced what will, in some circles, be remembered as the Year of the Toxic Recall. In the spring of 2007, Chinese-made pet food was recalled because it contained melamine, a toxic synthetic used in cleaning products, plastics, fertilizer, and paint that killed some 4,000 American dogs and cats. In China, melamine found in baby formula and in chicken eggs killed four babies and sickened tens of thousands of others.[17]

In May, almost a million tubes of Cooldent toothpaste imported from China were recalled because they were found to contain diethylene glycol, a solvent, typically found in antifreeze, that can lead to kidney damage or liver disease. The toothpaste had been distributed to jails as well as to expensive hotels. No deaths were reported from the tainted toothpaste, but Panama claimed that hundreds of people died, and hundreds more were poisoned, after using cold medicine imported from China that contained the same chemical, diethylene glycol.[18]

But The Year of the Toxic Recall will be remembered most for the astonishing number of contaminated toys. In June, a toy eyeball made in China was recalled after it was found to be filled with kerosene. Around the same time, RC2, the company that makes Thomas and Friends wooden railway toys, recalled 1.5 million toys because of lead contamination—a small number, really, when you consider that in the previous three years some 20 million pieces of children's jewelry had been recalled because of lead. In August, Toys "R" Us offered customers refunds for about one million baby bibs after tests showed that some, made in China, had also been contaminated with lead. A month after that, Target recalled 350,000 gardening toys because of lead, and Target and RC2 announced the recall of an additional 550,000 train toys, also because of lead contamination. RC2's chief executive apologized for the "burden that recalls create for parents."[19]

A burden indeed. Most Americans thought lead had disappeared as a consumer threat thirty years ago, when it was phased out of gasoline and banished from things like paint. The day after the Target recall, a group called the Center for Health, Environment and Justice tested 50 plastic toys and discovered high lead levels in 11 of them. Ten were made of PVC plastic, and three others contained "extremely high lead levels": a Go Diego Go backpack, a Superfly monkey, and a pair of Circo Lulu boots. The backpack had lead levels nearly eight times the health standard set by the Consumer Product Safety Commission.

"It's absolutely astonishing to us that lead continues to be found in children's toys, despite the fact that consumer and environmental groups have been warning the government about the issue for more than 10 years," a group spokesman said.[20]

So what was going on? In 1973, car fumes were considered the biggest source of lead in the air, dust, and dirt. A year later, with the Clean Air Act, the EPA set a timetable to phase out lead in gas, and within a few years average lead levels in children plummeted. What was it doing, creeping back into our lives like a shadow from the past? A toy train is made of wood (or plastic) and a bit of rubber and metal, all held together with glue and painted green or blue or red. Pretty simple. But what's in the plastic? What's in the paint? What's in the glue? What happens when the whole thing is in your child's mouth? Do you have a right to know the answers to these questions?

Children put toys in their mouth that are "intended" to go in their mouths, and they put things in their mouths that are not intended to go in their mouth. What we've discovered, in recent years, is that neither category guarantees that a product is made without hazardous chemicals.

The hazards of lead have been described in medical writings for 2000 years, and concerns over lead-contaminated water were acknowledged in England as far back as the late 1700s. Lead is known to be toxic to the reproductive system, the liver and kidney, and the immune system. Studies throughout the 1970s and 1980s showed that even low-level lead poisoning can cause neurological damage in the developing brain, and that children exposed to lead are at higher risk of developmental deficits. And although the link between lead and cancer in humans is less clear, lead has been shown to cause kidney and brain tumors in animals. Recent studies indicate that lead may increase the risk of cancer by compromising a cell's ability to protect or repair its DNA that has been damaged by other chemical exposures.[21]

Yet during the Year of the Toxic Recall, it wasn't just mothers in cities who were worried about lead poisoning. It was everyone. If American laws had removed lead from paint and gasoline, but we were buying our toys from a country with less regulatory muscle than our own, had we traded one peril for another? For a child, the peril of lead paint is the same, after all, whether the paint is flaking off a windowsill or sucked off a toy train.

Here, at least in part, is what happened. In just the last decade, imports of Chinese consumer products nationwide have surged from $62 billion to $246 billion. Nearly 20 percent of the consumer products for sale in the country today are Chinese-made, compared to 5 percent in 1997. China now makes roughly 80 percent of the toys sold in the United States, and the toy companies that sell them here are largely—does this sound familiar?—self-regulated. A month after the recall, RC2 launched a "Multi-Check Safety System" to reassure consumers that the company's products were safe. This would include greater scrutiny of its manufacturing partners, frequent lab tests of paint, and random plant inspections. "Going forward, the truest measure of our success is and always will be the trust parents place in our products," the company reported on its website. "We are working very hard to preserve and strengthen that trust. And, we hope that you and other parents recognize that our products have been subjected to intense internal scrutiny and testing and are the safer for it."[22]

What federal oversight there is for toys—and it isn't much—is offered by the Consumer Product Safety Commission, a beleaguered regulatory body that, ever since it was created by Congress in 1972, has been seen as an onerous bureaucratic obstacle by manufacturers and business groups. Until last year, it hadn't adopted any major regulations in nearly two decades. The staff in 2008 was just 400—half what it had been in the 1980s. Charged with monitoring the unimaginably wide conveyor belt of goods coming into this country every year (in 2007 it was worth $614 billion) is a staff of—wait for it—fifteen people.[23]

Not only that, but in the two years prior to The Year of the Toxic Recall, the Bush Administration cut the budget and the number of inspectors overseeing the country's vast network of ports, warehouses, and stores. The commission's shrinking budget was just 62 million USD in 2007, even though the agency regulates an industry that sells 1.4 trillion USD worth of toys, tools, and televisions ever year. The Food and Drug Administration, with a 2 billion USD budget, spends nearly twice as much monitoring the safety of animal feed and drugs. All told, the CPSC has just 81 field inspectors, who work out of their homes, compared with a network of field offices with 133 employees in 2002. Among their missions? Oversee tens of billions of dollars' worth of toys and other consumer products sold in the country each year. Here's what that looks like: In Los Angeles area ports, through which 15 million truck-size containers move a year, a single agency inspector, working two or three days a week, spot-checks incoming shipments.[24]

Here's what else it looks like: When *The New York Times* sent a reporter to the agency's product testing lab, which operates out of a former missile defense radar station in Gaithersburg, Maryland, he found a single lab worker used a magnifying glass and a mechanical stop watch to help conduct a fabric flammability experiment—the same equipment she had used for three decades. The toy laboratory, down the hall, was an office so cramped that the only space dedicated to a drop test to see if toys will break into small pieces and cause a choking hazard is the spare space behind the office door. "This is the toy lab for all of America—for all of the United States government!" said Robert L. Hundemer, the one agency employee who routinely tests toys, as he held up his arms in the air. "We do what we can."[25]

AFTER THE SAFARI, WHAT?

So what, then, are we to do? Given the world we currently inhabit, it's easy to feel overwhelmed. Synthetic chemicals are literally everywhere; they seem hard to name, harder to avoid, and even harder to replace. So what choices should we make? Where do we even begin?

Some answers to these questions are simple, and some are quite complex. Some require only small changes, and some could, if taken seriously, lead to deep adjustments in our personal lives and the way we think about entire systems. Changing brands of toothpaste or throwing out the roach spray is easy. Learning how to paint our houses—and our faces—with products that won't harm our health is a bit harder. Firing the lawn service and planting native species—an action that would improve the health of your family *and* your watershed—requires an even bigger shift. Getting toxins out of our food? Making our rivers clean enough to swim in? How far do you want to go?

When it comes to my experience in a Big Box store, the wisest words might well have come (as they often do) from my wife:

"For a store that's trying to sell to people who are trying to save money, there's so much here that people just don't need," Katherine said. "There's another way to save money: don't buy anything."

NOTES

1. "Top 10 U.S. Retailers: Walmart, Kroger and Costco Lead List," *Retail Info Systems News*, December 15, 2009. See http://www.risnews.com/ME2/dirmod.asp?sid=E2F9E0FBAE98430896F0B62A8F1C95B9&nm=&type=MultiPublishing&mod=

PublishingTitles&mid=2E3DABA5396D4649BABC55BEADF2F8FD&tier=4&id=7AA7E9B218804F47BE51E12DA16D752A

2. Douglas Fischer, "What's In You," first of a three-part series in *Oakland Tribune*, March 10, 2005.

3. The Washington study can be found at http://www.pollutioninpeople.org/. The Oregon study can be found at http://www.oeconline.org/our-work/kidshealth/pollutioninpeople. The Maine study can be found at http://www.cleanandhealthyme.org/BodyofEvidenceReport/Tabid/55/Default.aspx

4. The CDC quote comes from the CDC's *Fourth National Report on Human Exposure to Environmental Chemicals. Updated September, 2013.* (see http://www.cdc.gov/exposurereport/)

5. In 2002, New York's Attorney General released a report showing that commercial pesticide applicators had applied 4.1 million pounds of dry pesticides and 820,000 gallons of liquid pesticides to apartments, schools, parks, day care centers, senior centers, hospitals, offices, and office buildings across New York State. Homeowners, landlords, and apartment dwellers purchased many additional thousands of pounds of pesticides for private application. The pesticides used in New York include carcinogens, endocrine disruptors, chemicals capable of causing birth defects, and chemicals that can cause brain damage. Among the findings: none of the schools surveyed warned parents or students about pesticide applications; illegal or restricted pesticides were frequently for sale and in wide use, even by schools. The Attorney General's survey discovered that some very dangerous pesticides are used by governmental agencies in places where people live, work, and play. For example, the New York City schools, the Syracuse schools, and the Albany Housing Authority used hydramethylnon, a pesticide classified by the U.S. EPA as a "possible carcinogen." The Syracuse Housing Authority used baygon, a "probable carcinogen." All of these chemicals are applied in areas frequented by infants and children. By reducing or eliminating toxic pesticides, New York could save billions of dollars in health care costs each year, the report said. See Michael H. Surgan, Thomas Congdon, et al., "Pest Control in Public Housing, Schools and Parks: Urban Children at Risk," Environmental Protection Bureau, Office of the New York State Attorney General, August 2002. The full report can be found at www.oag.state.ny.us/bureaus/environmental/pdfs/pest_control_public_housing.pdf

6. See http://www.epa.gov/iaq/voc.html

7. Manuela Gago-Dominguez et al., "Use of Permanent Hair Dyes and Bladder Cancer Risk." *International Journal of Cancer* 91(2001): 575–79. Europe has banned the use of paradioxane in all personal care products and recently recalled all contaminated products. Not so the United States, where synthetic ingredients, in the words of one industry spokesman, are like "salt." "A little salt on your peas or tomatoes can be good," says John Bailey, executive vice president for science of the Cosmetic, Toiletry and Fragrance Association. "But a lot of salt can have adverse health effects on your blood pressure, and too much can be fatal." See Devra Davis, "A Thousand Threats: Cancer-Causing Chemicals Don't Work Alone, but in Tandem." *Newsweek International*, March 5, 2007; Natasha Singer, "Skin Deep: Should You Trust Your Makeup?" *The New York Times*, February 15, 2007.

8. http://news.google.com/newspapers?nid=1356&dat=19620211&id=UpEUAAAAIBAJ&sjid=MwUEAAAAIBAJ&pg=6077,1540065. See also Nancy Irwin Maxwell, "Social Differences in Women's Use of Personal Care Products: A Study of Magazine Advertisements, 1950-1994." Silent Spring Institute, November 1, 2000.

9. Zhu Hao and John Xiao, "Uptake, Translocation and Accumulation of Manufactured Iron Oxide Nanoparticles by Pumpkin Plants," *Journal of Environmental Monitoring* 10 (2008): 713–17.

10. Sandra K. Cesario and Lisa A. Hughes, "Precocious Puberty: A Comprehensive Review of Literature," *Journal of Obstetric, Gynecologic and Neonatal Nursing* 36, no. 3 (2007) 263. For the full NIH report, see www.niehs.nih.gov/health/topics/agents/endocrine/docs/endocrine.pdf). See also Diana Zuckerman, "When Little Girls Become

Women: Early Onset of Puberty in Girls," *The Ribbon*, a newsletter of the Cornell University Program on Breast Cancer and Environmental Risk Factors in New York State, 6, no. 1 (2001); Maryann Donovan et al., "Personal Care Products That Contain Estrogens or Xenostrogens May Increase Breast Cancer Risk," *Medical Hypotheses* 68 (2007): 756–66. "Ten-Year-Old Bravely Battles Breast Cancer," CBS News, May 19, 2009.

11. Theo Colburn, Dianne Dumanoski, and John Peterson Myers, *Our Stolen Future* (New York: Plume Books, 1996), 240.

12. http://www.cpsc.gov/businfo/frnotices/fr96/frsleeplg.html

13. T. McDonald, "A perspective on the potential health risks of PBDEs," *Chemosphere* 46, no. 5 (2002): 745–55; Darnerud et al., "Polybrominated Diphenyl Ethers: Occurrence, Dietary Exposure, and Toxicology," *Environmental Health Perspectives* 109, supp. 1 (March 2001):49–68. See also P. O. Darnerud, "Toxic effects of brominated flame retardants in man and wildlife," *Environment International* 29, no. 6 (2003): 841–53; Darnerud et al., "Polybrominated Diphenyl Ethers: Occurrence, Dietary Exposure, and Toxicology," *Environmental Health Perspectives* 109, supp. 1 (March 2001): 49–68; I. Branchi, F. Capone, E. Alleva, L. G. Costa, "Polybrominated Diphenyl Ethers: Neurobehavioral Effects Following Developmental Exposure," *Neurotoxicology* 24, no. 3 (2003): 449–62; T. A. McDonald, "A perspective on the potential health risks of PBDEs," *Chemosphere* 46, no. 5 (2002): 745–55; Darnerud, "Toxic effects of brominated flame retardants in man and wildlife," *Environment International* 29, no. 6 (2003): 841–53. See also H. Stapleton, M. Alaee, and J. Baker, "Debromination of Decabromodiphenyl Ether by Juvenile Carp (Cyprinus Carpio)," *Organohalogen Compounds* 61 (2003): 21–24; M. LaGuardia, R. C. Hale, and E. Harvey, "Are Waste Water Treatment Plants Sources for Polybrominated Diphenyl Ethers?" presented at the Annual Meeting of the Society of Environmental Toxicology and Chemistry (SETAC), 2003; and Watanabe et al., "Formation of brominated dibenzofurans from the photolysis of flame retardant decabromidiphenyl etherin hexane solution by UV and sunlight," *Bulletin of Environmental Containment Toxicology* 35 (1987): 953–59.

14. National Geographic Society, *The Green Guide: The Complete Reference for Consuming Wisely* (Washington, DC: National Geographic, 2008).

15. Penta, Octa, and Deca are three different formulations of polybrominated diphenyl ethers, commonly used as flame retardant compounds. Penta and Octa are no longer manufactured in the United States, but can still be found by the millions of pounds in consumer products in American homes. Deca is still made, with some 50 million pounds a year going into things like television casings. See the Washington Toxics Campaign website, http://watoxics.org/chemicals-of-concern/toxic-flame-retardants-pbdes. See Rebecca Renner, "What Fate for Brominated Flame Retardants?" *Environmental Science and Technology* 34, no. 9 (2000): 223A–26A; A. Bocio, J. M. Llobet, J. L. Domingo, J. Corbella, A. Teixido, C. Casas, "Polybrominated Diphenyl Ethers (PBDEs) in Foodstuffs: Human Exposure through the Diet," *Journal of Agricultural and Food Chemistry* 51, no. 10 (2003): 3191195; R. C. Hale, M. Alaee, J. B. Manchester-Neesvig, H. M. Stapleton, M. G. Ikonomou, "Polybrominated diphenyl ether flame retardants in the North American environment," *Environment International* 29, no. 6 (2003): 771–79; Meironyte et al., "Analysis of polybrominated diphenyl ethers in Swedish human milk. A time-related trend study, 1972-1997," *Journal of Toxicological Environmental Health* 58, Part A, no. 6 (1999): 329–41; K. Hooper and J. She, "Lessons from the Polybrominated Diphenyl Ethers (PBDEs): Precautionary Principle, Primary Prevention, and the Value of Community-Based Body-Burden Monitoring Using Breast Milk," *Environmental Health Perspectives* 111, no. 1 (2003): 109–13.

16. Sweden is the only nation with a comprehensive breast milk monitoring program, so it has been difficult to track these trends elsewhere. However, in regions where bans and restrictions have not been established, available studies are showing that concentrations of flame retardants in breast milk have risen far past Sweden's 1997 peak. See P. O. Darnerud, M. Aune, S. Atuma, W. Becker, R. Bjerselius, S. Cnattingius, A. Glynn, "Time trend of polybrominated diphenyl ether (PBDE) levels in breast

milk from Uppsala, Sweden, 1996-2001," *Organohalogen Compounds* 58 (2002): 233–36. At Sweden's urging, the European Commission banned the sale and use of Penta and Octa, in 2004, and began phasing out the use of Deca in electronics a couple years later. The International POPs Elimination Network, an alliance of non-governmental organizations from 65 countries, is working to get them added to the "dirty dozen" chemicals listed by the Stockholm Convention, a global treaty designed to protect people and the environment from toxic chemicals. For more information about the International POPs Elimination Network, see http://www.ipen.org/; European Union (EU), Directive of the European Parliament and of the Council on the restriction of the use of certain hazardous substances in electrical and electronic equipment. Document PE-CONS 3662/02, Brussels, November 8, 2002. Official Journal C 127E, 29.5.2003: 510–15. http://europa.eu.int/. In the U.S., no federal regulatory action has been taken to ban or restrict flame retardants. The EPA reached a voluntary agreement with Great Lakes Chemical Corp., the compounds' only manufacturer, to cease production of Penta and Octa in 2004, but products containing the stuff still abound—both in older products and in new ones imported from places like China. As with other toxins, laws restricting their manufacture in the United States do very little if most of the products are coming in from other places. Some of the chemicals replacing PBDEs are themselves suspect. Foam once made with Penta is now made with chlorinated Tris, a chemical banned from children's pajamas in the 1970s because it was shown to cause cancer. In the summer of 2008, reporters from the Milwaukee *Journal-Sentinel* examined the EPA's oversight of Tris, which has also been linked to reproductive and developmental problems. The paper found that the EPA's program set up to warn the public about toxic chemicals relies on studies that were at best decades old, and at worst had been paid for by the very industries they were supposed to oversee. "This lopsided assessment is the latest example of how the EPA gives preferential treatment to the chemical industry," the newspaper reported. "Instead of conducting independent reviews of chemicals, the EPA allows chemical manufacturers to characterize the safety of the products they make. The EPA then posts those claims on its Web site, often without verifying or correcting the information." Arlene Blum, a scientist from the University of California-Berkeley whose work led to the chemicals being taken out of children's sleepwear in the 1970s, told the paper she was astonished to learn that chlorinated Tris is back in such widespread use in other consumer products, particularly couches and places where children play. "We are going from one toxin to another with no requirement to tell people about the threats to their health and safety," Blum said. "It's been more than 30 years and the chemical industry hasn't bothered to come up with alternative? We can't do any better than this?" See Susanne Rust and Meg Kissinger, "Hazardous Flame Retardant Found in Household Objects," Milwaukee *Journal-Sentinel*, July 13, 2008.

17. James E. McWilliams, "Our Home-Grown Melamine Problem," *The New York Times*, Nov. 17, 2008.

18. Walt Bogdanich, "From China to Panama, a Trail of Poisoned Medicine," *The New York Times,* May 6, 2007. See also the Associated Press, "2 Companies Charged Over Tainted Toothpaste," *The New York Times*, March 6, 2008; Louise Story and Geraldine Fabrikant, "4 Executives Are Charged Over Tainted Toothpaste," *The New York Times*, March 7, 2008.

19. "New Toy Recalls As Group Finds High Lead Levels," *The New York Times*, Sept. 27, 2007.

20. Jad Mouawad, "550,000 More Chinese Toys Recalled for Lead," *The New York Times*, September 27, 2007.

21. Ellen Silbergeld, Michael Waalkes, and Jerry M. Rice, "Lead as a Carcinogen: Experimental Evidence and Mechanisms of Action," *American Journal of Industrial Medicine* 38 (2000): 316–23.

22. See the company website at http://www.rc2corp.com/company/multicheck.asp

23. In 1983, the Consumer Product Safety Commission determined that substantial exposure to DEHP, a common phthalate, could put children at risk for cancer, but the

agency didn't issue a regulation. Instead, it reached an agreement with the Toy Industry Association to keep DEHP out of pacifiers, rattles, and teethers. The agreement left unregulated all other toys that babies put in their mouths. See Jane Kay, "San Francisco Prepares to Ban Certain Chemicals in Products for Kids, but Enforcement Will Be Tough—and Toymakers Question Necessity." *San Francisco Chronicle,* November 19, 2006; Jane Kay, "Supervisors Tweak 'Toxic' Child Products; City Will Test Up to 100 Items a Year, List Those Illegal to Sell." *San Francisco Chronicle,* April 11, 2007. See also Stephen Labaton, "Senate Votes to Strengthen Product Safety Laws," *The New York Times,* March 7, 2008.

24. David Barboza, "As More Toys Are Recalled, Trail Ends in China." *The New York Times,* June 18, 2007.

25. Eric Lipton, "Safety Agency Faces Scrutiny Amid Charges," *The New York Times,* September 2, 2007. Joel Ticknor, a professor of environmental health at the University of Massachusetts-Lowell, considers federal protection against toxins in toys to be "weak at best and dysfunctional at worst. Consumers would be astonished if they knew that federal laws regulating chemicals in children's toys all require balancing the benefits of protecting children with the costs to industry of implementing safer alternatives." See Jane Kay, *San Francisco Chronicle,* April 11, 2007, September 5, 2007, November 19, 2006.

NINE

Secondhand Learning

Using Secondhand Consumerism in the Classroom

Helen Sheumaker

> I wear your granddad's clothes
> I look incredible
> I'm in this big ass coat
> From that thrift shop down the road.
> —Macklemore and Ryan Lewis, "Thrift Shop"[1]

Secondhand consumerism is part of a cycle of production, consumption, waste, and reuse around the globe. Residents of the United States play a central role in this cycle, particularly in the circulation of used clothing globally. When clothing is donated for resale, local thrift stores, for example, become a nexus in which the local and the global meet. Clothing deemed unsuitable for resale in the United States is purchased by middlemen who export the used items to other countries for resale there. Theoretical arguments about the effects of global trade are instrumental in understanding these processes, but it is in real, lived experience that the materiality of clothing melds with economic roles. This chapter describes an experiential pedagogical approach that helped undergraduate students understand theoretical arguments about the globalized circulation of used clothing originating from the United States through a service learning exercise in a thrift store.

THRIFT SHOPPING AS ECONOMIC STRATEGY AND SELF-EXPRESSION

For most Americans, there really is a "thrift shop down the road," as rapper Macklemore's lyrics from his hit song "Thrift Shop" maintain.[2] Thrift shops are, as he argues, local stores. But whether resale, consignment, or nonprofit retail stores, thrift shops are where the global and local intersect.[3] Clothing is imported into the country, sold, worn and used, donated, and then if not resold within the country, exported back out to flow into other nation's economies.

Shopping for secondhand clothing is also both in the United States and around the world, about creativity, self-expression, and self-identity. The thrift shopper takes clothing, decontextualized and removed from the original owner's wardrobe, and invests it with a different taste and value. Granddad's clothes are assigned new cultural significance when the wearer is a rapper in a "big ass coat." Economic need is sometimes present, sometimes not, but this creative process is always at play.[4] As Macklemore's lyrics point out, "But shit, it was ninety-nine cents! (Bag it)/ Coppin' it, washin' it, 'bout to go and get some compliments."

GLOBALIZATION AND SECONDHAND CLOTHING

As Arjun Appadurai argues in his landmark text, "Disjuncture and Difference in the Global Cultural Economy," the process signified by the term "globalization," as it has developed over the past twenty-five years, is not a seamless, propulsive shift to a new state of economic exchange. Rather, globalization is a term that describes a disjointed, disjunctive, complex series of simultaneously occurring and disparate processes of change. In particular, Appadurai cautions against concluding that this ongoing complex of change is uniformly resulting in the homogenization or heterogenization of cultural groups. These processes are not somehow benign; he warns that "Americanization" may be a special concern to lesser-developed nations.[5]

In light of Appadurai's and other's analyses of the emergence of a global cultural economy, some researchers have focused particularly on the role played by the exchange of secondhand goods from the United States. Karen Tranberg Hansen's *Salaula* (2000), for example, argues that American secondhand goods have dominated the clothing trade in Zambia, largely due to World Bank policies that ironically favor the importation of used clothing rather than the domestic production and consumption of clothing. Moreover, as in the United States, people in Zambia look to used clothing for material self-expression. Tranberg Hansen's findings are also demonstrated in two documentary films. One is *T-Shirt Travels*, a 2001 video by Shantha Bloemen, a filmmaker who served as an aid worker in Zambia. It shows villagers and townspeople, from sophisticated city workers to impoverished farmworkers, wearing secondhand clothing imported from the West, usually the United States, and ties the decimation of the clothing manufacturing industry and the debt load of the country to international monetary policies that forced Zambia to accept the Western secondhand trade.[6] Another, *Secondhand (Pepe)* (2007), examines how American secondhand clothing has weakened Haitian manufacturing and how Haitians have adapted to the used clothing market, including overcoming spiritual beliefs against used clothing and using dressmaking techniques to tailor American goods for Haitian stylistic and fit preferences.[7]

Economist Luz Claudio provides helpful data about the role of American charities in processing donated clothing. In 2007, he noted that ten pounds of donated clothing comes from each American household (this represents about 15 percent of the clothing discarded by each American household in one year) and that about one-fifth of the clothing donated to charities is used or sold.[8] The rest of the clothing either becomes rag waste or is baled and then purchased by middlemen, who sell it internationally. As Pietra Rivoli, another major economist interested in the secondhand clothing trade, suggests, there are "nowhere near enough poor people in America to absorb the mountains of castoffs, even if they were given away."[9] To deal with this excess, Americans give it away to charity stores, either local ones or regional or national chains, such as Goodwill Industries or the Salvation Army. Despite its mass scale, however, as Rivoli points out, the secondhand clothing trade relies mainly on independent, small-scale exporters and resellers; it is "a global industry for the little guy."[10]

Anthropologist Lucy Norris remarks that "[t]he used clothing economy brings into one frame the links between the market, materiality, and morals, revealing complex connections as gifts of clothing are commodified by charities in the Global North, sold onto the international market, and become a resource for developing local livelihoods in the Global South."[11] Well schooled in charitable giving, Americans donate used clothing to better their community, to benefit those less fortunate, and to alleviate the material wants of others with their own excess. While seeing themselves as benevolent and distinct from the imagined beneficiaries, most Americans do not recognize, however, that giving used clothing can result in the crippling of other nation's economies.

On a local level, donors may consider themselves engaged in the recent "living local" movement to center one's economic activity where one lives. Farmers' markets, local shops, and other consumerist activities reflect a self-conscious effort not to purchase goods or services produced from afar. One study of Salvation Army stores in Australia found that charity stores "reflected and co-created a local secondhand market . . . [that] was highly social, with customers donating not just from a moral imperative, but also because the thrift store formed a local point of social contact."[12]

THE ROLE OF HUMAN LABOR

From the donors' point of view, the process of secondhand consumption may seem to end with their donation; its further circulation may be not only invisible, but unimagined. In particular, the labor of those who handled the clothing may be hidden. Consider the sorters, that is, the workers who touch each item of donated clothing, judging its likelihood to retain or accrue value. Norris points out that "[i]t is the work of sorters to create exchange-value," and sorters are positioned at every exchange nodule of the secondhand good's life.[13] Once an item donated in the United States finds its way to, say, Zambia, at least four individuals have touched and judged the garment: the original donor who sorted through her clothing and selected those items deemed worthless to herself but of potential value to another, the store volunteer or employee who sorts the clothing, the recycler who purchases the bundles from the charity store, and the importer.[14]

EXPERIENTIAL LEARNING: MAKING THE ABSTRACT REAL

While the globalized trade in secondhand clothing has so far been described mainly in immaterial terms, the process is deeply material. In the remainder of this chapter, I describe a pedagogical approach I developed that helped students understand their role as agents in this circulatory process. They learned theory in the classroom and lived the experience of secondhand consumption outside the classroom, in thrift stores not only as shoppers but also as laborers.

They also, significantly, reflected on their learning in discussions and written assignments based on field notes. A course goal for students was to develop critical self-awareness by contextualizing their beliefs, values, and experiences in the framework of American culture through a combination of scholarly perspectives, personal experience, and critical evaluation of that experience. In meeting this goal, the seminar aimed to position students as actors rather than simply as receivers of others' knowledge.[15] Even though I recognize that outcomes are uneven when one moves from transmitting a packaged set of facts or assertions to an experiential model, I felt that an experiential approach was best; as Kolb and Kolb note: "learning is a process of creating knowledge . . . whereby social knowledge is created and recreated in the personal knowledge of the learner."[16]

THE COURSE

Secondhand consumption was introduced within an American Studies honors seminar that I taught in 2010 at Miami University in Ohio. It enrolled twelve students, most with majors in the sciences or prelaw. Almost all were in the first semester of their first year, all but one self-identified as white, and most self-identified as being from upper middle to upper class families.

The course was linked to a large (150+ students) economic and cultural geography course. My American Studies seminar served as a gateway to the major and a general education service course, which at the honors level is a discussion-driven format. A material culture focus matched the interests of undergraduate students, who are often particularly gifted at analyzing and interpreting the things around them. Thrift shopping became a way to explore issues of globalism, structured markets, and consumerist practices. In addition, thinking about secondhand consumer goods encouraged students to think critically about their position in the social, economic, and cultural worlds. The various assignments in the class aimed to help students develop their observational skills in real-life situations and integrate those observations with information from their course readings.

Some background: the town in which our campus is located is sharply divided socioeconomically from the surrounding communities, with local residents being largely of the working class and with much greater ethnic and racial diversity than that found on campus. For most students, the town is an unfamiliar, vague place without discernible landmarks, history, or community. While students are, on average, from wealthy families, only 9 percent of families in the county have a total household income of $150,000+; the K–12 school district has a household poverty rate of 41 percent. The campus Foursquare™ site refers to itself as "The Bubble."[17] There is thus a wide disparity between the socioeconomic position of most students at the university and that of the residential community surrounding it, and this disparity became a subject of study as well.[18]

The students' family wealth also tends to isolate them from broader American socioeconomic life. Students' economic practices were bereft of thrift shopping experience: of the twelve students in this class, only one had visited a thrift store to purchase clothing to wear (as opposed to a costume). In part because of the relative youth and freshman status of the students, most had limited life experiences with "alternative" consumerist practices. They were unfamiliar with farmers' markets, local craft fairs, rummage sales, and other less-corporatized market experiences.

MAKING IT REAL: SHOPPERS

To prepare for their experiential exercise, students read the literature cited earlier in this chapter and viewed the documentaries; they also read scholarship about how clothing is used to construct identity, including Erving Goffman's landmark work on social roles and a brief essay about marketing to college students.[19]

The students visited two thrift stores that operated in different ways and they engaged in different activities in each store. In the first, a large thrift store in a nearby community, students acted as shoppers. This "soft" introduction to the retail environment of a thrift store proved necessary, given the students' lack of experience at such stores. To enhance their observations, students completed a worksheet and photographed one section of clothing. For each item in that section, they recorded the place of manufacture and estimated or placed the item in its original retail context (Limited, Gap, Old Navy, Walmart, and the like). They also noted the condition of the clothes and selected several items for closer observation. They then wandered around the store, observing its clientele, employees, range of products, and specific items being purchased. Several students ended up purchasing an item, something I had encouraged but had not expected they would do.

This store represents the socioeconomic decline of the region, the Rust Belt Midwest. Appropriately, given the perception of thrift stores as a hard-luck option for shopping, the store is located directly across from the now-shuttered, mammoth Fisher Automobile Body Plant (Chevrolet and Pontiac), which closed in 1988. The store is a freestanding building surrounded by an immense parking lot and empty fields, on a heavily traveled commercial strip of used car lots and discount groceries.

Students agreed with Claudio's findings, arguing that the "best stuff" remained within the country for secondhand sale, and they wondered about the quality of the goods sent overseas. We were engaged in analyzing both what remained (that is, was offered for sale) and what was absent (that is, the lower-quality goods that did not make it onto the sales floor). Above all, they were stunned by the variety of clothing brands, the dominance of specific brands, the wide array of national origins of manufacture of the clothing, and the high quality of the clothing that was placed on the sales racks. They were impressed with the store itself, finding that it was cleaner, tidier, and more organized than they had expected. Cataloguing brands and country of manufacture for one rack section of clothing made clear to the students that the secondhand trade in the United States was a dynamic nexus of global exchanges.

MAKING IT REAL: WORKERS

The next thrift store we visited, at the Family Resource Center (FRC), provided a different experience. Since service learning was a university-mandated component of the course, students became workers there. The FRC provides indigent dental care, rent vouchers, school supply bags, and other needed social services. Before this exercise, no student in the class had visited the FRC as either a volunteer or client. The FRC site is composed of three temporary buildings: a main office and donation center, a small classroom for ESL and job training courses, and a very small thrift store open six days a week to the community. Students heard a presentation by the two staff members about the various outreach activities of the organization. Then they were put "to work" in the small store, as a staff member termed it, sorting donated clothing and furniture as either "saleable" or rejects. Students gamely sorted through the bags of donated clothing. According to the store manager, rejects were "trashed," that is, bundled and donated to the Salvation Army. These bundles presumably in turn were sold with other rejected donated clothing to brokers for international delivery. Like others in similar positions in many thrift stores, the manager was unaware of the practice of baling the clothing; he had always assumed the bundles being donated to the Salvation Army were unbundled and re-sorted for sale elsewhere in the United States.

An assignment based on this experience led students to consider how the arguments about globalized trade affected their material life. For example, the prompt for an essay was "You performed routine, even boring, tasks processing used clothing and other goods that would be sold in the shop, given away, or provided to the Salvation Army for free. How was this activity both *local* and *global*?" What resulted from this prompt, however, was a rich discourse, especially in response to the first element, the "routine, even boring tasks," which many students deemed humiliating. The phrases about used clothing that "would be sold in the shop, given away, or provided to the Salvation Army for free" prompted comments about the supposed dirtiness of the work they participated in. Students had unforeseen visceral reactions to the store and the donated items, characterizing them as "gross" and "dirty." One student commented that the clients "made me very sad because they just didn't care." Students were not interested at this point in developing discussion about globalized trade; their attention was on how working within this system affected them.

MAKING IT REAL: REFLECTIONS

In recognizing these sharp reactions of discomfort and even anger, students took a step toward developing a critical self-awareness. The psychic and intellectual distance from the consumer economy they usually enjoyed as shoppers with certain socioeconomic advantages diminished in this exercise. It was unnerving for students to have the globalized processes they had read about become a part of their own experience.

In class, we had a lengthy discussion about the connotations and denotations of "dirtiness" in popular usage and in the *Oxford English Dictionary*. The concepts of Mary Douglas, the anthropologist and cultural theorist, especially her analyses of the cultural constructions of "dirty" and "clean," became pertinent.[20] We discussed how clothing can connote "dirtiness" or "grossness" without actually being dirty (most, if not all, clothing processed by students was clean, that is, laundered, before handling).[21]

When students were shoppers, as in the first, larger store, they were impressed with the quality of the clothing and the tidy racks. That store presents the donated clothing in an impersonal, wholly familiar retail setting, with signage, price tags, and commercial retail racks. The employees at this store wear hospital scrubs and latex gloves to suggest a high level of cleanliness to customers, an element that had an impact on students' impression of the store. In the FRC store, as workers, not shoppers, they handled clothes in a way that made other people's use more apparent. They realized, too, that the consumer retail experience often masks the human labor inherent in the production and sale of commodities.

These students were seemingly not influenced by some contemporary views of thrift shopping in which it is seen as an optional form of consumerism devoid of the connotations of uncleanliness or poverty.[22] As one recent study of thrift store customers in the United Kingdom noted, "the *old* perception of thrift stores is that they are unorganized, dark, smelly, and dirty [emphasis added]."[23] For this group of under-21-year-old students, however, the "old perception" was in fact their overwhelming perception. Almost every student used a term like "dirty," "smelly," or "gross" in both written and oral reflections on their experience at the FRC. These descriptors indicate the materiality of secondhand clothing, to be sure, although the items were often freshly washed and smelling of no more than strongly scented fabric softener. But the students were using these terms mainly to discuss an experience they found unsettling. The literature on trash and discard helps to explain the students' reaction. Historian Susan Strasser argued in 1999 that "trash is a dynamic category," and the students were placed within the cycle of definition in which goods move from consumable to trash and back to consumable in the secondhand market.[24] At the FRC, the students confronted the low point in the cycle.

The location of the FRC also contributed to the students' negative reaction. Local thrift stores, including well-known nonprofit corporations, such as Salvation Army stores, often serve a social purpose for the community. The FRC store laid bare some uncomfortable realities behind the circulation of goods in the students' own neighborhood, while the more conventional retail atmosphere of the larger store obscured those processes.

In addition, being a worker in the store presented an uncomfortable reality. To my surprise, most students had not worked for pay before. Obviously, they were not working for money in this situation either, but I surmised that for most of the students, working a menial, laboring position was a new and unwanted experience. Moreover, at the FRC store, students were engaged in the same labor as those sorting clothes in the film *T-Shirt Travels*. Ironically, it was this parallel between the documentaries of secondhand clothing economies in Zambia and Haiti and the "labor" the students would perform that I, as the instructor, was the most excited about. While I recognized the potential for reflective contrast between the secondary sources and the primary source of actual experience, the students were not as thrilled by this intellectual frisson.

This issue of labor thus turned out to be crucial to the students' experience. The position of power in a philanthropic relationship is invested in the giver, not the taker. Students were accustomed to the role of volunteer—in class discussions they revealed experiences serving in homeless shelters. But the combination of reading essays about globalized circulation of used goods and viewing documentaries that showed individuals in less-developed parts of the world sorting secondhand clothing meant that these students (and myself, who also helped sort clothing) found themselves in the position of "worker," not consumer or donor, in this larger economic system. That role has social implications the students rejected: they did not enjoy handling and sorting materials, and they framed their dislike in Westernized terms of cleanliness and dirtiness.

THE CHALLENGES OF PROBLEM-BASED LEARNING

These experiences forced students to encounter the challenges of problem-based learning. Faced with an unfamiliar, uncomfortable experience, they reacted in visceral ways. In-class discussions were tense right after the FRC experience, but students were eventually able to proceed with a critical analysis of their own reactions as they examined the broader structural issues of secondhand consumerism as a global phenomenon and explored how their two experiences revealed the culturally constructed ways in which being a customer differs from other forms of labor.

Americans exist within a consumer culture overflowing with goods, such as clothing, much of it produced in other parts of the world at extraordinarily low cost. For students in the seminar, the material characteristics of used clothing (physically present, used in appearance and feel, creating a certain smell in a store filled with such items) brought home important aspects of that consumer culture. Studying the full cycle of production, consumption, waste, and reuse, students began to recognize that mini mountains of used clothing grew because consumers individually, and then on a mass scale, partly in response to a social system that encouraged such purchases, bought, used, and discarded those items. Overconsumption in the United States may be seen as mitigated somewhat by the charitable impulse. Providing material aid is a benevolent activity, helping to assuage poverty and demonstrate, on the part of individuals or the nation, charitable intent. The role of the United States, and by extension its citizens, in acting as a self-defined benevolent power has been critiqued by other nations but is less questioned by its own citizenry. The circulation of secondhand clothing, especially from the United States to developing countries, however, is not an unquestionable good, and charitable organizations often have the problem of too many donated items rather than too few.

On another iteration of this seminar, I might extend students' work at the FRC store to an entire semester. The students made two visits, one for orientation and the other to serve the charity. I did not foresee some students' negative reaction to the physical labor they were asked to do. Those students would gain from additional time working at the store and reconsidering their assumptions. Most students, however, participated at high levels in their role of charitable volunteer even if they were not familiar with problematizing that position.

I was surprised that students bought an array of goods from the high-volume thrift store; our university rental vans were quite full on our return trip. When we arrived at campus, the students proceeded to lug their new, used stuff to their dorm rooms and apartments, energized by their own thriftiness. And I carted to the van a vintage chair, which I later struggled to fit into my already overly furnished living room. No students purchased anything from the FRC store, although they did share a bottle of hand disinfectant on the way home from that field trip. Both trips engaged students as actors in a consumer culture of material goods. As shoppers, students were at home in the first store, attracted by the range of desirable brands, interested in the international sources of manufacture, and hardly aware of the secondhand quality of the merchandise. As workers at the FRC store, some students were horrified at the sheer volume of used goods and surprised at the ways human use was evident in smells, worn fabrics, and crumpled fabric. Yet, there, too, students noted that globalized production was evident in ways they had not been aware of before this experience. The power of material culture in making tangible the abstract discussions of globalized culture, economic hierarchies, and social and economic privilege lies in part in the traces of "dirtiness" inscribed in its prior use by others. For these consumers, secondhand shopping was a way to investigate the local and the global, the theoretical and the real. The experience and their intellectual work broadened their understanding of their role in the vast, nearly unknowable circulation of goods that forms the basis of their everyday lives.

NOTES

1. Macklemore (Benjamin Haggerty) and Ryan Lewis, "Thrift Shop," August 28, 2012, digital download release, Macklemore LLC. Lyrics quoted in this chapter are used with permission of copyright holders and Inside Passage Management.

2. For more about "Thrift Shop," see Natasha Chandel, "Macklemore 'Pops Some Tags' While Thrift Shopping," December 21, 2012, MTV, Viacom International, http://www.mtv.com/news/articles/1699304/macklemore-thrift-shop.jhtml, one of several recent online profiles in which Haggerty discusses his lifelong experiences thrift shopping. The song may be best read as a descriptive narrative rather than as a prescriptive entreaty; see Rebecca Nelson, "People Listening to 'Thrift Shop' Not Going to Actual Thrift Shops," *Time Newsfeed*, March 8, 2013, http://newsfeed.time.com/2013/03/08/people-listening-to-thrift-shop-not-going-to-actual-thrift-shops/print/.

3. I use the terms "thrift shop" and "thrift store" interchangeably in this discussion. "Secondhand merchandise stores" is the most precise term. The term "store" often denotes a large-scale retail operation, whereas "shop" denotes a small-scale retail operation. For this discussion, the difference between the two is minimal. Likewise, I use "secondhand shopping" and "thrift shopping," and "used" and "secondhand" interchangeably. See the National Association of Resale Professionals, http://www.narts.org/i4a/pages/index.cfm?pageid=3310, for definitions of each term and see the U.S. Department of Commerce, "Industry Standards Statistics: NAICS 453310, Used Merchandise Stores," http://www.census.gov/econ/industry/def/d453310.htm, which provides definitions from 2007.

4. This intersection of economic strategy and creative self-expression emerges in the twentieth century. Jennifer Le Zotte has recently argued that "creative" thrift shopping occurred as early as 1899, in her article "'Not Charity, but a Chance': Philanthropic Capitalism and the Rise of American Thrift Stores, 1894-1930," *The New England Quarterly* 86:2 (June 2013), 169–95. In 1988, Angela McRobbie's *Zoot Suits and Second-Hand Dresses: An Anthology of Fashion and Music* (Boston: Unwin Hyman) provided the impetus for other researchers to examine the recontextualization of mass-produced culture through the practice of secondhand shopping. Tim Christiansen and David J. Snepenger examine the specific issue of motivations for secondhand clothing shopping in "Information Sources for Thrift Shopping: Is There a 'Thrift Maven'?" *Journal of Consumer Marketing* 22:6 (2005), 323–331, while Marie-Cécile Cervellon, Lindsey Carey, and Trine Harms, "Something Old, Something Used: Determinants of Women's Purchase of Vintage Fashion vs. Second-Hand Fashion," *International Journal of Retail and Distribution Management* 40:12 (June 2012), 965–74, examines the intersection of the practice of vintage shopping (with connoisseurship and collecting motivations) and secondhand shopping (with economic issues driving the activity). Another study of the economic needs that drive secondhand shopping is Susan Porter Benson's "What Goes 'Round Comes 'Round: Secondhand Clothing, Furniture, and Tools in Working-Class Lives in the Interwar United States," *Journal of Women's History* 19:1 (Spring 2007), 17–31, which examines the historical practice of secondhand shopping.

All studies of secondhand clothing shopping in the global South point to the same conclusion that secondhand shopping—no matter the nation—is a combination of economic need and creative self-expression.

5. Arjun Appadurai, "Disjuncture and Difference in the Global Cultural Economy," *Theory, Culture & Society* 7 (1990), 295–310.

6. Lucy Norris, "Trade and Transformations of Secondhand Clothing," *Textiles: The Journal of Cloth and Culture* 10:2 (July 2012), 128–42, citing Andrew Brooks and David Simon, "Untangling the Relationship between Used-Clothing Imports and the Decline of the African Clothing Industry," *Development and Change* 43:6 (November 2012), 1265–90, suggests that this causal link is problematic. Karen Tranberg Hansen, *Salaula: The World of Secondhand Clothing and Zambia* (Chicago: University of Chicago Press, 2000); Shantha Bloemen, *T-Shirt Travels: The Story of Secondhand Clothes & Third World Debt* (New York: Filmmakers Library, 2001); and Lucy Norris, *Recycling Indian Clothing: Global Contexts of Reuse and Value* (Bloomington: Indiana University Press, 2010) have all explored the global and globalized contours of the trade in secondhand clothing.

7. *Secondhand (Pepe)* (2007), directed by Hannah Rose Shell and Vanessa Bertozzi, 24 min., examines the impact of U.S. secondhand clothing in Haiti; Karen Tranberg Hansen, "Second-Hand Clothing Encounters in Zambia: Global Discourses, Western Commodities, and Local Histories," *Africa: Journal of the International African Institute* 69:3 (1999), 343–65, examines the impact of U.S. secondhand clothing in Zambia.

8. Luz Claudio, "Waste Couture: Environmental Impact of the Clothing Industry," *Environmental Health Perspectives* 115:9 (September 2007), A448-–54.

9. Pietra Rivoli, *The Travels of a T-Shirt in the Global Economy*, Second Edition (Hoboken, NJ: John Wiley & Sons, 2009), 216.

10. Rivoli, *Travels*, 218.

11. Lucy Norris, abstract of "Trade and Transformations of Secondhand Clothing," *Textiles: The Journal of Cloth and Culture* 10:2 (July 2012), 129.

12. Aneta Podkalicka and James Meese, "'Twin Transformations': The Salvation Army's Charity Shops and the Recreating of Material and Social Value," *European Journal of Cultural Studies* 15:6 (2012), 725. See also Julie Botticello, "Between Classification, Objectification, and Perception: Processing Secondhand Clothing for Recycling and Reuse," *Textiles: The Journal of Cloth and Culture* 10:2 (July 2012), 164–83.

13. Norris, 135.

14. Norris argues four; see also Tranberg Hansen, *Salaula*.

15. Marilla D. Svinicki and Nancy M. Dixon, "The Kolb Model Modified for Classroom Activities," *College Teaching* 35:4 (Fall 1987), 141–46; and Alice Y. Kolb and David A. Kolb, "Learning Styles and Learning Spaces: Experiential Learning in Higher Education," *Academy of Management Learning and Education* 4:2 (June 2005), 93–212.

16. Kolb and Kolb, "Learning Styles," 194.

17. "The Miami University Bubble," https://foursquare.com/v/the-miami-university-bubble/4e6bc4c01495acb0c753781e, accessed December 30, 2012.

18. "About the CIRP Freshman Survey," http://www.units.muohio.edu/oir/Surveys/CIRP/index.htm, accessed September 2009; "Ohio County Profiles: Butler County," http://www.development.ohio.gov/research/files/s0/Butler.pdf, accessed September 2009; Miami University Students for Staff, "Living Wage Presentation to the Classified Personnel Advisory Committee," March 2, 2006, available at http://www.musfs.org/sfs/wp-content/uploads/2007/08/cpac_3_2_06.pdf, accessed March 1, 2010; James Lin and Jared Bernstein, "What We Need to Get By—A Basic Standard of Living costs $48,778 and Nearly One-Third of Families Fall Short," Economic Policy Institute, Briefing Paper #224, October 29, 2008, available at http://www.epi.org/publications/entry/bp224/, accessed February 21, 2010.

19. Erving Goffman, "Performances," in *The Presentation of Self in Everyday Life* (New York: Anchor Books, 1959); Jennifer Edson Escalas and James R. Bettman, "You Are What They Eat: The Influence of Reference Groups on Consumer Connections to Brands," *Journal of Consumer Psychology* 13:3 (2003), 339–48.

20. Mary Douglas, *Purity and Danger: An Analysis of Pollution and Taboo* (New York: Praeger, 1966).

21. I do not pretend that all thrift shop items are clean; they are not, at least in their initial donated state. I will not quote Macklemore's lyrics due to the profanity, but he acknowledges in the song's lyrics that sometimes the clothing in a thrift store is soiled. However, in this instance, the clothing was freshly washed and often folded neatly before being donated to the store and thus was physically "clean" before the students began sorting.

22. Keep in mind this reaction was in a retail store environment (albeit a thrift store). An experience that potentially could have taken our group into the realm of "rubbish" would have been a visit to the local landfill. See Joshua Reno, "Your Trash Is Someone's Treasure: The Politics of Value at a Michigan Landfill," *Journal of Material Culture* 14:1 (2009), 29–46.

23. Mark Mitchell and Rob Montgomery, "An Examination of Thrift Store Shoppers," *Marketing Management Journal* 94-107 (Fall 2010), 95.

24. Susan Strasser, *Waste and Want: A Social History of Trash* (New York: Henry Holt and Company, 1999), 3. The landmark study that defined trash as a topic worthy of study is Michael Thompson, *Rubbish Theory* (Oxford: Oxford University Press, 1979). See also Couze Venn, "Rubbish, the Remnant, etcetera," Theory, Culture & Society 23:2-3 (May 2006), 44–46.

TEN

In Conversation

Community, Women, and Work in the American Garage Sale

Gretchen Herrmann with Martha Rosler

EDITOR'S NOTE

The following "In Conversation" originally appeared in *Garage Sale Standard, Issue 1*, a newspaper (and .pdf file) available to accompany an installation at the Museum of Modern Art (MoMA) in November 2012. The installation, the "Meta-Monumental Garage Sale," was one in a series of such exhibitions in Europe and the United States created by photographer and performance artist Martha Rosler and based on the institution of the American garage sale. In this "conversation," Rosler interviews Gretchen Herrmann, an anthropologist who has written extensively about such sales, attended over 3,000 sales, interviewed hundreds of shoppers and sellers, and conducted more than a dozen sales of her own. A selected bibliography of her writings on the topic follows this interview.

Garage sales originated in part in the backlog of consumer goods acquired by American householders after the deprivations of World War II, as Gitlin describes this period in chapter 7. Products were designed for disposability; marketing encouraged shoppers to buy the latest version. Garage sales also reflected suburbanization and a change in cultural values that erased any earlier stigma attached to selling personal items in the yard or driveway. The sellers, often women, were themselves consumers and in turn sold what they no longer needed. Reflecting those driveway conversations, Rosler negotiated with customers as she presided over the event at MoMA. The exhibition included real stuff (from Rosler, museum staff, local artists, earlier sales, and the public), really for sale, as well as materials about the role of commodities in suburban life, including a video of earlier such installations. If visitors agreed, their pictures (with purchases) were taken by a professional wedding photographer and then became part of the accumulating items for the next exhibit in this ongoing series.

In the following interview, *Rosler* precedes the questions posed by Rosler, and *Herrmann* precedes Herrmann's responses. To learn more about the context of this conversation, see what the exhibit looked like, and examine further the significance of garage sales, visit the exhibit website: http://www.moma.org/interactives/exhibitions/2012/garagesale/ We are grateful to Martha Rosler and Gretchen Herrmann, and to Sarah Resnick, editor of the newspaper, for permission to reprint this conversation.

Rosler. Your research locates the emergence of the garage sale in a contradiction in American life: Prosperity brings families the ability to replace domestic items regularly, but long-term decline in spending power puts stresses on that ability. The two processes of consumerism and survival help drive the behavior of families and individuals. *The New York Times*, right after the collapse of the housing bubble in 2008, noted the rise in garage sales in affected communities and the detachment from "sentiment" this involves.

When were the first garage sales, and how would you characterize the economic conditions and the changing nature of consumerism during that time period?

Herrmann. Garage sales as we know them—sales of a diverse allotment of household goods, decorative items, clothing, and other belongings from the home at an advertised date and time—are a product of the 1960s. There has always been some informal selling from the home, but never with the variety and amount of miscellaneous items that we see in garage sales. Several factors converged to allow this front yard trade to thrive. One was a backlog of consumer goods. The 1930s were the "make-do" Depression, the 1940s were the Second World War, and it was only in the late 1940s, the 1950s, and the early 1960s that the average American householder could have built up enough consumer goods to sell. In part the upsurge of acquired material possessions resulted from "planned obsolescence," by then introduced into product design, encouraging shoppers to purchase the latest styles of an increasing variety of household commodities.

Another factor was a change of architecture from multistory houses with an attic for storage to ranch style homes in suburbia with far less storage space. Unused belongings became clutter. Cars enabled the move to the suburbs and the U.S. became a more mobile society, forcing families to sell possessions rather than move them as they sought the American dream in places like California. Finally, the liberalization of cultural values in the second half of the 1960s and early 1970s swept in a generalized ethos that it was perfectly OK, even cool, to buy used stuff. For many the Depression-era stigma attached to the sale and use of secondhand goods diminished or disappeared. So, by the end of the 1960s and especially at the start of the 1970s garage-sale trade took off. It was abetted by numerous women's magazine articles and Sunday supplements that legitimized holding garage sales to proper suburban housewives "for fun and profit." During the 1970s, the numbers of garage sales exploded all over the country and they became firmly established as means to clean house and garner some savings. Also, to have fun.

Underlying these cultural and lifestyle changes was an economic shift. Starting in 1969, and accelerating with the recession of 1973-74, the real spendable income for workers in the U.S. began to drop. Families that could live on one salary now needed a second, usually contributed by the wife. So, the extra money garnered through selling unwanted household items or money saved through purchasing garage-sale bargains has assisted American families struggling to maintain a foothold in the middle class. In this way, garage sales act as a kind of "survival strategy." Many claim they wouldn't have made it economically without garage sales.

Rosler. Before the late sixties, the common term for a residential sale was "rummage sale." At some point the term "garage sale" emerged. What about American life occasioned the change, and what cultural values would you ascribe to this linguistic shift?

Herrmann. Good point. There was a linguistic shift as garage sales took hold. Initially the term "rummage sales" was used, likely modeled after sales held by religious and civic organizations to raise money and to assist those in need. "Rummage" describes undifferentiated goods of small value; it has a rather low-rent connotation. But in the late 1960s, the name for sales from private residences shifted to where sales were held, i.e. the driveway, porch, lawn, yard, carport, and, of course, the garage. These are all terms that speak of owning property and carry the implications that the seller is a respectable homeowner with desirable consumer goods to sell, better than mere rummage. These sales reflect the suburbanization of American culture of the time, with a fondness for single family homes, PTAs and other community organizations, and automobiles.

Rosler. When I was growing up in Brooklyn, New York, people would not have considered selling their used goods in a public place, for several reasons, the least of which, it seemed to me, having to do with the lack of privately controlled yet publicly frequented spaces in which to lay out the goods. Rather, there were expectations about the virtuousness of charity donations, on the one hand, and the shame of revealing one's unwanted possessions in a kind of unwilled portrait, on the other. (Not to mention the shame of appearing to need to sell your things at all.) In fact, a German interviewer asked me just the other day why anyone would consider exposing one's castoffs to the scrutiny of one's neighbors. When I first came across garage sales in the early 1970s in Southern California, I too was amazed and appalled.

Herrmann. You are an insightful observer! Garage sales are a uniquely American institution dependent on values of openness and friendliness. Aside from Canada and a few "Ameriphile" enclaves around the world, people don't sell used possessions from their homes. Europeans, for example, have different notions of privacy and traditionally furniture has passed down through the family. Most other parts of the world, such as much of Latin America, have long had a larger polarization of wealth, gated houses, and marked class stratification such that used goods would be donated to domestic help.

There has always been an element of exhibitionism on the part of garage-sale sellers, and a corresponding element of voyeurism on the part of shoppers, who can take stock of the sellers while literally pawing through their used underwear. Books, music, clothing, pet paraphernalia, art, and decorative items all say something about the seller, and many shoppers admit they love to frequent sales so they can look into other people's lives. Some sellers try to "edit" their sales so that they reveal only relatively non-embarrassing things about themselves in the items they put out to sell.

You are right that there was a shift in previous notions about charity, and about guilt and shame at selling and buying used things. But they have not shifted entirely or, rather, they have not shifted for everyone. Some feel that garage sales detract from the goods that might go to charitable organizations to help those in need, while sellers at sales feel that they can more directly help those in need by selling to them at their sales. Besides, sellers often donate goods that have not sold to charitable organizations. Even today some people have a shame-related hesitation to engage in garage sale trade because others might think that they actually need the proceeds or savings they derive from garage sale involvement. The very notion of buying some cast-off from someone else is also still repugnant for some. Others participate along class lines. Those who are secure in their middle-class status often feel free to purchase secondhand items and to wear used clothes, whereas those who are trying to gain a foothold into middle-class respectability may signify their earning power by consuming only new goods. But most Americans feel unconstrained to buy and sell at garage sales with little concern about what others may think of them. Indeed, for shoppers there is often the cache of unique finds and amazing bargains that they flaunt as "garage sale chic."

Rosler. In my experience, most garage sales are held by women, and most of the shoppers are women. You've written that of the five hundred garage sales you observed in and around Cortland and Ithaca, New York, over two-thirds of both sellers and shoppers are women. How are traditional gender roles inscribed in the garage sale or, on the contrary, subverted by it? What does participation in garage sales reveal about how women understand their worlds, especially with respect to patterns of work and consumption, and the still-prevalent assumption that women are the keepers and maintainers of the domestic sphere? Can you relate this to the inclusion of caring, or the caring community, as an element underlying the garage sale?

Herrmann. Yes, garage sales can be described as a women-dominated trade. Even today when I do spot checks of participation by gender, there are still around two-thirds of sellers and buyers who are female. There are lots of reasons that this form of trade is female-dominated. Garage sales take place in and around the home, traditionally women's domain, and involve activities that are extensions of traditional women's domestic duties: cleaning house and managing possessions; selecting items for disposal; cleaning and arranging the items; sorting and organizing belongings; creating an attractive display; and assigning prices (values) to the goods up for sale. Women still do most of the household shopping and are more aware of going prices and styles. Given that women are the primary domestic shoppers, they comprise most of the garage sale shoppers, particularly when they are seeking goods for domestic consumption.

When holding a sale, the gender division of labor tends to follow traditional lines. Men are likely to be the ones charged with lifting, carrying, and setting up heavy and/or bulky items. They put up the signs, help to set up, and price the "guy" stuff such as tools, sporting goods, electronics, music, and recreational items. Women still preside over children's items, clothing, housewares, decorative items, linens, and various crafts. There are of course many exceptions to these stereotypes, particularly as men have increasingly taken on more household responsibility and involvement in raising their children. For example, I often see younger men with small children as sellers and men of retirement age actively engaged in downsizing sales.

Since women comprise the majority of garage sale shoppers and sellers, this style of trade, coming as it does from the home, is informed by "women's values." What I mean by that is that women's traditional role in caring for the family, promoting the health and well-being of the community, and nurturing others, shape the style and substance of garage-sale exchange. Thus, garage-sale trade invokes mythical depictions of community in which things go from where they are no longer of use to those in need, at little, sometimes no, cost. Shoppers are nurtured through commodities. Sellers will often reduce the price if something especially suits the buyers, the buyers demonstrate special appreciation for the item, or if the buyers appear in need. Children are often given things outright. Thus something of a "moral" trade emerges, one that is based on semi-gifts or quasi-commodities. Money and profit are not necessarily the point of the trade. Women create ties with shoppers through the items circulated, in part because the goods in garages sales are used, and carry something of the seller with them (even if only in the form of scratches and dents). There are also numerous sales held for good causes, whether for a school trip or a dog rescue group, which helps to build community.

Rosler. You've written that the garage sale is typical of a wide range of informal social institutions that allow participants to feel a greater degree of power over their lives than is felt in the formal economy and in regular social institutions. How would you characterize this sense of empowerment? What motives can we attribute to the garage sale buyer and/or seller that are not directly economic?

Herrmann. Participants in many informal economic and social institutions feel empowered through their involvement in them. One salient theme, especially for shoppers, is that of "beating the system." Shoppers can get loads of good stuff for next to nothing; they may even vie with their friends to see who can get the best or most stuff for the least amount of money. The ability to get so many great things can be such a rush that shoppers may overdo it, and end up with living spaces chock-full of great garage-sale finds (and thus ensuring that they will need to, in turn, hold their own garage sale). Shopping economically for needed goods is probably most empowering to those who are struggling to make ends meet, but all garage-sale shopping vastly stretches the value of money.

Another notion is that of claiming one's own labor. Although setting up and holding a sale is physical work, and sellers do complain of the effort it requires, it is *their* work: They set up goods in their own little store, they decide when to sell and to whom, they decide the prices, and they are experts in the history and peculiarities of the goods. The sellers are in control and they do not have a boss over their shoulders telling them what to do. Besides, the efforts involved are often fun. Friends and family members get together to stage a sale, and it ends up being part sale and part party, especially when other neighbors and acquaintances join in the fun. Most, but by no means all, garage-sale participants find shopping a lot more fun than selling because there is considerably less physical effort and time commitment involved.

Garage sales also allow participants to assign value and price according to a sense of justice and proportion. The very act of offering articles for sale (re)values them, and sellers can determine what items are worth to them. Because sellers often do not need to make a profit on their used items, they have enormous flexibility in what they can charge for their goods. Overall, everyone wins in garage-sale exchange because sellers get a little cash for things they have already paid for and used, while shoppers get a really good deal on something that they need. Prices can also be created interactively through bargaining.

Rosler. You define transactions at garage sales as occurring along a continuum from profit maximizing to gift giving. You argue that even the most commercial of these interactions are more gift-like than in a store, since the parties to the transaction are linked in a fundamentally social way. What are the characteristics of garage sales that make them gift-like?

Herrmann. There is one overarching factor about garage sales that establishes the social conditions and practices that make them such a rich and hybrid phenomenon: that is, commercial activity takes place in private residences. This means that there is always a tension between notions of hospitality and desire for profit, between gift-giving and maximizing economic behavior. And the goods at a garage sale, although sold for money, may be sold for next to nothing, or at full-retail price.

Another gift-like aspect of garage sales follows from the fact that items sold are used belongings. They are "possessions" that are "singularized" or endowed with personal affect and frequently with signs of use. Social ties, however slight, are formed among shoppers and sellers through the trade of garage sales goods, especially when memories and stories are passed along with the objects that change hands. Many shoppers prefer garage sales to buying new because they acquire things with a history, and because something of the seller is passed along.

Rosler. You've written about barter economies like Ithaca dollars and the way they can facilitate sharing and play. In what ways do garage sales promote a sense of community, imagined or otherwise? Would it be fair to characterize garage sales as doing so in part by enacting social rituals that increase visibility and a sense of identification among neighbors, thereby decreasing anonymity?

Herrmann. Garage sales are a natural gathering place for building community. They provide a temporary site for neighbors, friends, relatives, and strangers to congregate, swapping advice on canning tomatoes and passing along outgrown children's clothes or never-used yogurt makers. People generate conversations and pass on news and gossip. Multi-family and neighborhood sales are enhanced cases of this sale-as-social-event form of community, and they often end up with a party-like, high-spirited atmosphere. Shoppers and sellers joke, play with the stuff for sale, listen to music, and amuse themselves by interacting with other participants. Neighborhood sales are often one of the few times of year, especially in northern climates, where those who live in close proximity are out of their houses and socializing face to face. Annual neighborhood sales may be the only event that brings neighbors together.

Rosler. How might you compare shopping at garage sales to shopping online, whether through eBay or Etsy, or even Craigslist, which is divided into communities? Do you recognize the influence of the garage sale on these digital marketplaces, and is the influence reciprocated?

Herrmann. This is a great question and I'll do my best to answer. I have only done a limited amount of buying and selling through these channels. The first thing I would note about all these venues is that initial contact between the parties is not face to face, but rather mediated through the computer. In the case of eBay, there is almost never a face-to-face interaction or even a voice interaction, but there can be some limited email interactions between buyers and sellers. There are also feedback mechanisms rating the seller. Craigslist, depending on the category of use, can involve interactions through email, telephone, and in person. There is more direct opportunity for taking in the information afforded by personal exposure, i.e. through writing style, voice, and presentation of self, and for greater interaction. Another possibility for the exchange of used goods is Freecycling. Interactions in this venue begin rather like those on Craigslist, but instead of meeting with a seller to see about purchasing items, Freecyclers often leave goods outside their homes to be picked up by a person they don't know, located through Freecycling.

At garage sales, shoppers and sellers engage in face-to-face interaction from the start, and derive a great deal of information about one another through this contact. Sellers, especially, reveal a lot about themselves through the goods they sell, their home surroundings, and their presentation of self. Sales also generally promote an open, friendly atmosphere for the trade of goods, and this reduces anxiety about any possible misrepresentation of goods for sale. The ability to actively see (and touch, hear, smell) the merchandise at a garage sale is also a relative advantage for purchasing in that venue, as opposed to eBay, or even catalog sales. Touching the fabric, checking to see if all the parts are present, or trying on the shoes, along with an (often unconscious) assessment of the seller(s), provide much more information for the shopper. Prices can also be quite low at garage sales—perhaps more so than in these online venues—and there is no delayed gratification in waiting for shipping.

Rosler. We tend to see economic exchanges through frames provided by neoclassical economics: utility maximization and rational choice. You argue that the garage sale provides a counterexample and cite bargaining, or haggling, as a process in which cultural values are factored into pricing. What determines bargaining at garage sales? How does bargaining reinsert elements of the personal into economic exchange? Does the injection of personal narratives into exchange reduce the aura of impersonality or alienation attached to industrially produced goods?

Herrmann. You are quite right that neoclassical economics elevates the market as the measure of value for so-called rational agents who are trying to maximize their economic positions. Behavioral economics has been challenging the universality of those views for some time by looking at how actors actually make economic decisions, and economic anthropology, the approach I take, looks at how value is culturally and contingently constructed, and at the social relations of exchange. Economic sociology takes a similar approach. The garage sale flourishes under the metaphor of the market, yet, as noted previously, retains elements of gift exchange in the form of give-away prices, histories of used possessions, and outright gifts, which personalize the transaction. The stories, memories, and enthusiasms that often accompany the items changing hands provide additional dimensions, far removed from rationalized exchange, to the act of valuing items.

From a strictly rational economic perspective most garage sales would not be held at all. Sellers rarely derive enough cash from the sales to justify all the time, effort, and in some cases, investment in price stickers, advertising, and the like. It is often more economically advantageous to donate the items to charity and to take the tax write-off for doing so.

Ultimately, sellers want to make sure that their used belongings go to "a good home," and garage sales enable sellers to match up with shoppers who will appreciate what is on offer. It can be a very intimate form of exchange. I have often seen sellers hold back from selling to a dealer something like an antique wood dresser, in hopes of selling it directly to a shopper who would love and appreciate it. And as a shopper, I have experienced certain purchases as genuine gifts with something of the sellers passed along with them.

The prevalence of bargaining at garage sales also personalizes and distinguishes the exchange. Sales are one of the few places in American culture where shoppers can haggle over low to moderately priced goods. The fact that most goods for sale have been bought and used once already renders the monetary "value" of the merchandise highly variable and open to mutual negotiation by the shoppers and sellers; many sellers price a little high to allow room for bargaining. Since the monetary value of the goods tends to diminish over the course of a sale—since the venue is temporary, and sellers generally intend to get rid of as much as possible—bargaining later in a sale, or over a group of items, or over damaged goods is very common.

In general, Americans prefer a soft or respectful approach to bargaining, with something like, "Will you take a little less for this?" Some sellers bristle at aggressive bargaining, especially early in the sale. They may refuse to sell to someone who contravenes their sense of protocol given that sales take place on their property and concern their belongings. In general, men bargain more than women, and, because bargaining is a learned behavior, foreign-born participants from more rigorous bargaining cultures often haggle more than those who are U.S. born. But for many, one of the chief attractions of garage sale shopping, and a form of empowerment, is the ability to interact with the seller through bargaining to create a mutually agreed-upon price.

Rosler. What survives the transplantation of a garage sale into an exhibition space? What comes to our attention when we consider the garage sale as a portrait? What sort of self-image are we assembling here?

Hermann. This is a totally fun question in which I get to peek through your artist's lens for a bit. I would imagine that bringing a garage sale into an exhibition space foregrounds the goods for sale over what in a home-based sale would be the ambiance of the surroundings. That is, in an exhibition space we don't see the lawn, the gardens, the tools in the garage not for sale, the neighborhood of the home. We don't see the wind kicking up and blowing things off tables, the rain dampening the clothes, nor the beating sun forcing the seller to seek shade in the garage. We don't hear the street sounds, and car doors closing with engines starting, nor do we smell the outdoor air. We don't feel the affective qualities of individual sales in their specific milieus.

In the exhibition hall, our focus is primarily narrowed to the selected and arranged assemblage of goods. Is it organized or just a jumble of goods? Have shoppers rearranged things? We look at what goods are presented for sale. How are they made? What do they represent? Do they reflect the artist personally as her belongings, or are they donations by others? Is clothing important? Books? What authors? What subjects? What do these say about the artist, either as owner or assembler? Is there music? What formats? What genres? Cooking implements? What parts of the exhibit space are used and are they integrated creatively?

When the seller is present, she breathes life into the assemblage and becomes its focus. Where does she put herself in the exhibit? Is she standing on the side or sitting in the middle? Do the goods arrayed about her reflect her tastes and personal presence? How is she involved with the goods? Does she tell stories about the goods for sale? Or does she let the shoppers tell her how they want to use their purchases? With the seller present, the exhibit becomes interactive and vital, especially as shoppers become engaged with the sale.

Although the exhibition hall privileges the visual, it also allows for interaction and for the purchase of the goods. Sounds of shoppers and their conversations may start to vie with the visual primacy and become another focus of interest. Participants can touch the wares, examine the items, and haggle over the price. I'd say it's probably a good place to find a bargain!

SELECTED BIBLIOGRAPHY: GRETCHEN HERRMANN

Herrmann, Gretchen M. "New Lives from Used Goods: Garage Sales as Rites of Passage." *Ethnology* 50, no. 3 (2011): 189–205.

_________. "Garage Sales Make Good Neighbors: Building Community Through Neighborhood Sales." *Human Organization* 65, no. 2 (2006): 181–191.

_________. "Special Money: Ithaca HOURS and Garage Sales." *Ethnology* 45, no. 2 (2006): 125–141.

_________. "Haggling Spoke Here: Gender, Class and Style in U.S. Garage Sale Bargaining." *Journal of Popular Culture* 38, no. 1 (2004): 55–81.

_________. "Negotiating Culture: Conflict and Consensus in U.S. Garage-Sale Bargaining." *Ethnology* 4, no. 3 (2003): 237–252.

_________. "Gift or Commodity: What Changes Hands in the U.S. Garage Sale?" *American Ethnologist* 24, no. 4 (1997): 910–930.

_________. "Women's Exchange in the U.S. Garage Sale: Giving Gifts and Creating Community." *Gender & Society* 10, no. 6 (1996): 703–728.

_________. "His and Hers: Gender and Garage Sales." *Journal of Popular Culture* 29, no. 1 (1995): 127–146.

_________ and Stephen M. Soiffer. "For Fun and Profit: An Analysis of the American Garage Sale." *Urban Life* 9, no. 4 (1984): 397–421.

Soiffer, Stephen M. and Gretchen M. Herrmann. "Visions of Power: Ideology and Practice in the American Garage Sale." *The Sociological Review* 35, no. 1 (1987): 48–83.

Index

advertising, 34, 143, 147; grocery stores, 95, 98, 101–102; marketing research, 65–66; promotional spaces, 77
arcades, xii, 13, 63, 64, 73–82
Arcades Project, 73–74, 81
art of shopping, xv–xvii, 205
automobiles and shopping, 19–27, 65, 70

Baudelaire, Charles, 76–77, 80
Benjamin, Walter, 73–76, 79, 81, 82, 83, 84, 85, 86, 87
bookstores, 83–84
box stores, 26–27, 87, 127, 159–176
brands, 22, 24, 29, 36, 47–48, 51, 98

capitalism, x, 73–74, 76, 77, 80, 82, 86
chain stores, 23, 44–48, 83; opposition to, 44–48
children and shopping, 132, 138–140, 149–150, 150, 153
clothing, used, 182–184
community shopping centers, 59; Roland Park, 59; Country Club Plaza, 59
convenience stores, 150–151
consumption, x–xi, 8, 35, 74, 79, 80, 150; secondhand consumerism, 181–184
Crystal Palace exhibition, 14–15

Dahl, Roald, 149–150
Defoe, Daniel, 8
department stores, xi, xvi, 15–18, 37–40, 58, 60, 61–62, 79
"dialectics at a standstill", 74–76, 84, 87

farmers' markets, 111–128, 183
flaneur, 76
food: production and distribution, 94, 97, 113–117, 126–127; food safety, 97, 127. *See also* farmers' markets; grocery stores; supermarkets; public markets
Foucault, Michel, 84

garage sales, 195–205; "Meta-Monumental Gar[b]age Sale", xv, 195, 205
Golden Age of Shopping, 13–18
grocery stores, 59, 89–107
Gruen, Victor, xii, 25, 62–65, 68, 70; Gruen effect, 62, 65–66

Hine, Thomas, 133, 153n1. *See also* populuxe

James, Henry, xiii

Le Bon Marche, 15–16, 18

Macklemore, 181, 182
mail-order shopping, 41–43
malls. *See* shopping malls
mass merchandising, 37–40
material culture: definition of, ix; effervescence in, 131–132, 150
Middle Ages, shopping in, 3–6
Miller, Daniel, x
Mister Selfridge, xvi
modernity, 73, 79; hoarding as a characteristic of, 80
modernization of grocery stories, in cities, 101–106
Museum of Modern Art (MoMA), xv–xvi, 195

online shopping, 1–3, 27–29, 80–81, 82–87, 202–203

pinball effect, 57–58, 65–67
populuxe, 131, 150
public markets, 90, 119; Boston, 118–119; Philadelphia, 119–123

Red Balloon, 144–145
regional shopping centers, 60
Rouse, James, 68

self-service, 23–25, 48–50; stores, 27
service learning, 181; secondhand consumption, course in, 185–190
shopping malls, 19–27, 57–70, 82; Forest Park, 61; hierarchy, 67–68; in decline, 82; in-town, 68; mixed-use and megamalls, 69; Northgate, 25, 61; Northland, 61–62, 62, 63; Shopper's World, 61; Southdale, 62, 63–64, 65, 151
Shopzilla, 86
suburbs, 25, 58–59, 59, 60, 69–70, 132–133, 145–146, 197; edge cities, 65; streetcar, 59; suburban sprawl, 70
supermarkets, 25, 59, 125; A&P, 45, 48–49; Ralph's, 25

thrift shops, xiv, 182, 186–189
toxic consumer products, 159–176. *See also* food safety

Walmart, 26–27, 33, 50–53
Wedgwood, Josiah, 9
Wharton, Edith, xvi–xvii
women and shopping, x, xiii, xvi, 18, 23, 60, 62, 63, 136–138, 199–200
Woolworth, 23, 33–34, 52

About the Contributors

David Ames, professor of urban affairs and public policy and geography at the University of Delaware, also directs the university's Center for Historic Architecture and Design. A leader in incorporating twentieth-century suburban historic resources into the field of historic preservation, he has published widely on the evolution of urban and suburban landscapes, preservation, and sustainable planning policy.

Deborah C. Andrews, professor of English at the University of Delaware, directs the university's Center for Material Culture Studies. The author of articles, book chapters, and texts on professional communication, she has combined that specialty with her material culture research in publications that address such topics as banking architecture in Philadelphia, nineteenth-century household management guides, Chicago novels with an architectural bent, and changes in workspace design that accommodate new definitions of work, new relationships among workers, and new technologies.

J. Ritchie Garrison is director of the Winterthur Program in American Material Culture and professor of history at the University of Delaware. He is the author of several books addressing vernacular architecture and early American material life, including *Two Carpenters: Architecture and Building in Early New England* (2006), which won the Abbott Lowell Cummings Prize from the Vernacular Architecture Forum and the Historic New England Book Prize in 2007.

Jay Gitlin is associate director of the Howard R. Lamar Center for the Study of Frontiers and Borders at Yale University, where he has taught courses on the American West, Québec and Canada, suburbanization, and—with Sandy Isenstadt—the history of shopping. In addition to his publications, including *The Bourgeois Frontier: French Towns, French Traders, and American Expansion* (2010), he has been an on-camera commentator and consultant for several television shows on the History Channel and Connecticut Public Television, including *Suburbia: The Good Life in Connecticut.*

Gretchen Herrmann is an anthropologist and bibliographer for the social sciences at SUNY Cortland, where she also teaches women's studies. Over the past twenty years, she has presented and published numerous academic papers on various aspects of the garage sale experience centered on related topics of women, work, and community. She has also recently published on the white elephant Christmas game.

Sandy Isenstadt is professor of art history at the University of Delaware. His writings span post–World War II reformulations of modernism by émigré architects such as Richard Neutra, Josep Lluis Sert, and Henry Klumb and visual polemics in the urban proposals of Leon Krier and Rem Koolhaas, as well as histories of American refrigerators, picture windows, landscape views, and real estate appraisal. His book, *The Modern American House: Spaciousness and Middle-Class Identity* (2006) describes the visual enhancement of spaciousness in the architectural, interior, and landscape design of American domestic architecture.

McKay Jenkins, Cornelius Tilghman Professor of English, Journalism, and Environmental Humanities at the University of Delaware, is the author of *What's Gotten Into Us: Staying Healthy in a Toxic World* (2011), from which his chapter in this anthology has been adapted. His other books include *Bloody Falls of the Coppermine: Madness, Murder and the Collision of Cultures in the Arctic, 1913* (2005); *The Last Ridge: The Epic Story of the U.S. Army's 10th Mountain Division and the Assault on Hitler's Europe* (2003); and *The White Death: Tragedy and Heroism in an Avalanche Zone* (2000).

Anne Krulikowski is assistant professor of history at West Chester University. Before joining West Chester, she worked at Rockwood Museum in Wilmington, Delaware, and was visiting assistant professor at Dickinson College. She has published articles and given numerous talks on suburbanization, housing, real estate and land use, urban farming, country club design, and the Colonial Revival.

Martha Rosler is an artist whose work centers on the public sphere and landscapes of everyday life, especially as they affect women. Using video, photo, photomontage, posters, and collaborative actions, she addresses matters from housing to the national security state. She has held garage sales in and around the art world since 1973, most recently in 2012 at New York's Museum of Modern Art.

Helen Sheumaker teaches American studies, public history, and US history at Miami University of Ohio. Her research focuses on the processes of identity formation and expression through material culture, and in particular, the role of consumer goods that aren't quite normal in their manufacture, production, distribution, and sale in these processes. Her publications include *Love Entwined: The Curious History of Human Hairwork* (2007) and *Material Culture in America: An Encylopedia* (2007), coedited with Shirley Wajda.

Susan Strasser, Richards Professor of American History (emerita) at the University of Delaware, has been praised by the *New Yorker* for "retrieving what history discards: the taken-for-granted minutiae of everyday life." Her books include *Never Done: A History of American Housework* (1982); *Satisfaction Guaranteed: The Making of the American Mass Market* (1989); and *Waste and Want: A Social History of Trash* (1999).

Lance Winn, professor of art at the University of Delaware, is an artist whose personal work searches for the language embedded in processes of reproduction. His academic research is directed most specifically toward a dialectic of modernity, best represented by Benjamin's *Arcades Project* and extending into material culture, architecture, and the effects of time on objects. He has lectured on his work at universities across the United States. His art has been shown nationally and internationally and has been included in a range of recent books.